RELIGION, POLITICS, AND LAW

RELIGION AND NORMATIVITY
VOLUME 3

RELIGION, POLITICS, AND LAW

Edited by Peter Lodberg

Acta Jutlandica
Theological Series

Aarhus University Press |

Religion, politics, and law
Religion and normativity vol. 3
© Aarhus University Press and the authors 2009

Cover, design and typesetting by Jørgen Sparre
Printed by Narayana Press, Gylling
Printed in Denmark 2009

ISBN 978 87 7934 425 9
ISSN 0065 1354 – Acta Jutlandica
ISSN 0106 0945 – Theological Series

Published with the financial support of
Aarhus University Research Foundation
The Learned Society in Aarhus
The Theological Faculty at Aarhus University

Aarhus University Press
Langelandsgade 177
DK-8200 Aarhus N
www.unipress.dk

INTERNATIONAL DISTRIBUTORS:
Gazelle Book Services Ltd.
White Cross Mills
Hightown, Lancaster, LA1 4XS
United Kingdom
www.gazellebookservices.co.uk

The David Brown Book Company
Box 511
Oakville, CT 06779
USA
www.oxbowbooks.com

TABLE OF CONTENTS

PREFACE

In 2005 the Faculty of Theology, Aarhus University, chose as its research priority area *Religion and normativity*. This research priority area builds on existing research on topics covered by the faculty's strengths, and is divided into three themes:

Theme 1: The discursive fight over religious texts
Theme 2: Bible and literature – receptions and transformations of the Bible
Theme 3: Religion, politics, and law.

The research priority area has contributed to a deeper understanding of the role played by religion in defining past and present cultures and societies. Its participants have compared Judaism, Christianity, Islam and antique religions in the light of exegetical, historical and systematic perspectives. In a contemporary context, they have explored whether religion is still normative.

The result of their research is presented in a three-volume work entitled:

The discursive fight over religious texts in antiquity, Religion and normativity, Vol. 1, ed. by Anders-Christian Jacobsen.

Receptions and transformations of the Bible, Religion and normativity, Vol. 2, ed. by Kirsten Nielsen,

Religion, politics, and law, Religion and normativity, Vol. 3, ed. by Peter Lodberg.

The three editors wish to express their sincere thanks to the participants in the research area for many stimulating discussions during the research period, and for their contributions to these three volumes.

The Faculty of Theology, Aarhus University, has provided excellent working conditions and financial support, for which we are most grateful.

Thanks are also due to Aarhus University Press for taking care of the publishing in a very professional way.

Finally we wish to thank the University Research Foundation and Det Lærde Selskab (the Learned Society) Aarhus for financial support.

Anders-Christian Jacobsen, Peter Lodberg, Kirsten Nielsen
Aarhus, April, 2009

INTRODUCTION

Peter Lodberg

This book is about the relationship between religion, politics, and law, and their role in modern discussions concerning the role of religion in the public sphere. The authors work at Aarhus University, Denmark, in the field of theology, religious studies, and political science. The idea is to discuss different aspects of religion in relation to the public debate beginning with the most fundamental question: is the so-called 'return of religion' real, or is it a self-increasing and self-affirming truth? One could also ask whether religion had ever really disappeared from the global political scene, or whether it had taken forms that made religion look like a hidden resource in the lives of many people.

However, today – at least in a Danish and North European context – religion plays an important role in political debates and in the public discourse. But global changes and political conflicts around the globe also involve serious religious issues and important religious players. The Iranian revolution has helped to unleash the potential for religiously legitimised religious violence; the political conflict in the Middle East has been 'desecularised'; Hindu nationalism plays an important role in the conflict between India and Pakistan; and in the US the Christian Right is mobilising political pressure on issues like abortion, same-sex marriages or the invasion of Iraq. In December 2005 the public and political debate on religion, politics, and law exploded in Denmark because of the publication in a Danish newspaper of a series of cartoons depicting the prophet Mohammed. The violent reaction in many countries around the world against the Danish government and the state of Denmark created the most serious international crisis for Denmark since the Second World War – the so-called 'cartoon crisis'.

These and many other examples show that one of the most important areas of research today is the area of theology and religion, because this is an area that involves a public dimension about the normative role of religion in politics and law. This book does not – of course – solve the issue. Some authors would like religion to be modest and humble in the field of politics and law in order to respect the idea of a common secular arena for all citizens irrespective of creed and religious affiliation. Others point to the resources in religion that can help to establish open and democratic societies for everybody. This involves respect for religious freedom, and dialogue among religious believers and their religious institutions regarding issues of common concern and disagreement. As revealed by some of the articles in this book, the discussion of religion and normativity in a Danish context also involves an important re-formulation of the Lutheran heritage, because the Evangelical-Lutheran Church plays an important role in Danish society and the majority of the Danish population (approx. 85%) are still members.

One possible reformulation of Lutheran political ethics is suggested in the first article by Svend Andersen. This includes a secular, general theory that is complementary to a Christian ethics of neighbourly love, and can be interpreted as a natural law theory. As a source of inspiration Svend Andersen draws on John Rawls' theory of justice and Jürgen Habermas' Kantian republicanism.

Lars Albinus views the topic of 'religion in the public sphere' from the perspective of rationality and power. He introduces a range of thoughts from the works of Michel Foucault and Jürgen Habermas. Lars Albinus warns against the free reign of traditional or religious communities and their interaction by whatever means they see fit, because this will create a situation of chaotic conflict. He appeals to secular standards or communicative reason, backed up by non-religious institutions and political processes of religiously 'neutral' decision-making.

Vagn Andersen presents a critical analysis of references to 'the return of religion' in the public sphere. He argues that in the modern media society this kind of headline is becoming a self-increasing and self-affirming truth. Vagn Andersen finds that the empirical question about the growth of religion and the critical philosophical question about the reality of religion need to be answered, and among others he refers to the work of Jürgen Habermas, Max Horkheimer and Theodor W. Adorno in his critical assessment of the way religion is presented and presents itself to the public today.

Johannes Adamsen discusses the issue of freedom of expression in relation to religion, censorship, and citizenship. He points to the fact that recent discussions of freedom of expression tend to contrast religion with free speech. The Danish cartoon crisis is interpreted as a recent example of how freedom of expression can clash with religious feelings. To avoid similar clashes in the future, Johannes Adamsen calls for the establishment of a democracy with moral courage and a clear understanding of citizenship for all.

Henrik Reintoft Christensen analyses representations of religion in the Danish parliament in the wake of the cartoon crisis, an event which left the Danish politicians bruised and battered. The debates in the parliament revealed disagreement about the private and public role of religion in Danish society. The Prime Minister argued that religion was a private matter, while several MPs argued that religion might necessitate affirmative action in some form or another.

Morten Brænder deals with the dimensions of civil religion in war accounts. For a long time the political speech has been regarded as the archetypical medium for expressing this kind of religion. In his analysis Morten Brænder understands civil religion from the perspective of traditional religion, but his focus is on those who put their life at stake in the name of the nation: US military personnel participating in the global war on terror.

John Møller Larsen takes a close look into the work of Sayyid Quṭb, the Egyptian teacher who has become a major source of inspiration for Islamist radicals and for modern Islamism. Special attention is given to Quṭb's view of democracy and public participation in the governing of society. John Møller Larsen concludes that the best Quṭb could offer to his followers in terms of society was a vision of past greatness and dangerous dreams of a future utopia.

Karen-Lise Johansen Karman demonstrates the way in which the European Council for Fatwa and Research contributes to legal pluralism and assists Muslim minorities to manoeuvre in multiple systems of legal order. She examines the Council's fatwas and the way it guides Muslim minorities in navigating a public sphere with diverse social and legal norms.

The second section of the book concentrates on issues relating specifically to ecclesiology and the role of the Church in society.

Johannes Nissen opens the second section by discussing the question of the Bible's authority in relation to private and public life. He highlights the fact that the authority of the Bible is disputed in both personal ethics and social ethics. Johannes Nissen's emphasis is on concrete issues such as the church-state relationship, peace and violence, and justice.

Peter Lodberg deals with the relationship between nation and empire from an ecclesiological point of view. He claims that a modern understanding of the identity of the Church – not least in Europe and North America – and its role in society involves examining the idea of 'empire lite'. The idea of the nation and the empire in its present form as an empire lite is central to the biblical narrative and its interpretation throughout the history of theology.

Per Ingesman analyses the way in which the Church tried to reform its lay members by means of cathecising instruction and clerical control during the great reform period from 1050 to 1250 in Europe. The idea was that true Christians should live up to the requirements of the Church in both thought and deed. The aim was to create a Christian society, and three large fields in medieval society were handed over to the ecclesiastical domain: education, poor relief, and marriage.

Against the background of a recent resurgence of the term 'crusade' in public debate, Else Marie Wiberg Pedersen describes the Second Crusade (1146-1148) and the role of the Cistercian abbot and prominent 'church politician' Bernard of Clairvaux. She paints a comprehensive picture of the relationship between religion and politics in Europe in one of its important formative periods, a picture which outlines a future understanding of religion and politics.

Jens Holger Schjørring examines various types of totalitarian ideologies and regimes after the Second World War, such as Communism, Nazism and Apartheid. They are seen against the background of the role played by Christian churches, which were forced into the struggle for survival as they faced the seemingly inexhaustible determination of those in power to eliminate open opposition and even silent reservation.

Viggo Mortensen shows what happens when faiths collide and states meet in the multireligious world of today. The question is how interreligious dialogue can function in states which are in principle secular. Three government-sponsored, consecutive interfaith dialogues are analysed; and it is clear that in these conversations religion can be treated either as an ideological force or as pure window-dressing. It is argued that interfaith dialogue is of importance when pluralist states organise their international relations.

Ulrik Nissen reflects on the role played by the church, democracy, and ethics in the light of the Lutheran tradition. His starting point is the Danish cartoon crisis, and the question asked is whether Martin Luther's understanding of temporal authority means that religion should play a subordinate role in society. Ulrik Nissen compares Martin Luther to the Lutheran theologian Dietrich Bonhoeffer, who opens the way for a Lutheran theology in society by arguing for the mysterious role of religion.

PART I

Democracy, religion, and modernity

DEMOCRACY AND MODERNITY – A LUTHERAN PERSPECTIVE

Svend Andersen

Can we imagine a Lutheran politics for the 21st century, or is this by definition an impossible dream? There are several reasons why I think we should make the attempt.

First, there are theological reasons. I think we need a Lutheran alternative to what I see as a strong tendency towards Christian political self-overestimation. Let me just mention Radical Orthodoxy, Stanley Hauerwas' militant pacifism and Oliver O'Donovan's Anglican triumphalism. We need Lutheran modesty and realism in political theology. But there are also reasons connected with domestic politics. The so-called Danish cartoon crisis – which has now appeared for a second time – has prompted the wish that religion should take up less public space. In this connection Luther's 'two kingdom' distinction was mobilised. In this situation we theologians have an obligation to think through the Lutheran heritage in order to contribute to the public discourse in a qualified way.

But the question is: Is it possible to reformulate or reconstruct Lutheran political ethics in such a way that it can match the conditions of today, both intellectually and politically? I will try to answer the question by first giving a very short presentation of Luther's political thinking, as I see it. Then I will give a few examples of the way in which Lutheran theologians have reacted to political modernisation. And finally – and most extensively – I will discuss John Rawls' and Jürgen Habermas' political philosophy as possible allies of Lutheran political ethics.

Martin Luther's political ethics

I should like to draw attention to a few of the main points in Martin Luther's political ethics as found in *Von weltlicher Obrigkeit* (On Secular Authority). Luther's distinction between the two kingdoms – two ways in which God rules over humans – is a distinction between the means by which faith is established and sustained on the one hand, and the means by which profane human social life is sustained on the other. A significant difference is that in the latter case the use of human power is absolutely indispensable, whereas in the spiritual sphere it is absolutely out of place. In the secular, profane domain political authority – Obrigkeit – is necessary, and the very structure of authority is an ordinance installed by God in Creation. The function of authority is negatively to restrain evil and destruction caused by sin, and positively to protect the good human life. Luther sometimes summarises the positive function as keeping peace.

As political authority is an ordinance of Creation, God is the sustainer of the socio-political order. But this order includes an office filled by humans, so leeway is given for human contributions to the political world. This is the place for political ethics. Without being systematic, Luther operates with different types of authority. The most common is tyranny, which Luther describes very much like Machiavelli. But there is also a Christian way of ruling, and this is actually the main subject of *Von weltlicher Obrigkeit*.

It may sound surprising that Luther assumes Christian political authority as he makes the remarkable claim that "you cannot govern the world with the Gospel". The explanation is to be found in his view on the relation of faith and love.

As mentioned above, the spiritual domain, free of domination, has to do with the establishment and maintenance of faith. This is exclusively God's affair, and the function of the spiritual cannot be transferred into the secular realm. But faith necessarily manifests itself in the form of neighbourly love. The relation of faith and love has the structure of a double role exchange which Luther describes this way:

Siehe, Christus, der oberste Fürst, ist kommen und hat mir gedienet, nicht gesucht, wie er Gewalt, Gut und Ehre an mir hätte, sondern hat nur mein Not angesehen und alles dran gewandt, daß ich Gewalt, Gut und Ehre an ihm und durch ihn hätte. Also will ich auch tun: nicht an meinen Untertanen das Meine suchen, sondern das Ihre, und will ihnen auch also dienen mit meinem Amt (Luther 1900, 273).

These are the words of the Christian prince: he has experienced that Christ exchanged the prince's misery with his own justice. This enables the prince to put himself in the position of his subjects in a similar fashion, and to act for their benefit.

Now neighbourly love is a complex phenomenon with various modes of expression. In some situations it has the character of suffering and renouncing; whereas in other situations it is simply beneficence. The latter is the case when a Christian acts in the secular realm for the sake of his neighbours. According to Luther, Christian political ethics is a way of acting by Christians that realises governance in such a way that other people profit from it and created human life flourishes. There is congeniality between Christian neighbourly love and the function of political authority. This is also made clear by Luther:

Aber weil ein rechter Christ auf Erden nicht ihm selbst, sondern seinem Nächsten lebt und dienet, so tut er von Art seins Geistes auch das, des er nicht bedarf, sondern das seinem Nächsten *nutz und not* ist. Nun aber das Schwert ein *groß nötiger Nutz* ist aller Welt, daß Fried erhalten, Sünd gestraft und den Bösen gewehret werde, so gibt er sich aufs allerwilligst unter des Schwerts Regiment (Op. cit., 253. My italics).

This kind of Christian political ethics exists, so to speak, in both a ruler and a subject version.

Luther's typology of authority is not exhausted by the two types mentioned: the tyrant and the Christian ruler. There is a third ruler whom we could call the reasonable and righteous ruler. The foundation of this type is given with Luther's theory of *natural law* that he introduces in an interesting way. A Christian ruler also has to apply the law as a judge, and in the first place he will apply 'Recht der Liebe', the law of love, which implies (among other things) restraint with regard to punishment and claims for compensation. However, not all sides are willing to accept such an adjudication. But confronted with such stubborn parties the Christian prince-judge can make the following appeal:

> ... die Natur lehret, wie die Liebe tut, daß ich tun soll, was ich mir wollt getan haben. Darum kann ich niemand also entblößen, wie gut Recht ich immer habe, so ich selbst nicht gern wollt also entblößt sein; sondern wie ich wollt, daß ein anderer sein Recht an mir nach ließe in solchem Fall, also soll ich auf mein Recht verzichten (Op. cit., 279).

Luther's version of natural law theory differs significantly from the Thomistic. Nature in the biological sense does not play any role in Luther. Rather, the law is 'natural' in that it is known to natural man, i.e. it does not rest on revelation. And the natural human capacity for recognising natural law is reason. In reason Luther emphasises the freedom of judgment. In contrast, both in Thomas Aquinas and later in Phillip Melanchthon lex naturalis consists of a number of principles, from which concrete norms of action can be deduced. In Luther, natural law is the same as rational reciprocity, so to speak.

These are what I regard as the most important basic political thoughts in Luther. From this we have to distinguish time-conditioned assumptions. These include the necessary difference between superior and subject, and the impossibility of organising political rule on the basis of freedom and equality. But these are precisely the assumptions that are rejected by political modernity.

Political modernity

Among other things, political modernity means that the concept of Creation ordinance is replaced by the concept of social contract, and it means a revision of the understanding of natural law.

As to the first point, Thomas Hobbes has been called the first philosopher of modernity – also because of his contractualism.[1] And as to the second point, there is a clear difference between the Danish theologian Niels Hemmingsen, for instance, and Hugo Grotius. According to Hemmingsen, all kinds of law (ius) are founded in nature, more precisely in the Creator of nature. But natural law is not purely secular, for religion is part of what is demanded by natural law: "God is to be worshipped in religion" (Deum religiose colendum). In addition, the ultimate aim of the political order is God. And it belongs to the task of the secular government to support spiritual

---

1   Hobbes is claimed to be modern in the sense that for him self-conservation is the rational principle of both individual and state life. See Henrich 1976, 99.

life (vita spiritualis) (Hemmingsen 1993, 151). In contrast to this religious concept of natural law, in Grotius we find the well-known thought that natural law would be valid even if "we should concede ... that there is no God, or that the affairs of men are of no concern to him" (etsi deus non daretur). Grotius formulates a secular concept of natural law. On this line of thought I would place Kant's rational ethics and political philosophy.

In spite of the significance of Hobbes, I think it is fair to regard Kant as the main philosopher of political modernity. As a justification for this point of view, I can only make the following claims:

1. Kant transforms the Christian commandment of neighbourly love into his rational ethics of the categorical imperative; and he modifies the Golden Rule, because being an obligation against all others, it is not really universal.[2]
2. He defines law as a coercive norm that makes the free choice (Willkür) of everybody compatible with the freedom of all others.[3]
3. The principle of law is the general will of the people in the original contract; the principle is instituted in a republican constitution of free and equal citizens.[4]

The question now is: is Lutheran Christianity compatible with political modernity?

Lutheran theology and political modernity

In so far as we can talk about modern political theology in a Lutheran context, it has developed not so much in pure theory but rather in reaction to real political changes. I have looked at two phases of democratisation: the adoption of the Danish constitution of 1849, and the German situation at the time of the Weimar Republic.

19th century Denmark is normally associated with two theological heroes, Søren Kierkegaard and N.F.S. Grundtvig. But when it comes to theological reflection on political modernisation, I find Hans L. Martensen a much more intriguing figure.

In his ethics Martensen tries to combine Luther and Kant. Humans are free, but not autonomous. The moral law is an expression of God's personal will, but it is a law intended for free obedience. Obedience to the law is also the virtue of love created through justification in Christ. The aim of both law and love is the establishment of the earthly kingdom of God, the highest good. In his social and political ethics, Martensen makes a crucial step beyond Luther. He regards human freedom – the Protestant principle – as a basic social idea:

---

2   "Ich will jedes anderen Wohlwollen (benevolentiam) gegen mich; ich soll also auch gegen jeden anderen wohlwollend sein." (Kant, *Metaphysik*, 120).
3   "Das Recht ist also der Inbegriff der Bedingungen, unter denen die Willkür des einen mit der Willkür des andern nach einem allgemeinen Gesetze der Freiheit zusammen vereinigt werden kann." (Kant, *Metaphysik*, 33).
4   The republican constitution is: "Die erstlich nach Prinzipien der Freiheit der Glieder einer Gesellschaft (als Menschen); zweitens nach Grundsätzen der Abhängigkeit aller von einer einzigen gemeinsamen Gesetzgebung (als Untertanen); und drittens, die nach dem Gesetze der Gleichheit derselben (als Staatsbürger) gestiftete Verfassung ..." (Kant, *Frieden*, 20).

From the person's infinite value before God, from the concept of personality free in God, also springs the demand for a person's right in the secular sphere, for civil and political freedom, for freedom of religion, freedom of scientific investigation etc. and above all the demand that no human being should be a mere means for others (Martensen 1878, 45. My translation).

According to Martensen, Christianity is the origin of an emancipated Christendom, marked by liberation with regard to human rights. These are expressions of a modern personality, emancipated in terms of humanity and universality, but presupposing religious dependence.

Martensen endorses individual liberty rights, but not political rights in the sense of popular sovereignty. He does not hold a Kantian contractarian view of the state, but rather adopts a Hegelian holistic understanding, with the state consisting of a number of estates. Martensen rejects universal suffrage, but defends political participation in the form of estate representation. He expects the abandonment of the state church as the constitution requires, but still the state should be Christian by supporting the Lutheran church, for instance.

"No, politics is not my issue", says Søren Kierkegaard in a letter of 1848. We know that he talks about "the catastrophe of 48". So it is natural to regard Kierkegaard as an extreme individualist reactionary, an anti-democrat etc. But that is of course too simplistic. In *A Literary Review* in 1846 he praises the age of revolution at the expense of his own age. This is not because of the actual political events in question, but because the age of revolution was an age of passion. Passion means that the individual is both self-related and related to others. The political aspect of this consists of the fact that both the individual and the union relate themselves to an idea. Now this politics of passion can degenerate in two ways. If the individual's relation to the idea is annulled, we have a relation to the idea en masse, a riotous relation to the idea. But the attitude is still idealistic. If the relation to the idea is totally abolished riot becomes rudeness. Then we have levelling, community degenerating to the mass, and the press as the medium for the abstract public. This of course was Kierkegaard's view of his own time. There is no positive relation between Christian faith and the politics of the mass, least of all in a Lutheran sense. Actually Kierkegaard blames Luther, because he became "too much involved with the worldly, so that the fruit of the Reformation was politics and political development". But there is a negative relation between degenerated politics and Christianity: mass politics can be a starting point for the individual to become an individual.

Grundtvig's reaction to political modernisation was complex. Unlike his two contemporaries, he actually took part in the political process as a member of the constitutional assembly. He was not a democrat in the strict sense, but rather supported a kind of constitutional monarchy. Here, I will only mention his ideas of popular participation. Like Martensen, Grundtvig emphasises the Protestant idea of the freedom of faith. But this freedom is not purely individual; it is freedom in the context of the people. Christianity therefore presupposes freedom of the people. In many ways Grundtvig's concept of the people is a reformulation of Luther's concept of secular life as guided by natural law. But for Grundtvig, the natural laws of human life express themselves in different ways in different people. And if people are to take part in the political process, they have to be enlightened about their own character. This is the essence of Grundtvig's idea of the folk high school.

As mentioned above, Grundtvig does not support democracy in the sense of popular sovereignty. Of the key ideas of democracy he rejects equality but strongly defends freedom, primarily in the sense of freedom of conscience and faith, personal freedom and economic freedom.

Ernst Troeltsch's political thinking can be seen as a parallel to Martensen's, Kierkegaard's and Grundtvig's reaction to democratisation in Denmark. As a professor in Berlin Troeltsch experienced the First World War, the German Revolution and the end of the German Empire. And he participated in the establishment of the Weimar Republic.

Troeltsch deals with the issue of Protestantism and politics in two different theoretical contexts. One is sociology and the philosophy of history, and the other is his theological ethics.

Troeltsch's main work, *The Social Teaching of the Christian Churches*, belongs to the former context. In this book he places Lutheran social and political thinking within a comprehensive historical framework. His main thesis on Lutheran political ethics is that in Luther we find a contradiction between two kinds of ethics: the radical ethics based on Jesus' preaching on the one hand, and a natural-rational ethics on the other. The first ethics is personal dispositional (Gesinnungsethik), whereas the second is an ethics for the social world. Troeltsch regards this ethical dualism as a manifestation of a contradiction within the basic religious thought itself, which is irreconcilable with a political sense. In contemporary Lutheranism Troeltsch does not find much potential for contributing to social reform. Its political activity primarily takes place within conservative parties.

According to Troeltsch, Christian ethics is basically a personal ethics of love, founded in the kingdom of God. So there is no Christian political ethics in a straightforward sense. Troeltsch takes four types of secular political ethics into account: nationalism, liberalism, democracy and conservatism. He thinks that Christianity can support both democracy and conservatism. They correspond to two different thoughts in Christianity. One is the idea mentioned above of the individual personality as being devoted to God, which can support the democratic ideas of participation and distributive justice. The other thought is redemption, the picture of the Christian as being freed from the structures of the sinful world, but submitting him or herself to the conditions of the world. This thought supports conservatism in the sense of aristocracy.

Troeltsch sees the time after the First World War as 'planetaric', and as the hour of Christianity. Christians should support an international order based on Western ideas of inalienable human rights and organised within a league of peoples. As a final remark I want to claim that the political theology of Troeltsch is much more fruitful than the ethics of Bonhoeffer. In our situation we have much more to learn from the constructive attempt to unite Protestant Christianity with a democratic order than from a theology of resistance.

Allies for a modernised Lutheranism: John Rawls and Jürgen Habermas

The points made above have shown that there is a line of development in Lutheran theology that differs radically from the degeneration of ordinance theology in 20th century Germany. The compatibility of Lutheran Christianity and democracy was established no less than a hundred years ago. How then can a Lutheran political ethics be developed today? The reconstructive enterprise would have two elements: the presentation of Lutheran theology – and the search for a secular, general theory of the political that is complementary to a Christian ethics of neighbourly love, this theory being interpretable as a natural law theory. I have now come to the latter part. There are of course a number of possible candidates. Luther himself often talks of the utility (Nutzen) of the political order, and one could of course argue that utilitarianism actually corresponds with the basic Lutheran view on secular authority: society could be regarded from the viewpoint of a 'sympathetic observer', who wants the best for all, wishing to fulfil people's needs to the maximum extent. However, my thesis is that John Rawls' theory of justice or political liberalism is a more convincing candidate. Rawls' political philosophy bears many similarities to Jürgen Habermas' Kantian republicanism. I will therefore present the two together and try to make clear the strength of Rawls as compared with Habermas. I shall move in two steps. First, I will sketch the two similar understandings of the democratic political order. And then I will discuss their view on the political role of religion.

According to Habermas, the disagreement with Rawls has the character of a family quarrel. They both take a modern view of the political, i.e. they reject the idea that the basic institutions of society are given by nature or creation. Thus without mentioning it they reject the Lutheran concept of creation ordinances. In addition, both Rawls and Habermas defend a normative understanding of the political as distinct from, say, economic or system theoretical approaches.

The principles of modern democracy

Let us now take a closer look at *John Rawls'* political philosophy. Rawls sees the political as a framework for people's social cooperation to their mutual advantage, and thus rejects the theory of Carl Schmitt, who makes enmity the core political concept. From this starting point, it seems obvious that the main political-ethical problem is the problem of *justice*. According to Rawls, we are to conceive of justice as fairness: justice meaning the fair terms of social cooperation. A concept of justice is necessary for various reasons: people have different interests so conflict lurks, resources are scarce and knowledge is limited. For reasons that I will put aside for the time being, Rawls claims that justice as fairness consists of two basic principles:

1. Each person is to have an equal right to the most extensive basic liberty compatible with a similar liberty for others.
2. Social and economic inequalities are to be arranged so that they are both (a) reasonably expected to be to everyone's advantage [in particular for the worst off members], and (b) attached to positions and offices that are open to all.[5]

Justice as specified in the two principles is a property or virtue of the basic institutions of society such as the constitution, the economic regime and the legal system. Institutions are the subject of justice, because it is they that distribute goods and burdens to citizens. The principles of justice are implemented in the constitution, form the basis of legislation and guide the decisions of administrators and judges. In other words, they form the normative basis of all state powers: the legislative, executive and judicial.

The liberties of the first principle are on one hand individual liberties such as freedom of conscience and thought, the right to hold property, and the freedoms of the rule of law. On the other hand, they also comprise political liberty and freedom of speech and assembly.

As to the second principle, the so-called difference principle, it is important to be aware of Rawls' point of view on material inequality. What is to be distributed is not quantities of 'happiness' or quality of life, but rather what Rawls calls primary social goods, the means every person needs in order to realise his or her individual life plan. These are means like power, opportunity, income and wealth, but also freedoms and rights. Incidentally, some people have debated whether health service should be counted among the primary goods. If we are slightly more concrete, we can see that the inclusion of the difference principle gives Rawls' liberalism the character of social liberalism. The difference principle could be seen as a principle supporting a welfare state.

Citizens in a democratic state regard each other as free and equal. The stability and cohesion of such a state rest not on religious or national unity but on the fact that citizens mutually expect each other to comply with the principles of justice. This mutual expectation creates a bond of civic friendship. As free and equal they all share in the coercive power constitutive of the political order. And they are all entitled to participate in the debate taking place in various public fora.

As a starting point for my sketch of *Jürgen Habermas'* reconstructive picture of the democratic political order, I take his view on human sociality. This is marked by what he calls discursive socialisation (diskursive Vergesellschaftung): the working of a human society rests on features of linguistic communication. The political dimension of sociality is introduced by Habermas via the concept of *law*. The legal system is a crucial condition of social integration – we could also say of social cohesion. Law is marked by the duality that appears in the title of Habermas' main work of political philosophy: *Faktizität und Geltung*, facticity and validity. Legal norms are enforced on

---

5   Of the various formulations of the principles, see Rawls, *Theory* 1999a, 53, for instance.

us as a matter of fact, but they also presuppose that we rationally comply with their legitimacy or validity. Like Rawls, Habermas sees citizens in a democratic society as free and equal; and from these properties, together with the fact of discursive socialisation and the medium of law, he develops a system of rights that can be seen as a parallel to Rawls' two principles of justice. Habermas orders the basic rights (Grundrechte) into five groups: (1) Individual or subjective liberty rights; (2) Rights of citizenship; (3) Rights of the rule of law/due process; (4) Rights of political participation; (5) Rights of life conditions that secure equal exploitation of the first four groups of rights. Roughly, we could parallel these first four groups with Rawls' first principle, and the fifth group with Rawls' second, the difference principle.

Now, one very essential claim in Habermas is that in democracy there is a necessary connection between liberty rights and participation rights, between individual and collective autonomy. A state marked by the rule of law (Rechtsstaat) is not only a state that grants its citizens the rights of individual freedom. It is also a state where citizens – via their rights of political participation – are the collective author of the law. Or, as Habermas also puts it, in a democratic state there is an essential link between human rights and sovereignty of the people. The two are co-original, gleichursprünglich. In mentioning the state I have indicated that according to Habermas the state with its coercive power is necessary in order to sustain the legal system. But the political power is subject to the law, as the exercise of political power has to follow legal rules. And again, in order to be legitimate in the democratic sense, the legal rules for the exercise of political power originate in the collective autonomy of the citizens.

Habermas emphasises the participation of citizens in the political process more than Rawls does. This process has the character of communication, and through deliberation, debate etc. communication creates its own form of power. Communicative power is distinct from political power in the ordinary sense – what Habermas calls administrative power. But in deliberative democracy communicative power is channelled into the system of administrative power via the medium of law. The creation of communicative power takes place in *civil society*, which is in turn closely linked to the so-called *life-world*, which also consists of culture and structures of personality. Popularly speaking, the life-world is where ordinary people lead their ordinary lives. It is in the life-world that the effects of political decisions are experienced, and it is important that these effects are fed into the political communicative process so that they can influence political decisions in legislation and administration.

The political discourse has a threefold character: it includes pragmatic, ethical-political and moral arguments. One example of the pragmatic aspect is the negotiation process involved in finalising the state budget. The meaning of the ethical-political has to do with Habermas' distinction between ethics and morality. Ethics consists of the norms and values of a particular community, its tradition, culture and identity. So political-ethical arguments answer the question: how do we as a community organise ourselves? One example of this aspect is a decision taken in order to protect the Danish language. Morality, on the other hand, consists of universal norms and principles such as the prohibition of torture. Habermas' emphasis on citizens' participation gives his understanding of democracy a more republican than liberal stamp – republican in the sense of citizens forming a political community. The republican interpretation is also connected with Habermas' emphasis on the ethical aspect of politics, the fact that a political and legal order is embedded in a particular community.

One essential aspect of the communicative political process is that it takes place in the *public*. Referred to by metaphors like 'forum', 'arena', 'stage' (and 'square'), the public is where every citizen is entitled to take part in the political process of forming meaning and will. The public in this sense is distinct from the institutionalised political process, which involves parliamentary debate and decisions among other things. I will return to this later.

Both Rawls and Habermas also deal with international politics, and they both take a liberal as opposed to a realist position. Let me just mention a few of the points made by Rawls, based on his book *The Law of Peoples*. As to international politics, Rawls wants to reformulate Kant's view in *Vom ewigen Frieden* (On Perpetual Peace). He extends the contract theory from individuals to peoples, thus reaching a number of well-known principles such as independence of peoples, equality, self-defence, non-intervention and human rights. In the first place these principles are formulated for liberal peoples. But Rawls wants to include some non-liberal peoples as well, viz. those he calls 'decent'. Decent peoples may be hierarchically organised – they do not necessarily grant equality to all religions, and they only endorse some human rights.

Finally, both Rawls and Habermas regard pluralism as an essential fact about modern democracy, but this fact has very different consequences in their theories. And this is where I turn to the second point: the role of religion within the democratic order.

The role of religion

In Rawls, the fact of pluralism causes a significant change in his theory, something which is revealed in the difference between his two main works, *A Theory of Justice* and *Political Liberalism*. Rawls bases his theory on the assumption that moral and political agents are rational persons, or better: they are persons endowed with two 'moral powers': a conception of their own good – and a sense of justice. The question for such persons is: how can it be justified that these two principles of justice should guide political cooperation? Rawls answers by creating two devices for rational justification, viz. the original position and reflective equilibrium. I will not go further into this now. But granted these means of justification, we can imagine an ideal situation where all members of society reach a state of equilibrium in which the two principles of justice are rationally accepted by all. This would constitute a normative consensus, and would largely contribute to social stability. In *A Theory of Justice*, Rawls calls this situation one of a well-ordered society.

But this is where a number of problems appear. In order for the idea of a well-ordered society to be realistic, Rawls' theory about persons as rational and moral agents has to be true. In other words, a specific philosophical doctrine about the character of human beings, of social acting etc. is supposed to be true. Such a doctrine is what Rawls calls a comprehensive doctrine, because it comprehends all important aspects of human life and the world. Religions are obvious instances of comprehensive doctrines.

But as mentioned above, modern societies are pluralistic not least in the sense that their members adhere to different comprehensive doctrines. According to Rawls, this pluralism is not an anomaly – on the contrary: given freedom of thought and religion, a pluralism of comprehensive doctrines is unavoidable. Rawls' reason for taking this view is his understanding of the very nature of comprehensive doctrines. A key concept in this respect is the *burdens of judgment*. The burdens of judgment are a number of factors lying behind *reasonable disagreement*. In many cases, Rawls claims, disagreement cannot be explained by lack of insight, dominance of prejudices etc. in some of the disagreeing parties. Rather, there are a number of limitations to our knowledge: complex and conflicting evidence, uncertainty about the weight of different considerations, vagueness of concepts, the influence of a person's whole experience and life for his or her judgment etc. One place where the burdens of judgment are obvious is comprehensive doctrines. This means that

… many of our most important judgments are made under conditions where it is not to be expected that conscientious persons with full powers of reason, even after free discussion, will all arrive at the same conclusion (Rawls 1996, 58).

If a comprehensive doctrine is adhered to in acceptance of the burdens of judgment, Rawls calls it a reasonable doctrine. So here we have a new aspect of human reason. By reasonableness Rawls means on the one hand the readiness to propose and adhere to fair terms of cooperation, provided that others do the same. This aspect of reasonableness we could call reciprocity. But on the other hand, a person is reasonable if he or she accepts the burdens of judgment. The second aspect means that reasonable adherents of comprehensive doctrines or adherents of reasonable doctrines accept the freedom of religion. In other words, even if they are convinced that their own doctrine is true they regard it as unacceptable to use political power to force their doctrine upon others.

Adherents of reasonable doctrines are also reasonable in the sense that they endorse the principles of justice as principles for their political life. And they endorse them not as a kind of modus vivendi or compromise, but because the principles are founded within the doctrines themselves. If the reasonable doctrines represented in a society all endorse the principles of justice, the result is what Rawls calls an overlapping consensus. The consensus is overlapping in the sense that the principles of justice only form one part of the normative content of the comprehensive doctrines. Probably the most important parts cover the non-political aspects of life. The attitude of religious citizens is thus marked by a dualism: their worldview consists of both a publicly recognised conception of justice, and their religion as a comprehensive doctrine (Op.cit., 38).

In the mature theory of *Political Liberalism*, then, the principles of justice are on the one hand justified because they are supported by a number of reasonable comprehensive doctrines – but on the other hand, according to Rawls they are 'freestanding'.

The picture emerging above may be surprising to some, because it portrays Rawls as being much more open and affirmative towards religion than is normally assumed. It is a widespread perception that Rawls is a restrictive secular hardliner, whereas Habermas is more open towards religion. In order to make this clear, we have to look at the way the two think about the public.

In *Rawls* the concept of the public appears in at least three forms: (i) the publicity condition, (ii) the public forum and (iii) public reason.

(i)   The principles of justice are subject to a *publicity condition* in the sense that citizens know that others obey the same principles. The principles of justice are essentially

… conceptions of justice as publicly acknowledged and fully effective moral constitutions of social life (Rawls 1999a, 133).

(ii) The *public forum* is important in different ways. It is a necessary condition for political participation. The first principle of justice includes a principle of (equal) participation, and this requires:

If the public forum is to be free and open to all, and in continuous session, everyone should be able to make use of it (Op.cit., 225).

Also, by definition civil disobedience is a manifestation occurring in the public forum, which is why it is essential that it is understood (Op. cit., 376)

And finally, *self-respect*, regarded by Rawls as a basic social good,

… is secured by the public affirmation of the status of equal citizenship for all (Op. cit. 545).

So far the meaning of 'public' is something like: known by all citizens. Public is a feature of the status of citizenship and of mutuality.

(iii) But we probably find a more important aspect of the public in Rawls in his concept *public reason*. Habermas translates this into 'öffentlicher Gebrauch der Vernunft'. But this, I think, is misleading. What Rawls means by public reason corresponds less with the German 'Öffentlichkeit' or the Danish 'offentlighed', and more with 'die öffentliche Hand' ('det offentlige' in Danish). This should become clear through Rawls' own explanation.

A political society always has a reason in the sense of a formulation of plans and priorities of aims and decisions. Public reason exists in a democratic society, in persons who share the status of equal citizenship. The content of public reason is the principles of justice. How does public reason differ from the publicity condition and the public forum?

[The idea of public reason] is a view about the kind of reasons on which citizens are to rest their political cases in making their political justifications to one another when they support laws and policies that invoke coercive powers of government concerning fundamental political questions (Rawls 1999b, 165f).

Public reason, then, concerns constitutional essentials and basic justice, items typically dealt with by the Supreme Court. More broadly public reason is exercised by judges, legislators, members of government and candidates for political offices. But importantly, public reason is also exercised by citizens who place themselves in such roles. So public reason is closely connected with democratic legitimacy and reciprocity:

Our exercise of political power is proper only when we sincerely believe that the reasons we would offer for our political actions – were we to state them as government officials – are sufficient, and we also think that other citizens might also reasonably accept those reasons (Op. cit., 137).

It is in relation to public reason that Rawls places relatively strict restrictions on religion. Religions and other comprehensive doctrines claim to possess the whole truth, but

Political liberalism views this insistence on the whole truth in politics as incompatible with democratic citizenship and the idea of legitimate law (Op. cit., 138).

This does not mean that every appeal to comprehensive doctrines is excluded from public reason. Such appeals are acceptable under the proviso that we are later able to give public reasons.

We may think of the reasonable comprehensive doctrines that support society's reasonable political conceptions as those conceptions' vital social basis, giving them enduring strength and vigor. When these doctrines accept the proviso and only then come into public debate, the commitment to constitutional democracy is publicly manifested (Op. cit., 153f).

Rawls emphasises that public reason is something quite different from the public sphere as part of the 'background culture' of civil society. Public reason is secular – not as an expression of a secular comprehensive doctrine, but rather as a purely political conception.

Habermas' considerations about the public take place against the background of the thorough analysis of the genesis of the concept, presented in *Strukturwandel*

der Öffentlichkeit. Here he points out the seeming paradox that the civic public was constituted by private persons. The concept emerged in the 18th century, i.e. during absolutism. The civic public was marked by equality, and it was a counter-concept to the representative public of monarchy. In absolutism political authority and publicity are not connected – on the contrary, in fact.

In the first place, civic publicity is literary – but it becomes political by subjecting the use of power to public critique. So in the last resort democratic rule is prepared:

In der bürgerlichen Öffentlichkeit entfaltet sich ein politisches Bewusstsein, das gegen die absolute Herrschaft den Begriff und die Forderung genereller und abstrakter Gesetze artikuliert, und schließlich auch sich selbst, nämlich öffentliche Meinung, als die einzig legitime Quelle dieser Gesetze zu behaupten lernt (Habermas 1971, 72).

Returning to *Faktizität und Geltung*, an important difference from Rawls is that Habermas makes a clear distinction between administrative and communicative power, and correspondingly between parliamentary opinion formation and opinion formation in the political public open to all. The communication structure of the public is relieved from decision making, as this is reserved for decision-making institutions.

Gegen die Verselbständigung illegitimer Macht dient … nur eine misstrauische, mobile, wache und informierte Öffentlichkeit, die auf den parlamentarischen Komplex einwirkt und auf den *Entstehungsbedingen legitimen Rechts* beharrt (Habermas 1992, 532).

'Öffentlichkeit' watches and influences the genesis of legitimate law, but it does not take part in the process proper. That is left – so I would express it – to 'die öffentliche Hand'.

In the more recent book *Zwischen Naturalismus und Religion* Habermas takes a more positive stand towards religion than in his earlier writings. As freedom of religion supports religious forms of life, all believers cannot be expected to justify their political opinion independently of religious convictions. This strict requirement is only valid for politicians. At the institutional level authority has to be neutral as to its worldview – this is the basis of the separation between state and church. But this principle cannot be transferred to the opinion of citizens and organisations in the political public. That would be 'eine säkularistische Überverallgemeinerung'.

Aus dem säkularen Charakter der Staatsgewalt ergibt sich nicht für jeden Staatsbürger persönlich die unmittelbare Verpflichtung, öffentlich geäusserte religiöse Überzeugungen durch Äquivalente in einer allgemein zugänglichen Sprache zu ergänzen (Habermas 2005, 134).

According to Habermas, there is an institutional threshold between the informal public on the one hand and parliaments, courts, ministries and administrations on the other. It is within the latter that only secular reasons count. Habermas rejects Rawls' proviso: religious communities must not be deprived of their courage to voice themselves politically. Otherwise there is a risk of cutting secular society off from 'wichtigen Ressourcen der Sinnstiftung'. Secular citizens can learn from religious contributions, e.g. by recognising in the normative truth content of religious statements 'eigene, manchmal verschüttete Intuitionen'.

I want to conclude this section on religion and politics with the following observation. Rawls and Habermas do not disagree on the legitimacy of religious arguments in relation to political decisions. Rather, they draw the line between justifying political decisions and stating political opinions differently. In Rawls, not only officials like parliamentarians and judges justify political decisions – we all do when we justify the use of coercive political power. In such cases we make use of public reason. In Habermas, ordinary citizens argue politically only in the informal public. As Rawls notes: "The public reason of political liberalism may be confused with Habermas' public square but they are not the same." (Rawls 1996, 382).

Conclusion

In conclusion, I should like to briefly justify my claim that political liberalism as formulated by John Rawls is the most appropriate ally for a Lutheran political ethics suitable for a democratic political culture.

Rawls' principles of justice are an interpretation of democratic society that is compatible with a Lutheran political ethics. The two principles define the justice-counterpart of Christian love; neighbours are translated into fellow citizens.

Rawls' concept of overlapping consensus is analogous to Luther's distinction between the two kingdoms. The distinction between comprehensive doctrine and the political corresponds to Luther's distinction between spiritual and secular. The limitation of the political is crucial to Lutheran Christianity.

Rawls' concept of public reason draws a clear line for the legitimacy of religious arguments without excluding religion from the so-called public square.

Bibliography

Grotius, Hugo 1963. *The law of war and peace / De Jure Belli ac Pacis Libri Tres* (Transl. by Francis W. Kelsey). Indinapolis, New York: Bobbs-Merrill.

Grundtvig, N.F.S. 1847. 'Folkelighed og Christendom'. In: *Dansk Kirketidende* 107.

Habermas, Jürgen 1971. *Strukturwandel der Öffentlichkeit. Untersuchungen zu einer Kategorie der bürgerlichen Gesellschaft*. München: Luchterhand.

Habermas, Jürgen 1992. *Faktizität und Geltung. Beiträge zur Diskurstheorie des Rechts und des demokratischen Rechtsstaats*. Frankfurt/M.: Suhrkamp Verlag.

Habermas, Jürgen 2005. *Zwischen Naturalismus und Religion. Philosophische Aufsätze*. Frankfurt/M: Suhrkamp.

Hemmingsen, Niels 1993. *Om Naturens Lov 1562. 3. Del oversat og med forord og noter ved Richard Mott. Indledning af Alex Wittendorff*. Forlaget Øresund.

Henrich, Dieter 1976. 'Die Grundstruktur der modernen Philosophie'. In: H. Ebeling (Hg.): *Subjektivität und Selbsterhaltung. Beiträge zur Diagnose der Moderne.* Frankfurt/ M.: Suhrkamp Verlag.

Kant, Immanuel 1795. *Zum ewigen Frieden. Ein philosophischer Entwurf.* Königsberg: Friedrich Nicolovius.

Kant, Immanuel 1797. *Die Metaphysik der Sitten in zwey Theilen.* Königsberg: Friedrich Nicolovius.

Kierkegaard, Søren 1978. *Two ages: the age of revolution and the present age: a literary review* (Ed. and transl. with introduction and notes by Howard V. Hong and Edna H. Hong). Princeton, N.J.: Princeton Univ. Press.

Luther, Martin 1900. *Von weltlicher Obrigkeit. Wie weit man ihr Gehorsam sei* (D. Martin Luthers Werke. Kritische Gesammtausgabe. 11. Band). Weimar: Hermann Böhlaus Nachfolger.

Martensen, Hans L. 1878. *Den christelige Ethik. Den specielle Deel. Anden Afdeling: Den sociale Ethik.* Copenhagen: Gyldendalske Boghandel.

Rawls, John 1996. *Political Liberalism.* New York: Columbia University Press.

Rawls, John 1999a. *A Theory of Justice. Revised Edition.* Cambridge Mass.: The Belknap Press of Harvard University Press.

Rawls, John 1999b. *The Law of Peoples with "The Idea of Public Reason Revisited".* Cambridge Mass.: Harvard University Press.

Troeltsch, Ernst 1904. *Politische Ethik und Christentum.* Göttingen: Vandenhoeck & Ruprecht.

Troeltsch, Ernst 1994. Die *Soziallehren der christlichen Kirchen und Gruppen* (Neudruck der Ausgabe Tübingen 1912). Tübingen: J.C.B. Mohr.

FOUCAULT AND HABERMAS

THE DILEMMA OF POWER VS. RATIONALITY

Lars Albinus

Introduction

In this article I shall view the topic of 'religion in the public sphere' from a perspective of rationality and power. In order to reach this point, however, I will present a range of thoughts from the works of Michel Foucault and Jürgen Habermas, which will take up some space. I can only ask the reader to bear with me, as I hope this detour will pay off in the end.

In the year of 1983, Foucault and Habermas both agreed to participate in a conference on the theme of modernity. Foucault had some reservations, confessing that he was unsure what modernity really meant, but he was intrigued to engage in a dialogue with Habermas upon the matter. Actually, they had met earlier in Paris, where they had the opportunity to engage in some undisturbed conversation, and by the end of the day they had made quite an impression on one another (Miller, 1993, 338f). Still, Habermas was more than reluctant to appreciate the advantages of Foucault's view on history, philosophy and rationality. In Habermas' view, Foucault's approach was quasi-metaphysical and crypto-normative in a way that invited to subjectivism and relativism (Habermas 1985, 279-343). Foucault was more appreciative of Habermas' ideas, although he felt that the theory of communicative action included a utopian view of the absence of power (Foucault 1988, 18). Actually, Foucault fully agreed on the importance of ongoing dialogue, 'the serious play of questions and answers' (1997, 111), and even regarded this as the only way to minimise the dangerous influence of power relations. Habermas, on the other hand, came to appreciate, albeit with some unresolved reservations, the unsettling power of Foucault's critique and his attempt to unmask various delusions of rationalising self-consciousness (Habermas 1994, 149-154). This, however, was first acknowledged in the form of an obituary. In the end Foucault died in June 1984, and the proposed conference on modernity never took place.

Instead, books and other conferences on what came to be known as the Foucault-Habermas-debate replaced the real encounter (*Critique and Power,* 1994; *Foucault contra Habermas,* 1999). Notwithstanding the general quality of the many contributions to this 'debate', it is of course regrettable that the two philosophers never confronted each other in a real-life debate. In spite of differences which would probably always have been insurmountable, they would at least have had the chance to demonstrate the importance of open and ongoing dialogue as well as having the opportunity to clear up some misunderstandings which apparently hampered their understanding of each other. In fact, Habermas did not opt for a utopian ideal, as Foucault claimed, although it is true that – to this day – he insists on the anticipation of uncoerced dialogue as implicitly present in any communicative event which is actually communicative and not merely strategic. On the other hand, Foucault did not present any theory of power or believe that truth could be reduced to power as Habermas seemed to believe; although it is correct to say that in Foucault's eyes power is everywhere and that it can be dangerous to overlook it under the guise of rationality – particularly if this is done due to sheer self-complacency.

Foucault and Habermas both thought of the modern role of the philosopher as a modest one within the bounds of post-metaphysical thinking, and they both agreed on the obligation to speak the truth against the manifestations of power. The essential difference between Foucault's and Habermas' views on modern philosophy concerned the notion of rationality and consequently the means of critique.

In the following, I will try to elucidate some of the implications of this important disagreement. But instead of trying to resolve obvious tensions, which may indeed be a hopeless task anyway, and instead of hailing one or the other as the winner in a ghostly performance of a virtual dialogue, I will try to bring some basic critical insights from each one to bear on the other. If this sounds rather dialectical, I might add before proceeding that I do not by any means count on any final synthesis which would (incidentally) make both of them fall flat. Rather, I am going to suggest some critical remarks regarding the general outlook of Habermas' and Foucault's thinking, remarks which will hopefully have their own critical potential.

As stated at the outset, the focus of the juxtaposition will be 'religion in the public sphere' or, expressing this more generally, religion in modernity. Apart from giving away my main field of interest in the current global situation, this subject matter also leads us into the Foucault-Habermas debate through an angle that has been missed in most of the discussion. This may of course be due to the fact that neither of them was especially interested in religion, at least until late in Foucault's work, and now, as it appears, in the latest works of Habermas. Still, questions pertaining to religion actually permeated both of their works from beginning to end. The intention here is not to follow the trails of these questions systematically, but only to highlight the fact that the reality of 'religion', at least as a social phenomenon, certainly has an implicit and explicit influence on Foucault's as well as Habermas' view on modernity, rationality and power.

Rationality

The intention here is not to delve into the profound theory of communicative action that Habermas has gradually evolved and revised continuously over the years. I can only pinpoint a few important aspects of what Rawls even takes to be a 'comprehensive doctrine' on rationality in Habermas' work (Rawls 1996, 376). However, far from being due to a doctrine, in Habermas' own eyes his notion of rationality, which is intimately related to his notions of 'discourse' and 'communicative action', is developed from a laborious reconstruction of the historical and pragmatic possibilities of coming to a mutual understanding. Even so, what makes the comprehensive notion of rationality *look* like a doctrine is the fact that it is thought to pervade, implicitly or not, the communicative aspects of our whole life-world (*Lebenswelt*), and that it is thus claimed to abridge, as a matter of principle, the differences between the objective, the social (or intersubjective) and the subjective world which make up the three dimensions of a modern worldview in western communities. Consequently, the possibility of post-metaphysical claims to rationality, which is derived from this reconstruction, folds back upon itself in so far as the reconstruction itself must claim to be rational. Indeed, Habermas calls his own method a 'rational reconstruction' (*rationale Nachkonstruktion*); being conscious of the fallible premises of post-metaphysical thinking, he has given up the claim to any 'final justification' (*Letztbegründung*). So his theory of communicative action can only be regarded as a *reconstruction* of the premises that makes this action basically rational inasmuch as the means of reaching a 'mutual understanding' (*Einverständnis*) in questions of validity are shown to be implicit in the social function of language. In other words, the rational premises cannot be regarded as transcendental in the strong Kantian sense, but stand rather as anticipations extracted from a practice we are already part of as historical and social beings.

Habermas' notion of rationality is strong in the sense that he regards any given speech act as basically oriented towards mutual understanding, thus implicitly committing the speaker to be prepared to give reasons for its validity. This means that any speech act which is *not* directed at mutual understanding due to the possibility of raising validity questions is seen as violating the basic principle of language as a means of social interaction. It goes without saying that this does not imply a view of real-life communicative action as being perpetual discussions of validity claims. Most of the time our mutual understanding pertaining to speech acts passes unnoticed and unquestioned. However, the option of raising claims to validity is always present due to the grammar and nature of linguistic exchange. Every speaker implicitly takes upon herself an obligation to redeem claims of validity insofar as they may be raised against the speech act in question. By raising such claims the unproblematic communicative action turns into discourse, that is a confrontation of views which can only be *rationally* resolved by means of a dialogue in which it is presupposed that both partakers have an equal right to participate freely by submitting arguments to the discussion *and* that both partakers are willing to surrender to the better argument.

As this theory of communicative action concerns the formal conditions of reaching a mutual understanding, no scientific or moral theory can be deduced from it. In other words: Habermas renounces any substantial notion of rationality in order to insist – all the more forcefully – upon its procedural character and the indispensability of argumentation in matters of disagreement. Among the three types of validity claims,[1] how-

---

1   There are actually four, namely 1) understandability, 2) objective truth, 3) normative rightness and 4) authenticity pertaining to the following performatives: 1) kommunikativa, 2) konstativa, 3) repräsentativa, 4) regulativa, cf. Habermas, 1972, 111. 'Kommunikativa', however, serve to announce the pragmatic meaning of the utterance, whereas the others transgress the level of the utterance by presenting validity pretensions for the coordination of acts. Later on, as in his *Theory of the Communicative Action*, 1981, Habermas leaves out the 'kommunikativa' in his focus on the pragmatic conditions of these pretensions and the concomitant option of raising claims to their redemption.

ever, only two (statements regarding objective and social matters) are apt for discursive approval. When it comes to matters of the subjective world (experiences, feeling, values etc.), the pertaining validity claims are of a different nature. Statements about the physical world can be either true or false; moral statements about social, political and legal affairs can be either right or wrong; and the crucial point of justification can in both cases proceed discursively without semantic ambiguity. Subjective statements, on the other hand, implying the two other worlds and yet irreducible to them, can be sincere or insincere, honest or dishonest, authentic or untrustworthy, but this may very well escape transparency in any immediate discursive testing. Still, in so far as all speech acts, in Habermas' eyes, are intersubjective propositions or *offers* that surrender themselves to yes- or no-commitments on the part of the addressee, subjective statements can render themselves untrustworthy for various reasons, for instance if they do not seem to reflect implied consequences by way of action. They thus become suspicious regarding their authenticity and may eventually lose their appeal to any rational acknowledgement; and rational acknowledgement, so Habermas insists, *stands* as intrinsically linked to linguistically mediated coordination of acts among social agents.

The three types of validity claims: 1) the assertive, 2) the normative and 3) the expressive, regarding for instance 1) statements about objective reality, 2) statements about social reality, and finally 3) statements about subjective reality, reflect the consciousness of a post-traditional society inasmuch as no mythical or theological worldview can any longer identify 'the true' with 'the good' and 'the beautiful' other than within closed worldviews isolated from the general appeals to justification. The threefold dimension of our modern worldview is also reflected in general from Kant to Weber and Piaget, to name just a few of the authors who have had a great influence on Habermas' own thinking. Generally, this differentiation has been seen as: 1) making the physical reality of causality a subject matter for science, 2) making the social world of normative relations a subject matter for politics, morality and religion, and 3) making the subjective world a subject matter for art and personal lifestyles. For Habermas, though, the consequence of post-metaphysical thinking must be that religion can no longer claim any special authority in matters of normative validity. Questions of justice cannot be resolved by referring to traditional law or ethics as induced by revelation. Enhancing the Kantian ethics to include the free rational agreement of all who are involved by a moral judgment, Habermas shows how the linguistic turn must revise our notion of rationality to pertain not to the rational faculty of the human subject in and by itself, but to the use of linguistic, intersubjective means of reaching agreement. As a result, questions of morality can only appeal to the 'court of reason' in the community of competent speakers, and no longer to tradition as such, that is, traditional norms which are not at the same time acknowledged as rationally justifiable (and criticisable) validity claims. Thus, along the lines of Hegel's distinction between *Moralität* and *Sittlichkeit*, Habermas must insist on a difference between morality and ethics, in so far as questions of morality deal with justice and are universal in their pretensions; whereas questions of ethics (including religion) can only be judged within the confines of a community whose identity is formed by a particular historical background. In practice (and in this respect the similarity with Hegel falls short), this entails that if matters of evaluation regarding the good life (or the 'true existence of man' in terms of religion) come into conflict with matters of right and wrong in a legal sense (i.e. due to the common law), the moral judgment has the priority over the ethical stance. Thus, to put it rather briefly, Habermas clearly distances himself from neo-aristotelian or neo-wittgensteinian attempts to bring questions of norms and values on an equal footing. We shall return to the distinction between morality and ethics later, but for now a few words are needed by way of concluding this short exposition of Habermas' notion of rationality.

Habermas regards language as a means of communication which is primarily oriented towards reaching an understanding and only secondarily a tool to be used strategically. In other words, the use of language for a teleological purpose, where the addressee is treated as a mere object for the speaker's own interest, already implies the successful workings of a communicative action. A lie, for instance, depends upon communicative appreciation on the part of the addressee and is therefore strategic and parasitic. Habermas thus holds that communicative action is basic and that strategic action is parasitic. Before we can treat each other as objects for our own purpose, we must take an intersubjective attitude towards the other partaker in linguistic exchange for the sake of successful communication. Obviously, this crucial point in Habermas' theory reflects Kant's famous distinction between 'means' and 'purpose'[2], the difference being that Habermas does not pretend to speak in terms of deontology, but in terms of formal pragmatics. In this respect, Habermas' notion of rationality is, in some crucial respects, at odds with Foucault's.

Before turning to Foucault's notion of power, which also reveals his notion of rationality, it can be said that 'rationality', for Foucault, is interesting not due to its purely formal aspects but rather as a situated practice, that is, a regime of rules which determines, in the very possibility of a discursive event, what can count as true or false. In other words: Rationality, in Foucault's eyes, is either instrumentally linked to a discourse formation of possible utterances, or a way of rationalising what has already been said and done, which is, in principle, one and the same thing. In Foucault's view, to use language for the purpose of communication is always to be part of a particular game that you cannot hope to escape, but merely to change from within by playing it differently, that is, strategically, in order to keep relations of power from turning into a structure of dominance.

In Habermas' view, to use language for the purpose of communication is to engage in social life in a way that enables us to coordinate our actions by rational commitments (instead of merely subjecting each other to random power claims). In some respects this view of language can be said to reflect the pragmatics of the later Wittgenstein. A

---

2   The practical imperative thus sounds: 'Handle so, dass du die Menschheit sowohl in deiner Person, als in der Person eines jeden andern jederzeit zugleich als Zweck, niemals bloss als Mittel braucht.' GzMdS, 429.

crucial breach appears, however, when Habermas takes pains to extract the process of coming to a mutual understanding *from* the very use of language. As Nigel Pleasants has pointed out: "Wittgenstein's point is that people agree in what they do with language, but it is absurd to think that they must somehow *reach* an agreement/understanding *before* they can mean anything" (Pleasants, 1999, 160). Not surprisingly, though not entirely fairly, this comment is directed against Habermas' view of language. In linguistic communication, so Habermas says, we do not present each other with statements or meanings before anything else, but with proposals for the validity of statements or meanings (Habermas 1999, 176). In other words, Habermas seems anxious to identify, pragmatically, a notion of meaning with a notion of (communicative) rationality. To understand linguistic meaning is to understand what it takes to redeem validity claims which are either implicitly or explicitly present in a given proposition. The notion of speech and mutual understanding can only be interpreted interchangeably (1981, I, 387).

The question is, however, if this is as obvious as it may sound. Without being able to fully justify my view on the matter here, I would like to draw attention to a distinction between understanding a proposition – whether its validity claims can be redeemed or not – and understanding a proposal. A speech act which sets forth a power claim is just as much an illocutionary act as a speech act which implies a normative commitment (such as a promise). For Habermas the power claim fails as an illocutionary act inasmuch as it will take extra-linguistic sanctions to make it work (1981, I, 403f). This may be very true in so far as communication is directed towards coordination of actions, but not in the case of understanding the utterance as such. Making an utterance (*locution*), however, is by itself an action directed towards understanding, albeit not a mutual understanding in the rational sense of being prepared to offer a justification for a normative implication. The point is, however, that nothing forces us to presuppose such an implication if we accept that communication (in its basic functionalistic sense) is not exclusively directed towards normative 'Einverständnis', but towards the understanding of power claims as well. The lie may indeed be parasitic; the forthright power claim, however, may not. This leads us, naturally, to deal more systematically with the notion of power.

Power

For Habermas, power is due to teleological or strategic action and thus mediates the will and intention of the subject. In this respect, Habermas' notion of power seems to concord with the sociological outlook of Max Weber and Talcott Parsons. On the other hand, he is appreciative of Hannah Arendt's attempt to understand power as different from violence and force in the sense that power presupposes the capability of acting collectively by communicating subjects. Still, Habermas' theory of communicative action departs from the Aristotelian comprehension of action and *phronesis* which form the background for this notion of power. Power, in Habermas' formal pragmatics, pertains first and foremost to 'a power claim'. As such it denotes the position of an individual will.

Foucault came to his notion of power in the early seventies, inspired by Nietzsche's 'genealogy'. But instead of repeating a basically romantic notion of power as being due to a blind and unrestrained will to live, Foucault detaches it from the position of the individual subject and relocates it within the practical reality of social relations. Thus, power in Foucault's eyes no longer has a subject. Instead, he sees it as a vitality of strategic efforts, even as a microphysics of force relations. In his works on the birth of the prison (1975) and the history of sexuality (1976), power is basically bio-power, i.e., disciplinary techniques enacted over the body as a means of control and producing the (sexual, working, speaking) subject within a certain regime of truth. Later, in the final studies of 'the history of sexuality', which in reality became a history of 'the technologies of the Self' (Foucault 1984a; 1984b), Foucault reached a notion of power which no longer focused directly on force, but rather on a creative and formative potential, that is, power as mechanisms in forming one's life. The condition of possibility for power, Foucault now said, is freedom. Relations of power can only take hold within various possibilities for action. Thus, power is 'a set of actions upon other actions' (1983, 220).

Habermas takes Foucault's notion of power to betray a transcendental-genealogical historiography which aims to be pure description *as well as* a theory of constitution (Habermas 1985, 317). Thus by having the formation of power and the formation of knowledge composing an indissoluble unity ('unauflösliche einheit', op.cit. 320), Foucault has given up the ground from which it would be possible to meet a truth claim or even to answer a question about the motivation for resisting or criticising power in the first place. Thus, Foucault's genealogy or analytics of power ends in relativism and arbitrary partisanship similar to the philosophical enterprise of Nietzsche (op.cit. 324).

I will not deny the force of Habermas' critical arguments, but only suggest that they may not have captured all, or even the most important, connotations of Foucault's notion of power. First of all, it has to be stated against Habermas that Foucault did not intend to put forward a theory of power. It is not correct to claim that Foucault used the notion of power as a transcendental ground for describing relations between the production of truth and the practice, on a societal level, of dealing with insanity, criminality and sexuality. Rather, Foucault intended to describe the way in which a certain prevailing knowledge of the subject was produced within various disciplinary practices. He firmly states that it has never been his intention to reduce truth to power, which would have been ridiculous, but to understand, by way of careful and patient description, the relation between power and the practice of truth (Foucault 1988, 16; 1989, 444f; 462; 1994, 132f). Foucault was not interested in formal conditions of possibility for making a truth claim, but in the concrete effects of a 'discourse of truth' brought to its practical use. With respect to Habermas' idea of a communicative practice, Foucault was reluctant to buy into the possibility of conditions outside the grip of power, which may be seen as a logical consequence of the empirical outlook of his own notion of power. Foucault intends to describe 'what happens' (1983, 217), not to make a strong claim about the constitution of 'actions upon other actions'. Foucault hunts down any kind of historical self-rationalisation that cannot be shown to have been the only and necessary way of dealing with certain problems (as concerning madness, law-breaking and sexual behaviour); but he is not claiming that he can use a theory of power to *explain* what has been going on. It is unfortunate that we read, in Foucault's own text, that "each society has its regime of truth, its 'general politics' of truth" (1977, 131), if this is taken to mean that there is no truth without politics, for this would be the very reduction of truth to power which he has firmly disclaimed. What it means can only be that in social reality the production of truth is always involved with practical matters and political decisions, in fact with power, and that every society produces 'games of truth' in striving to establish hegemony (to speak in the vein of Gramsci). The driving force of Foucault's genealogical investigations is, as I see it, the conviction that this state of affairs needs our constant vigilance if we are to minimise the relations of power and prevent them from hardening into die-hard positions of dominance.

Habermas holds fast to a notion of power as that by which the subject has an effect on objects in successful actions (1985, 323), and claims that Foucault does not escape this kind of philosophical outlook (which resides unknowingly in a philosophy of the subject) merely by reversing power's truth-dependency (*Wahrheitsabhängigkeit*) into a power-dependency (*Machtabhängigkeit*) of truth (ibid.). But this power-dependency, which is indeed salient in Foucault's historical investigations, has to be appreciated in a specific context and not as a matter of principle. Furthermore, Foucault would not subscribe to Habermas' notion of power as resulting from the relation between subject and object, but rather as resulting from social relations as such. If Foucault actually succeeds, genealogically, in describing the effects of power without recourse to the will or intention of a subject, as strategies of exclusion (e.g. in cases of institutional confinement), then the accusation of buying unknowingly into a philosophy of the subject seems far-fetched.

I therefore suggest we appreciate the constructive element in Foucault's empirical notion of power-relations-as-*effects* (which does not imply a metaphysical notion of power). But it remains to be said that he owes us more than a simplistic notion of rationality as being just a generic term for concrete cases of rationalisation. In fact, no reader would be able to appreciate the critical impact of his genealogical research if it didn't appeal to standards of rationality that went beyond sheer rationalisation. In effect, Foucault draws on the communicative potential of rationality which is, at the same time, excised from the picture by his genealogical manoeuvres. Thus, by digging genealogically into a history of rationality, Foucault has paid the price of justificatory illegitimacy on a *general* level. Ultimately, whether one can live with this or not may be a matter of philosophical taste and temperament.

The strong justificatory claim has, at any rate, been given up by Habermas as well. Indeed the validity of his theory of communicative action does not even pertain to its own claims. Taken as a whole, the theory cannot be judged as being true, right or authentic, but must (merely) appeal to a criterion of plausibility. As long as no better alternative is offered, however, the theory stands. It goes without saying that a 'theory of power', accused of performative self-contradiction, cannot be regarded as such an alternative in Habermas' eyes. Be that as it may, both reconstructions of modernity (Foucault's history of the present and Habermas' universal pragmatics) claim to be plausible descriptions of the historical dimension of the world we currently inhabit. In my view, each description is only partially plausible although in different respects and at the cost of diverse deficiencies. In Habermas' theory of communicative action power is explained away too easily; whereas in Foucault's genealogical adventures the blind eye is turned to rationality (in the sense of coming to a mutual understanding). I am aware that no simple approach can mitigate the chasm between these two positions. But this is not to say that they cannot enrich each other in certain respects. One of these respects might be the question of religion in modernity, and it is now time we turned to this.

Religion in modernity

Foucault was a proclaimed atheist; but as demonstrated in recent years religion was definitely not a matter of indifference to him (see, for example, Bernauer, 1993; Carrette, 2000). On the one hand, he regarded confessed religion or the institution of religion (referring explicitly to the Catholic Church, which formed the background for his own upbringing), as a 'superb instrument of power' (Foucault 1978, 107). On the other hand he regarded modernity as an opening towards a new kind of spirituality. The rationality of the state (*la raison d'État*), prevalent in the modern world, can be seen to have turned the salvation of the soul into a security of life, which, as part of the inherent logic, reflects the transformation of spirit and immortality into language, labour and life, denoting the finitude of human existence. By this modern experience, spiritual transgression tends to inhabit the body instead of the soul (that is, a 'soul' which was hitherto caught in the dreams of a transcendent being). This means that spirituality, in Foucault's eyes, continues before anything else in the practice of the body, that is, in 'lived' religion. As a journalist in Teheran in late 1978 and early 1979 he felt he was witnessing exactly this spiritual corporality, the Shi'ite way of life, turning into a political spirituality (see Carrette, 2000, 129ff; Foucault, 2005, 209). The results of the Iranian revolution are well known, and Foucault was, of course, soon to regret the terror of the subsequent mullah regime; but we may be inclined to ask ourselves whether Foucault's notion of power, paired as it was with the notion of resistance or counter-power, did not lead him too easily to be impressed by the rise of unarmed people in the street (cf. Foucault, 2005, 210f). As I see it, Foucault's fascination with the revolutionary force of the people led him to view Shi'ism as an 'authentic' form of self-expression, not because of the promises of afterlife, but rather because of a spiritual way of living here and now (2005, 223; 255). What is of interest in this respect is that

Foucault's late perspective of power and his ethics of 'an aesthetics of existence' seem to be sympathetic to a religious way of life that simply manifests itself before and beyond any rational justification.

Exactly the opposite can be said of Habermas' view on religion. Habermas also understands himself as an atheist in the sense that he confesses to 'lack an ear for religion'. On the one hand, he has forcefully shown the evolutionary logics of communicative action by means of which we have developed the principles of a post-traditional society; on the other hand, he has come to believe that we will have to pay our due respect to the religious citizens amongst us and, in a reflected way, to the religious tradition of our own history. In fact, this is not at all contrary to the commitment of post-metaphysical thinking inasmuch as the rational procedure of uncoerced dialogue is strictly formal, defined by the structure of reaching an agreement on rational premises, but *not* defined by way of content. In principle, there is no issue that cannot constitute a topic for rational debate. Still, there are personal or ethical values that are not fit for rational discussion simply because they pertain to a form of life, or *Lebenswelt*, that are not shared by all. In this case, the values in question can only qualify for the status of mutual agreement if they are translated into secular norms which can be acknowledged by all involved parties. It goes without saying that many (though not all) religious norms will prove unfit to meet these criteria for reaching a rational agreement. As a matter of principle, then, religious norms are values that can only be brought to bear on the individual's own decisions, that is, as an instance of authenticity claims. Ethics, religious or not, concern groups and individuals for whom 'a good life' can only be a life (or a history of life, *Lebensgeschichte*) they choose and take upon themselves by way of uncoerced self-identification. As citizens in a democratic society, on the other hand, we are all committed before anything else to the obedience (and normative appropriation) of the law, which, among other things, means the freedom (though not necessarily the equality) of religion. For a democratic culture to function, it is also necessary that every citizen shows unconditional loyalty towards the premises of reaching a rational agreement which, although often counterfactually, constitutes the justification of political decisions. Whereas people are free to live by their own ethical standards in so far as they do not violate the law (including human rights), the institutions of a democratic, post-traditional and secularised (or even post-secular) society will have to be neutral in respect of world-views or particular values (Habermas 2005, 140). Thus, Habermas firmly disagrees with traditionalists (such as Millbank, MacIntyre, Neuhaus, Weithman, Wolterstorff and Hauerwas) that religious interests can be represented in a public debate pertaining to political decisions (see 2005, 138, for instance). A free exchange of views, including religious convictions, can easily take place in the public sphere on the condition that the level of moral justifications, that is, questions concerning all citizens as citizens, abides by secular standards of rationality. On this point Habermas sides with political philosophers such as John Rawls, Richard Rorty, Nancy Fraser and Seyla Benahbib; but not with more moderate liberals of a theological orientation such as Jeffrey Stout or Robert Audi.

Habermas does not believe that it is reasonable to ask every religious citizen to translate his or her own beliefs into a secular language. On the contrary, he appeals to the willingness, on each side of a religious and a non-religious worldview, to listen to what the other party is actually saying and show 'a readiness to learn' (*Lehrnbereitschaft*). Still, when it comes to decisions in respect of institutional rules (including the right to implement sanctions for breaking these rules) or political agendas, all parties are obliged to translate suggestions into reasons that can be accounted for on a rational basis (that is, a mutual exchange of arguments which renounces any reference to traditional or transcendent authorities).

Habermas appreciates a religious tradition for a 'sensibility' (*Senzibilität*) towards sufferings or pathologies in life forms that may pass unnoticed in a purely rational view of the premises for a just society. Religious traditions may indeed have something to offer by way of providing a 'meaning of life', but in the public and political debate they can no longer expect to be taken seriously by way of making *mutually exclusive* claims to a 'comprehensive doctrine' of truth (to borrow, once more, Rawls' term).

Let us try to work out what this means, as a matter of principle, for the premises of an actual dialogical encounter between, for the lack of better words, a 'religious' and 'a non-religious' citizen. Let us picture a scenario in which a religious citizen engages in a dialogue with a non-religious citizen on the topic of school education. Let us also say that the religious citizen, A, sees the whole range of values that make up her worldview as intimately connected with the authority of tradition; and that the non-religious citizen, B, subscribes to a secular and liberal society which leaves the question of values to be judged individually. At the outset A and B can agree that ordinary school education will have to include 'religion' as a subject, but then disagreement sets in. A sees the rationale for teaching this subject as involving the transmission of values to children; whereas B sees the rationale as involving informing children about the historical background of values that now occur in the form of norms. B might even refer to the fact that this friendly exchange of views between A and B is only possible due to the unchallenged resource of secular or post-traditional norms. A might answer that these norms would have no real value or driving force if they were not backed up by the authority of tradition and were not in some sense god-given. Here, the discussion might come to a dead end or become less than friendly (and this is before we have even considered the question of whose religion should be an obligatory part of the curriculum). But why can't religious citizens acknowledge the fact that it is only possible for everyone to speak his or her mind if there is respect for all values that do not conflict with norms, including the norm of speaking freely? Why can't religious citizens simply limit their traditional values to their personal, family or community lives within the identification of a particular cultural context? The answer that immediately springs to mind is: Because if they did so the values would no longer be the same values. Or to phrase it differently: They would be nothing more *than* values, placed on an equal footing with all other values and thus reduced to a pale apparition of their original truth pretensions.

But if such a de-sacralisation seems to be what is needed to live peacefully together in a multicultural society, then one might ask if the price that some have to pay for the 'common good' is at the risk of turning into resentment, which then makes the standards of rational justification seem rather like an invalid bill. This objection is not news to Rawls (2002, 149) and Habermas (2005, 128), who nevertheless insist on the indispensability of using arguments which transcend a privileged recourse to tradition. For Habermas there is no way to secure a peaceful co-existence and mutual respect other than through a kind of dialogue which does not prevent anyone from saying yes or no to *reasons*. However, this does not alter the fact that the religious citizen may *experience* such premises as discursive constraints which predetermine the outcome of communication to the benefit of secular reasoning, and more importantly that this condition of possibility for making valid statements (or presenting valid arguments) stands in a regime of rationality which, in effect, makes up a game of power relations. Let us say, hypothetically but not unrealistically, that the very core of a religious commitment for a given person consists in buying into the 'whole package', as it were, of revealed truths. How then can obligatory loyalty to dialogical reasoning on post-traditional grounds be grasped as anything other than, at best, a strategic necessity? If it is fair to say that the freedom of religion is secured by secular reasons, and that people committed to a religious confession must therefore realise that they cannot afford to dismiss the level of such reasoning, then this is not, by any means, the same as saying that these 'worldviews' will be able to prosper or even survive in any authentic form under these conditions. There is no guarantee that a religious or traditional self-interpretation can identify with the level of justice due to norms in a secular or at least post-metaphysical sense. So much the worse for that kind of self-interpretation, one might say, but then we might seem (suspiciously) to be including ourselves self-righteously among those who are simply wise enough to be on the right side of the gap.

Conclusion

All this can be boiled down to saying that 'a commitment to universal standards of reasoning' in Habermas' theory of communicative action draws relations of power with it, although this occurs unintentionally.[3] I am not trying to say that there are other ways which might be better suited to reducing the influence of power. If traditional or religious communities are allowed a free reign of interaction by whatever means they see fit, we might soon enough find ourselves in a situation of chaotic conflict or even warlike confrontations. I do not opt for any communitarian proposal to solve the problem, and I certainly do not opt for any impulsive fascination of contingent instances of resistance either (cf. Foucault's Iranian adventure). The dilemma is not an either/or between subscribing to an arbitrary will or subscribing to the communicative

---

3   Without being able to go into the matter here, I am inclined to say that the same goes for 'a justice of fairness' in an early Rawlsian kind of liberalism.

use of reason. The challenge is to refine the notion of reason in a non-exclusive way. I also suggest that we might gain some valuable insight from estimating the procedure of communicative rationality for what it is, namely a voice speaking from a traditional background which, among other things, secures itself by advocating for the obligation to redeem validity claims on a rational basis. Granted, this voice also speaks with a universal pretension inasmuch as these claims to validity appeal to anyone involved and thus direct themselves towards an understanding beyond the (historical, cultural, social) context of departure. But this does not mean that any traditional and valuable view of human existence is fit to survive by recognising itself (as far as possible) within these confines, and neither does it mean that what proves unfit also, automatically, proves irrational or dangerous. As a matrix for rationality as well as power, the appeal to secular standards or communicative reason, backed up by non-religious institutions and political processes of religiously 'neutral' decision-making, may be the best way to proceed, providing that we also keep a vigilant eye on certain rhetoric or real-life practices in which this 'appeal' is no longer power-minimising but rather serves to increase differences by stigmatising or expelling a vast area of self-identification as dangerous irrationalism.

Bibliography

Bernauer, James 1993. *Michel Foucault's Force of Flight. Toward an Ethics for Thought*. London & New Jersey: Humanities Press International, inc.

Carrette, Jeremy 2000. *Foucault and Religion. Spiritual Corporality and Political Spirituality*. London: Routledge.

Critique and Power, Recasting the Foucault/Habermas Debate 1994 (ed. M. Kelly). Cambridge; Massachusetts & London: MIT Press.

Foucault Contra Habermas. Recasting the Dialogue between Genealogy and Critical Theory 1999 (eds., S. Ashenden & D. Owen). London: SAGE Publications.

Foucault, Michel 1975. *Surveiller et punir. Naissance de la prison*. Paris: Gallimard.

Foucault, Michel 1976. *La volonté de savoir: Histoire de la sexualité 1*. Paris: Gallimard.

Foucault, Michel 1977. *Power/Knowledge. Selected interviews & other writings 1972-1977* (ed. C. Gordon). New York: Pantheon.

Foucault, Michel 1978. 'On religion'. In: Jeremy R. Carrette (ed.), *Religion and Culture – Michel Foucault* (transl. by Richard Townshend). London & New York: Routledge, 106-109.

Foucault, Michel 1983. 'The Subject and Power'. In: H.L. Dreyfus & P. Rabinow (eds.), *Michel Foucault. Beyond Structuralism and Hermeneutics* (2nd edn.). The University of Chicago Press, 208-226.

Foucault, Michel 1984a. *Historie de la Sexualité 2: L'usage des plaisiers*. Paris: Gallimard.

Foucault, Michel 1984b. *Historie de la Sexualité 3: Le Souci de soi*. Paris: Gallimard.

Foucault, Michel 1988. 'The ethic of care for the Self as a practice of freedom: An interview translated by J.D. Gauthier, s.j.'. In: M. Bernauer & D. Rasmussen (eds.), *Final Foucault*. Cambridge, Massachusetts: MIT Press.

Foucault, Michel 1989. *Foucault Live. Collected Interview, 1961-1984* (ed. Sylvère Lotringer). New York: Semiotext[e].

Foucault, Michel 1994. 'Critical Theory/Intellectual History'. In: M. Kelly (ed.), *Critique and Power. Recasting the Foucault/Habermas Debate*. Cambridge, Mass., 109-137.

Foucault, Michel 1997. 'Polemics, Politics, and Problematizations: An Interview with Michel Foucault'. In: P. Rabinow (ed.), *Michel Foucault – essential works of Foucault 1954 – 1984, Vol. 1*. London & New York: Penguin Books, 111-119.

Foucault, Michel 2005. 'Appendix' (including Foucault's articles). In: Janet Afary & Kevin B. Anderson (eds.), *Foucault and the Iranian Revolution. Gender and the Seductions of Islamism*. Chicago: The University of Chicago Press, 181-277.

Habermas, Jürgen 1972. 'Vorbereitende Bemerkungen zu einer Theorie der kommunikativen Kompetenz'. In: J. Habermas & N. Luhmann (eds.), *Theorie der Gesellschaft oder Socialtechnologie*. Frankfurt a.M.

Habermas, Jürgen 1981. *Theorie des Kommunikativen Handelns*, I-II. Frankfurt a.M.: Suhrkamp.

Habermas, Jürgen 1985. *Der philosophische Diskurs der Moderne*, Frankfurt a.M.: Suhrkamp.

Habermas, Jürgen 1994. 'Taking Aim at the Heart of the Present: On Foucault's Lecture on Kant's What Is Enlightenment?'. In: M. Kelly (ed.), *Critique and Power – Recasting the Foucault/Habermas Debate*. Cambridge; Massachusetts & London: MIT Press, 149-154 (translated by S.W. Nicholsen from 'Untiefen der Rationalitätskritik' in *Die Neue Unübersichtlichkeit*, Frankfurt, 1985).

Habermas, Jürgen 1999. *Wahrheit und Rechtfertigung. Philosophische Aufsätze*, Frankfurt a.M.: Suhrkamp.

Habermas, Jürgen 2005. *Zwischen Naturalismus und Religion*. Frankfurt a.M.: Suhrkamp.

Kant, Immanuel 1968. GzMdS = *Grundlegung zur Metaphysik der Sitten*, Kants Werke, Band IV, Walter de Gruyter & Co.: Berlin.

Miller, James 1993. *The Passion of Michel Foucault*. Cambridge, Massachusetts: Harvard University Press.

Pleasants, Nigel 1999. *Wittgenstein and the idea of a critical social theory*. London & New York: Routledge.

Rawls, John 1996. *Political Liberalism* (with a new introduction and the 'Reply to Habermas'), New York: Columbia University Press.

Rawls, John 2002. *The Law of the Peoples: with "The Idea of Public Reason Revisited"*. Cambridge, Massachusetts: Harvard University Press.

ON THE SO-CALLED RETURN OF RELIGION:

SOME CRITICAL REMARKS FROM A PHILOSOPHICAL POINT OF VIEW

Vagn Andersen

In recent years there has been much talk about 'the return of religion'. In the media society of today, such a headline tends to become a self-increasing and self-affirming truth. The following article attempts to look at this diagnosis from a somewhat critical point of view. Two questions remain unanswered: (a) the empirical, whether there are strong indications of growth in religion, and (b) the critical philosophical, whether what is perceived and presented as 'religion' under all circumstances deserves that name. The two questions will be dealt with here successively.[1]

Globalisation: the world moves closer together

As indicated, the modern media reality is not without its own ambiguities. I will revert to this point below. However, if we begin by taking a neutral position towards the issue, there is no doubt that, because of the electronic media, we now live in a 'global village' in which all the parts of the world are moving closer and becoming more visible to each other. Through television we are exposed on a daily basis to conditions and events around the globe which were previously remote and often completely unnoticed. In particular, the impressive range of communications facilitated by modern technology is bringing all parts of the world closer and thus also increasingly confronting people around the globe with realities of which they used to be more or less unaware or ignorant. The effect of rapidly increasing mutual attention may be two-fold: it *may* arouse a sense of global responsibility and solidarity, but it may also result in mutual misunderstandings and confrontation.

One element of what has been entitled 'the return of religion' is undoubtedly to be sought here. A largely secularised West is suddenly confronted on a daily basis with societies, cultures and ways of life that are still based on strong religious convictions and traditions. Things which had been forgotten or repressed in our own part of the world are suddenly visible and the focus of attention once again. But does it actually make sense to speak of the 'return' of religion? The thing that is reappearing suddenly has in all probability existed all the time, with the only new aspect being that what used to be foreign, remote and hidden is now the focus of attention thanks to a new global media

---

1   This article refers especially to the situation in Denmark. Comparable trends might be found in most of North-Western Europe.

reality. This process works both ways. To some extent, the previously underprivileged parts of the world have also benefited from the new media technology. Consequently, the economically privileged West has become visible to the people living *there*, which results in both attraction and repulsion. Especially since September 11th, 2001, it is well known to the world that global social inequalities which have become embarrassingly apparent can be religiously coded and instrumentalised. The danger that the West will jump on the bandwagon could turn out be one of the most unproductive countermeasures.

After all, what is known as globalisation is not just a universal media presence. Another point worth making is that due to technical and economic developments the world has also witnessed an ever-increasing mobility of its population. Migrant workers, immigrants, refugees and asylum seekers have become part of modern reality. As a result, people with different cultural backgrounds and religions are also becoming increasingly visible in our own societies. Again, we could ask if this phenomenon in itself gives rise to talk about 'the return of religion'. For the religion which has now become part of our own societies has simply arrived together with newcomers from other parts of the world, where it has always existed. What is most alarming – and disgraceful for us – is the hysteria caused by this new demographic reality.

Obviously, the different populations in relatively secularised Western European societies have reacted with varying degrees of liberal-mindedness towards such immigration, but everywhere there seems to be some level of xenophobia. Even though most of the problems in this connection are due to social factors, there is a very strong focus on cultural differences and, in particular, Muslim immigrants are often met with much fear and scepticism because of their religion. This is not to belittle the fact that cultural encounters may now and then result in a large degree of mutual mistrust and lack of understanding, but it would have been a credit to our societies if the problem had been tackled in a much more relaxed and pragmatic fashion. It is not surprising that the newcomers who have taken refuge with us for economic-social reasons also belonged to a social stratum characterised by relatively traditional and rooted religiosity in their home countries. Similarly, it would be only human if such newcomers tended to guard their inherent religious identity very carefully during a process of cultural transition involving radical changes. However, according to a domestic survey in the sociology of religion the vast majority of Muslim immigrants seem to have a relatively passive and distant relation to their own religion (Kühle 2006). If the receiving society had the patience to accept that changes to cultural identity do not happen overnight, it is indeed likely that a relatively smooth integration would happen over some generations. This, of course, would not mean that these people would lose their fundamental Muslim cultural identity. But it would probably mean a gradual adjustment to common modern norms for a critical and self-reflective view on their own traditions.

Unfortunately, Danish society in particular has not reacted like this. The high-blown rhetoric of a populist party, with some xenophobic undertones, has reached absurd heights of national chauvinism and self-sufficiency and achieved an alarming political power. Even the Evangelical Lutheran Church in Denmark has been taken hostage on this issue. There is no indication that the section of voters that this party appeals to has a particular religious commitment or a particular theological knowledge. When it comes to the mobilisation of all national traditions and symbols, though, Evangelical Lutheran Christianity can also be used for political purposes. However, this move may have counter-productive effects. The greater the emphasis placed on religion, the more the Muslim immigrants, who justly feel hated and humiliated, will also tend to interpret and articulate the polarity religiously. This is not an entirely Danish phenomenon, but it is to be feared that the more scare stories we hear about Islamic fundamentalism, the more risk there is that the warnings will contribute to a radicalisation and thus become a self-fulfilling prophecy.

Without any direct reference to the political party mentioned above, certain domestic cultural conservatives or ecclesiastical circles occasionally make optimistic assumptions that the presence of Muslims in Danish society will raise awareness among Danes 'of their own religious roots'. There is no weighty empirical evidence that these hopeful pleas have any particular effect. Of course, we cannot preclude the possibility that such considerations may have drawn some people closer to their own Christian roots, but there are no clear manifestations that the Danes are becoming increasingly active in support of their local churches. So current developments do not justify talk of a 'return of religion'. This lack of religious commitment obviously deserves no praise. On the other hand, however, there are no sure signs that a great number of Danes are currently leaving the church. However paradoxical it may sound, this half-heartedness could also in one sense be seen as a sign of health, which I will discuss in further detail below. Having said that, it is also true that half-heartedness is definitely not a sure and unambiguous sign of health. The only thing that is certain is that the Danes believe in *something*. But they rarely (if ever) attend church services, so it is no easy matter to work out *what* they believe in. There are some indications that they believe in all sorts of things: a bit of astrology, a bit of healing, a bit of yoga, a bit of re-incarnation, etc. If there is a 'return of religion' in Denmark today, these are the things it involves. The question is whether 'religion' is the right term to use.[2] In some ecclesiastical circles, the people interested in such phenomena are referred to as 'seekers' and regarded as potential true believers. My personal view is that it would be a good idea to carry out a critical sociological analysis of this area. This issue will also be discussed further below.

Religion, secularisation and historical consciousness

If we assume that the Danish people's lack of commitment and half-hearted loyalty to their church *might* be a sign of health, this means that they might also consider this church to be the best of all alternatives. Despite their poor commitment, they may deep

---

2   The Study of Religion, according to its empirical-descriptive self-understanding, does not distinguish between different values with regard to what is covered by its definition of religion. Philosophy, however, as long as it is guided by a normative concept of reason, maintains the right to distinguish between intellectually honourable religion and pseudo-religious ideology.

down have a feeling that Christianity is a fundamental part of their own history and has helped to make them what they are. It is very likely that the majority of Danes are so-called 'cultural Christians', which means that even though they are not very religious, they recognise Christianity and the church institution as being an influential and respectable cultural tradition to which there is no attractive or valuable alternative. It is important, however, to distinguish between cultural Christianity and true Christian confession. On the other hand, there is no need to neglect cultural Christianity or, in general, to treat it with disrespect.

Søren Kierkegaard distinguished between 'Christendom' and 'Christianity', and made it his task "to introduce Christianity into Christendom" (Kierkegaard 1964). This task also included a profound knowledge and recognition of the dialectics that the Christian Gospel at any given time can only be preached as topically challenging and radically relevant on the basis of the historical circumstances that it has itself helped to create. One interpretation of this dialectics in today's world could be that a Christian preaching of genuine theological quality only exists on the basis of the secularisation that it has itself helped to create. This has largely characterised the history of the Danish church. It is possible that a vague sense of this context could explain the Danes' cultural Christianity. Being modern North-Western Europeans, the Danes are not necessarily ignorant of the fact that Christianity, not least in its reformatory form, has helped to liberate the cultural and societal processes resulting in the modernity of which we ourselves are the children. Neither are they necessarily ignorant of the fact that theology has itself participated in this process and that the preaching in their churches over the last couple of centuries represents the very best attempt of each new generation to communicate the Gospel with intellectual integrity on the conditions of modernity. They may not even have completely given up the hope that they might still hear something of value to their contemporary world on their occasional visits to church.

These are all unlikely and idealised presumptions. They are based on the presupposition that as long as there is cultural Christianity, there will also be a certain amount of historical consciousness in the population. However, this hypothesis may seem to be increasingly unlikely and bold. Ecclesiastical circles are currently lamenting the so-called 'loss of tradition', and they may be quite right to do so. No matter how much biblical history and morning assembly are reintroduced, however, it is highly doubtful that this situation can be easily remedied. The lack of historical consciousness is much more encompassing, and can only be understood and explained through a critical sociological analysis of the modern media society. Fully as much as biblical history, it also comprises Europe's intellectual history. Much of what is naively perceived and greeted as the 'return of religion' is to be found here. When people believe in pyramid power, pendulum healing, crystal healing and spiritual energies, it is above all the memory of and respect for the Enlightenment that has been lost.

This issue has several angles. One aspect is the carefreeness with which so-called post-modernism has pronounced 'the collapse of the Enlightenment', proclaiming that 'anything goes'. What is particularly problematic is the power and primitiveness by which this message has spread among the general public. Post-modernism could be a useful warning against a scientific absolutism and a naïve and triumphalistic belief in progress but, most often, the relativistic consequences that it draws from 'the dialectics of Enlightenment' substantially overshoot the mark (Habermas 1985). Its philosophical arguments can be analysed one by one and often challenged. However, such a balancing scholarly debate seems to have had relatively little effect as regards the traces left in the public mind in the form of a more or less general zeitgeist. Again, the reason for this should probably not be found in the intellectual trends themselves, but rather in the new media reality. It does not take a genius to perceive that objective information and decent analyses in the electronic media are being replaced by 'infotainment' at an ever-increasing speed. The sensational set-up and sharp and clever 'angling' of a given 'story' seem to be an essential prerequisite for keeping market shares and audience ratings high. It is a very distinctive feature that for the sake of entertainment, 'debate' is reduced to heavily critical confrontations between people and views, with 'one-liners' and ultra-short 'statements' replacing argumentation. Each 'expert statement' in the first evening news on television is routinely followed by a statement by an expert holding the opposite view in the second evening news. In the light of this, it is completely understandable that people's respect for expert knowledge is gradually being undermined. The consequence is that people will eventually believe in anything – and feel that they have a clear right to believe in anything.

Recently, the general and uncritical acceptance of the 'return of religion' has been opposed. Due to a not unreasonable concern about increasing irrationalism, a quite aggressive 'new atheism' which puts its trust in science has taken the floor (Dawkins 2006, Dennett 2006). It is open to doubt whether this movement – with its rather naïve scientist belief that Darwinistic and cognitive science models of explanation can be used to undermine religion – is an adequate and successful countermove. In the words of Habermas, in their mutual opposition the new religious wave and scientist naturalism could also form a secret alliance (Habermas 2005). One common trait, at least, is a striking lack of historical consciousness and ability or will to see through and understand the historical and societal processes in which human religiosity is embedded. Therefore, they each, in their own way, lack a criterion for distinguishing between irrational obscurantism and intellectually reflected religion.

Reflected religion and popular culture

As mentioned above, the Danish church tradition has been characterised by the fact that the Gospel is always preached according to the cultural conditions that it has itself helped to create. Theology has therefore also participated in and reacted reflectively to the current secularisation process which characterises the history of North-Western Europe. Kant's critique of inherited metaphysics, Romanticism, German idealism and the later 19th-century critique of religion have all left their traces in theology. From

Schleiermacher via Kierkegaard to 20th-century dialectic theology, intellectual and critical standards have constantly been set up which neither church preaching nor the living religion has been willing or able to escape. As a *living* tradition, Evangelical-Lutheran Christianity at any time has gained a hearing and renewed itself precisely because it has expressed itself on the general cultural conditions of the given epoch. It has thus also expressed itself pari passu with modernity and its emancipatory gains. It is precisely in such a hermeneutical self-reflective religion that Jürgen Habermas places his trust when recently expressing the expectation that the semantic resources of a religious tradition currently being retranslated could also have something irreplaceable to offer the moral sensibility and extensive normative self-realisation in a modern secularised society (Habermas 2001/2005). This is the *only* kind of religion that can live in peaceful coexistence with modern post-metaphysical thinking. Its decisive characteristic feature is that in its own dogmatic self-reflection it has absorbed and treated three cognitive dissonances: (1) the pluralism of worldviews; (2) the monopoly of the sciences on world knowledge; and (3) the general positive nature of law and the necessary secular nature of social morality in a modern society. In brief, this is what characterises a religion which has mentally adopted the results of the Enlightenment and secularisation in its own self-understanding.

Due to its specific genesis, a great nation on the other side of the Atlantic has never actually been radically secularised. Modern as it may be in all other respects, its religious mentality has in many respects remained pre-modern. Being a technological, military and economic super power, however, it exerts enormous influence over the world's societies today – also culturally. What in our own societies is currently referred to as 'the return of religion' is to a great extent a cultural import from America. Phenomena which we could have sworn a few years ago would never reappear on European ground are now growing steadily. Evangelical fundamentalism, creationism and 'intelligent design' are no longer rare. Neither are glossolalia, exorcism and belief in miracles. It is to be hoped and also expected that such things will keep within certain narrow limits in Denmark. It is likely that the mentality of the population will erect a number of barriers preventing a regression to pure Middle Age. There is more reason to worry about the various forms of new spirituality spreading into therapy. To the spirituality emerging from the aftermath of the New Age wave, which pretends to be ultra modern, unorthodox and in opposition to traditional church religiosity, the population is probably much less resistant. The 'alternative' is interesting, precisely because it is alternative, no matter how much attention is drawn to the fact that the new 'holism' is more incompatible with post-metaphysical thinking than contemporary theology. At this point, it is probably completely fruitless to refer to Habermas and other philosophical authorities. Here we are up against social forces which are much more powerful and radical.

To explain this, we must again look towards the US. It is a deep-rooted element of the historical genesis and the fundamental democratic self-understanding of this society that it actually came into existence through a clash with the old world's hierarchies. In a way it has never known or, at least, always taken a critical attitude towards a European differentiation between elite culture and popular culture. Alexis de Tocqueville might have seen some of this, but the levelling certainly escalated with the explosive growth of market capitalism during the 19th century. At any rate, the market does not distinguish between high and low culture. One of the most paradoxical features of the youth revolution of the 1960s, which, incidentally, meant being in opposition to 'capitalism', is that in this respect it intentionally and happily followed the market trends. Even on the European continent, the protest against 'bourgeois society' also became a protest against 'bourgeois high art', despite Adorno's strong objections against it. What was triggered by the events at that time has influenced the whole youth culture to this day, when it has again been definitively conquered and swallowed up by the market.

As we all know, American popular culture – including the mentality which is inherent in it – is widely dispersed all over the globe. All qualitative distinctions and criteria are powerless against this. The distinction between true and false, reality and fiction, good and bad arguments, irrationalism and common sense becomes completely irrelevant. The only things that count are the effect, the aesthetic fascination and the commercial success. Against this present state of affairs, even gods fight a losing battle. It is probably useless to argue because arguments have no impact on economic and market dynamics. The only thing left to rely on may be a modicum of critical sociological insight into the social mechanisms creating and maintaining the current situation.

A central point in Horkheimer and Adorno's *Dialektik der Aufklärung* was that the 'culture industry' itself produces the minds which uncritically and unconsciously reproduce the given social reality (Adorno 1981, 141-191). Despite its ascetically positivistic abandonment of all value judgments, a recent Scandinavian investigation of Swedish conditions, viewed from the perspective of the sociology of religion, seems to agree with this picture based on all possible empirical and statistical evidence (Ahlin 2005). Both the losers and the winners in neo-liberal society seem increasingly to find the strength for their mental survival from new-religious currents, which we may rightly meet with considerable ideology-critical scepticism. It is no surprise that underprivileged sections of the population, feeling powerless towards social changes which they do not control or understand, seem to regress to a folk religiosity of belief in fate, which is today mostly manifested in the form of belief in horoscopes and other kinds of astrology. We get a more varied picture when it comes to the sections of the population who directly benefit from (or at least feel a certain spiritual power to cope with) such developments in society. The author of the investigation mentioned above, Lars Ahlin, in a generally individualistic turn away from traditional church religiosity characterising post-modernity, distinguishes between what he refers to as 'utilitarian individualism' and 'expressive individualism'. The former is not really religious, but makes a good team with general market liberalism and often also characterises its direct entrepreneurs. What is more paradoxical is that it also prevails among men of the lower social strata in particular, even though it is in direct opposition to their own objective self-interest. At this point the term ideology in its classical sense of 'false consciousness' is certainly appropriate. Expressive individualism, on the other hand, seems to flourish among well-educated women in particular. Here we find the whole spectrum of 'religious seeking' from yoga and meditation to more indefinite forms of psychological and 'spiritual' self-development. This religious search is not infrequently associated with a certain distance to or a clear dissociation from the market society's 'materialism'. In its individualistic concentration on inner self-development and the mobilisation of your own 'spiritual energies', however, it is not free of the dialectics of drawing attention away from the exterior and structural social processes and thus contributing to their continued and unchanged existence. Despite the frequent claims of the more meditative new religiosity to have its origin in the East, it is usually not difficult to spot the 'pizza effect' reflected in its pseudoscientific psychological vocabulary. In other words, such new religiosity has in most cases been on a trip around the US. Consequently, ideology-critical suspicion regarding an increasingly cumulative syndrome involving market liberalism, the culture industry and new religiosity does not seem far-fetched.

At one point, however, Horkheimer and Adorno's analysis must be revised or brought up to date. This does not weaken its strength, but rather topicalises and radicalises the idea of a tendentially 'all-encompassing connection of infatuation'. The sporadic conspiracy-theoretical undertones found in Horkheimer and Adorno's presentation might leave the impression that a cynical elite of capitalists and business people are consciously and instrumentally controlling 'the culture industry' for the purpose of mass stupidification. Such an idea is less likely today than ever before. With the growth of the 'experience economy', with yoga and astrology also having captured management offices, with management thinking such as 'coaching' assuming more or less autosuggestive shapes, and with the concept of 'corporate religion' not even intended to be a joke, nobody is a cynical and deliberate manipulator. Instead, everyone is an equally innocent and unconscious victim of what is starting to resemble a collective hallucination. The fact that all these areas are gaining ground at the expense of a religion which was once related to the Enlightenment is alarming.

Bibliography

Ahlin, Lars 2005. *Pilgrim, turist eller flyktning? En studie av individuell religiös rörlighet i senmoderniteten.* Stockholm: Brutus Östlings Bokforlag Symposion.

Dawkins, Richard 2006. *The God Delusion.* Boston: Houghton Mifflin Company.

Dennett, Daniel C. 2006. *Breaking the Spell. Religion as a Natural Phenomenon.* London and New York: Penguin Group.

Habermas, Jürgen 1985. *Der philosophische Diskurs der Moderne.* Frankfurt a.M.: Suhrkamp.

Habermas, Jürgen 2001. *Glauben und Wissen.* Frankfurt a.M.: Suhrkamp.

Habermas, Jürgen 2005. *Zwischen Naturalismus und Religion.* Frankfurt a.M.: Suhrkamp.

Horkheimer, Max & Theodor W. Adorno 1981 (1947). *Dialektik der Aufklärung*. In: Theodor W. Adorno, *Gesammelte Schriften*, Band 3, Frankfurt a.M.: Suhrkamp.

Kierkegaard, Søren 1964. *Synspunktet for min Forfatter-Virksomhed*. Søren Kierkegaard, *Samlede Værker* (3rd edition, vol. 18). Copenhagen: Gyldendal.

Kühle, Lene 2006. *Moskeer i Danmark – islam og muslimske bedesteder*. Højbjerg: Forlaget Univers.

FREEDOM OF EXPRESSION

RELIGION, CENSORSHIP, AND CITIZENSHIP

Johannes Adamsen

> 'None can love freedom heartily, but good men;
> the rest love not freedom, but licence.'
> John Milton

The modern idea and general perception of words is probably so much part and parcel of our whole being and worldview that we can only distance ourselves from it with considerable effort. In comparison, one could quote John Milton's excellent defence of the free press, *Areopagitica. A Speech for the Liberty of Unlicenced Printing to the Parliament of England*, in which he writes:

…almost kill a man as kill a good book. Who kills a man kills a reasonable creature, God's image; but he who destroys a good book, kills reason itself, kills the image of God, as it were in the eye. Many a man lives a burden to the earth; but a good book is the precious life-blood of a master spirit, embalmed and treasured up on purpose to a life beyond life (Milton 1644).

This quotation must seem strange to a modern mind. The exalted praise of books as being akin to reason itself, i.e. akin to the image of God, and the reference to the words of the creation of man are indeed strange. Compared with today's use of words, and not least compared with recent discussions of freedom of expression, something might be made more nuanced. In recent decades words and language have been seen in highly nominalistic terms – in other words, they are regarded as purely referential. But at the same time, Man's right to freedom of expression has been raised to new heights, implying that self-expression is the primary democratic right without regard for anything else.

In order to clear up some of the confusion, I shall first try to make explicit the meaning of the word in Milton's sense (1). Then, taking this perspective as my starting point, I shall briefly consider the use of words as a religiously inspired critique of power (2). I shall follow this by unravelling some of the unnoticed problems behind the Danish cartoon crisis in 2005-06 (3). And finally, based on the deeper understanding that has hopefully been gained, I shall conclude by outlining the consequences with regard to the responsibility of citizens (4).

1. Milton understood the word as creative in itself. In his defence of 'the liberty of unlicensed printing' he clearly set forward an understanding of words drawn from the Bible, and possibly also nourished by elements of classical philosophy. To liken a book to the 'image of God' is taken from Genesis 1:27, from the description of the creation

of man and woman. But Milton takes the simile an almost exaggerated step further in comparing a good book with reason itself. Behind this sort of rhetoric one can identify an old notion of the word, familiar in a great number of old cultures, namely that the word in itself is reality. The word is not just an instrument purveying an independent reality elsewhere – instead, it is simply indispensable and is itself reality. Indeed, it has the power to create reality, and like reality it cannot be withdrawn. To regret one's word cannot undo the reality of the word any more than regretting an action can make things undone.

This is demonstrated with all possible clarity in the tragic story in Judges 11, where Jephthah promises God that he will sacrifice the first person who meets him back home if God will grant him victory against the Ammonites. After the desired victory Jephthah returns only to find his daughter, his only child, dancing to welcome him, and he says: "Alas, my daughter! thou hast brought me very low, and thou art one of them that trouble me: for I have opened my mouth unto the LORD, and I cannot go back."

This idea of the solidness of words is of course well known from the Bible. Another example of this is the story of Jacob deceiving his blind father to bless him instead of his brother Esau (Genesis 27:35). Discovering the fraud, Isaac says: "Thy brother came with subtlety, and hath taken away thy blessing."

Notice that the blessing is taken away as if it were a camel or a lamb; it is as if the word is out there materialising itself, the word is reality. It does not matter that Jacob gained his father's blessing by subterfuge – the blessing cannot be withdrawn. A modern mind might ask why Isaac simply did not declare his blessing null and void because of Jacob's deception. But the question itself shows the difference between two notions of the relationship between word and reality.

I think that it is not quite this idea of the reality of the word that Milton expresses, although there is certainly some kinship present. The fact that words can be seen as a potent reality which is apt to create meaning is of course the reason why in some societies insults can only can be washed away with blood. Adam Seligman once called attention to the difference between the Western (American) saying "sticks and stones may break my bones, but words will never hurt me" and the Middle East proverb "wounds heal, but words hurt forever". This also nicely catches the distance to Milton, and is one main reason for defending unlicensed publishing.

But to understand the world of the Old Testament more closely, one can at least take the concept of the sacred into consideration. The sacred is dangerous, taboo, and one should be aware of the power of the sacred. When God chose to disclose himself to Moses on Mount Sinai, the strength of the sacred even made the mountain itself holy and untouchable:

… for the third day the LORD will come down in the sight of all the people upon Mount Sinai. And thou shalt set bounds unto the people round about, saying, Take heed to yourselves, that ye go not up into the mount, or touch the border of it: whosoever toucheth the mount shall be surely put to death (Exodus 19:11-12).

In itself this is commonly known, although it might not be obvious to everyone that the notion of the sacred and the notion of the word are interdependent. To perceive something as sacred, and hence as beyond discussion, and to consider the word as being itself reality, seem unavoidably to be two sides of the same coin. This might be shown negatively, then the idea of the sacred would be under attack at the same time as the understanding of language is being transformed for epistemological reasons. The epistemological breakthrough or new epistemological paradigm occurring in the days of John Milton desacrilised both the word and the world. John Locke, accepting the consequence of Newtonian physics, did understand language as instrumental: the meaning of the words is their reference (Locke 1690, chapter II). It unavoidably follows that the world becomes reduced to objects (it is objectified), and that the world can 'naturally' be seen as interdependent, i.e. that everything is relative to everything else, because the web of the world is reduced to sheer causality. The objectified world is no longer to be understood in terms of teleology. It can be explained, and what cannot be explained must be superfluous and therefore amount to superstition (Taylor 1995, 1-19). What is lost, or can no longer be seen as reality, is the idea of things participating in a kind of 'other' or transcendent world. To understand an object is to explain it, and not as in the past to see its intrinsic value in an order or hierarchy of things, the order of being. This, incidentally, could only end up in a shift in the very reason for studying nature – and later also the human world. The aim of study in the past was primarily contemplation, but the new idea of explanation resulted in a form of understanding in which technology or technological possibilities lurked in the background of all study.[1]

John Milton truly regarded the word as a kind of reality; but in order to understand his position accurately one must be aware of the word's connection to *freedom and truth*, and therefore to the possibility of character formation – known as virtue in Milton's terms.

Consequently, since the knowledge and survey of vice is so necessary in this world for the constitution of human virtue, and since the scanning of error is so necessary for the confirmation of truth, how can we more safely, and with less danger, scout into the regions of sin and falsity than by reading all manner of treatises and hearing all manner of reason? And this is the benefit which may be had of books promiscuously read (Milton 1644, 24).

The point is that only the freely understood message, which of course can endure examination, is worth its salt. The reason for this is that if one only takes truth for truth without even knowing an alternative, how then does one know truth from falsehood? So it appears that Milton defends freedom of the press because he basically believes in the power of truth; truth left alone, with no licensing or censorship, stands for itself and

---

1   It is important to be aware of the duality of this shift. The shift to explanation has its roots in a basic understanding of activity, hence the new focus on causality. The other side of understanding is connected to a new discipline, not to say a new worldview, namely the modern subject of history as human beings acting in a mostly self-created world.

is capable of creating a better world due to the connection of reason and virtue: truth talks to reason, and reason creates a virtuous man. Milton's attack on prior censorship has a background in his faith in the word as participating in truth. With regard to this particular point he may not be exactly congruent with the pre-Christian notion of the word.

2. Recent discussions of freedom of expression have tended to contrast religion with free speech. Referring to the Enlightenment, the Inquisition, Middle Eastern dictatorship or a variety of other phenomena, the defenders of free speech generally tend to contrast religion with freedom. Basically, so goes the modern prejudice regarding the fundamental freedom of human beings, freedom is natural and dictatorship as well as censorship are superimposed by a powerful clergy. Get rid of the clergy, and freedom will be restored to its pristine value. And with these arguments every organised religion is seen as just another form of coercion. Freedom being natural means that it comes from within, and henceforth every call to common opinion, not to mention preaching, is a priori regarded as being on the edge of violence.

However, just a quick glance at the Israelite religion might teach us something different. When King David (according to 2 Samuel) dared to take Bathsheba as his wife after he had sent her husband Uriah to a dangerous war so that he would be killed (a plan which worked), Nathan the prophet went to the king to tell him the truth. He told a parable in which a poor man with one lamb lost his lamb because his rich neighbour did not have the heart to take one of his own to offer his guest. When he heard this story David bridled and ordered: "As the LORD liveth, the man that hath done this thing shall surely die. And he shall restore the lamb fourfold, because he did this thing, and because he had no pity." (2 Sam 12:5-6). But Nathan famously replied: "Thou art the man".

This example shows clearly that there is a parallel institution to power, comparable with the philosophers of classical Greece. However, the connection to religion is explicit in the Israelite case, whereas it is thinner or more veiled in classical Greece. With some reservations it can reasonably be maintained that the church in medieval Europe had (and exercised) the option of 'speaking truth to power', even though the fact that it did so might be obscured because as a papal institution the church regarded itself not only as an institution of truth and truth speaking, but as another power which was quite often opposed to Caesar or kings.

3. It all began in 2005 when the Danish author Kåre Bluitgen said he could not find an illustrator for his book on the life of Mohammed (which has since been published with drawings and without attracting any specific attention). The editor of the Danish daily newspaper *Jyllands-Posten* felt that this was self-censorship and decided (allegedly) to look into the matter. In a bold, sensational rather provocative attempt to defend the right to free speech, *Jyllands-Posten* asked a number of newspaper illustrators to draw Mohammed, something which is forbidden according to Islamic philosophy. The consequences of this act have been dealt with often enough, and will not be elaborated on here. But it might be interesting to ask whether the initial view of the problem was

correct, and whether the newspaper actually analysed the matter before proceeding with its fight against 'self-censorship' and in favour of the right to free speech.

As far as I am aware, nobody knows how many artists declined to illustrate Bluitgen's book, and nobody actually knows why. How could they believe so firmly that this was self-censorship. For what is self-censorship, exactly? This is a question that has never been asked, and the answer may lead us in the right direction. *Jyllands-Posten* also regarded the banning of a work from an exhibition at the Tate Gallery for fear of offending Muslims as yet one more example of insidious self-censorship. The first time I came across the word self-censorship was in an essay by the author Danilo Kiš (1935-89) from the mid-80s, i.e. during the Cold War, from a voice behind the iron curtain. He writes about his experience of living in a country with censorship. He knows that he is being watched and that there are certain things that must not be expressed. He also knows that the punishment for doing so ranges from passages being crossed out and changes suggested to persecution and imprisonment. In his case, it was more the latter than the former. He knows that there is no clear definition of what is allowed and what is not allowed, and he also knows that he can give some interesting information by saying something apparently innocent – for censors usually have no sense of humour (cf. Zhang Yimou's film *Raise the Red Lantern*, 1991, which was initially passed by the Chinese censors). It is a fact, however, that because he is aware of censorship during the process of writing, he constantly tries to see his works through the eyes of the censor and thus avoid imagined or real interventions, the avoidance in itself being an effect of censorship. Danilo Kiš's analysis is that censorship is not just something external. Self-censorship will necessarily occur in all kinds of writing, and this self-censorship can be even worse than the actual consequences of censorship. *Self-censorship is the inherent consequence of censorship and it arises in a person's mind as an anonymous, suffocating restriction on his thoughts.* This is due to the fact that in a dictatorship there is no unambiguous legislation with courts of appeal. The rights and wrongs here depend on arbitrary attitudes and the exercise of power. What was all right yesterday may be 'illegal' tomorrow, or vice versa.

Returning to the cartoons, it is obvious that neither Bluitgen and the illustrators nor I are in this situation. According to the Danish Constitution we have freedom of speech in Denmark, and this is not just an empty statement on a piece of paper but political and legal practice. Censorship "can never be reintroduced" – but this certainly does not mean that Danes have unconditional freedom of speech, something which *Jyllands-Posten* as well as members of the government (including the Prime Minister) have maintained several times in their opinionated pronouncements. However, the destructive temptation to approach the debate as a black and white argument and to make unconditional what is conditional (the freedom of speech is subject to the law) has been too strong. Such politicians have assumed a considerable degree of power which bears some similarity to self-righteousness.

On the other hand, self-censorship – like language in general – is not a fixed term that cannot undergo a change of meaning. People are free to use it in a different sense than outlined above. I suppose that in September 2005 the editor of *Jyllands-Posten* thought that the reason why nobody seemed to want to illustrate a possibly critical book on Mohammed was due to the prevailing atmosphere of debate (partly self-created, incidentally) and, consequently, the fear of loud-mouthed people. The newspaper assumed that the reluctance of some illustrators was due to fear of the consequences of free expression, and therefore used the term 'self-censorship' to describe this kind of behaviour even though censorship was not being exercised in the legal sense of the word. The newspaper's reaction was that "This is really too bad, we must do something!"

My objection is that they came to the wrong conclusion. The illustrators may have declined to illustrate the book out of respect (or for reasons that they define as respect), or it may be true that some of them were in fact thinking about the possible consequences. The kind of consequences suffered by Salman Rushdie, for instance. This might then be termed care, due respect, prudence or cowardice. However, since we do not have censorship in Denmark but live in a society governed by law, and in a democracy, the following simple questions should be asked: (a) How, under realistic conditions, do we create a society in which everybody can speak freely about all matters? (b) Is there not always a risk of consequences from unforeseen quarters? (c) Are we not all aware that even local politicians and people who express themselves in public are regularly threatened with (and sometimes exposed to) attacks which may even be physical in nature by lunatics or desperate, marginalised individuals? In brief, is it realistic to imagine a society in which people are allowed to express their views without showing or being required to show some kind of *moral courage*?

I think that the journalists and editors reached the following erroneous conclusion: if just one person is subject to 'self-censorship', then it becomes possible to silence all criticism. And if the critics are silenced, we are already well on our way towards losing our freedom and towards dictatorship. So the problem must be solved, meaning that the right to free speech must be defended when self-censorship occurs. The short-circuit can be found at the boundary between apparent self-censorship (a matter of mind) and the threat to freedom of speech (a matter of law). We all refrain from saying things in certain cases, either because we are bound to secrecy (e.g. doctors, psychologists or Danish military intelligence officers such as Frank Grevil, a whistle blower who was certainly not defended by *Jyllands-Posten* for his right to free speech), or because we more or less deliberately (due to ethical reasons or cowardice), take care not to offend or hurt others. We are bound by a number of written and often unwritten rules,[2] the latter being the most difficult as well as the easiest to follow. Most difficult because they demand attention, and easiest because they may prove to be convenient. For example, it is easy for the Danish Prime Minister to refrain from using his freedom of speech to criticise the unfortunate drawings under cover

---

2   Montesquieu rightly pointed out that it is most likely in a democracy that opinion will be divided into two main blocks making even the understanding of history biased, cf. *l'Esprit*, book XIX, chap. XXVII.

of the right of *Jyllands-Posten* to free speech. Another short-circuit, at least as far as the argumentation is concerned.

The short-circuit is due to insufficient or non-existent analysis. If this kind of self-censorship derives from the fear of possible consequences, it is due to a lack of *moral courage,* and the solution is then *more* moral courage – not of course the right to freedom of speech that has already been granted judicially.

4. In other words, it would be desirable to find out what brings us moral courage. My assertion is that moral courage is motivated by love of democracy and a society governed by law, i.e. a love of justice which is founded in a critical understanding. Democracy, openness and a constitutional state rest on this understanding, and unlike mere knowledge the nature of this understanding is always critical. What we understand is a concept, an event, or a phenomenon in its context. This contextualisation is the real reason why we can defend and justify anything, and the reason why criticism and discussion are both necessary and positive. The only problem in this connection is that understanding cannot be enforced, but in a way only encouraged. At this point the prevailing opinion about democracy is to a great extent simply maladjusted. The general opinion is that if we talk about democracy (and especially the excellence of freedom) often and long enough, then everything in the garden will be rosy and anyone who might refuse to do the same is evil, dictatorial, fanatical etc. Moral – or civic – courage cannot simply be the wish to express oneself, but is usually something that has to be mobilised precisely because it is difficult.[3] In an ideal society it is hardly necessary. Neither is it motivated by group affiliation or the enthusiasm of claqueurs. Moral courage is unselfishly motivated by the understanding and respect of people and principles, and not least by an elementary sense of justice. So true moral courage cannot submit to threats or internal group pressure. It is demanding, also analytically demanding.

Democracy as a system is not enough to encourage moral courage, but can hardly survive without it. This applies to the somewhat uncompromising discussion which in its praise of freedom sometimes takes on the colourlessness of restraint and hardened polarisation. However, it also applies to contexts in which people are forced to turn against their fellow group members, whether they are Chinese, government officers, Muslims or politicians.

So the real question (also for democracies) is how to nurture moral courage, which is one of the main characteristics of citizenship alongside judgment. The answer – or answers – is unavoidably connected to upbringing, education and character, and in this respect the basic premise of course is recognition. It is no strange coincidence that thoughts on the formation of character occur simultaneously with the dawn of democracy, from Plato in Athens to Shaftesbury in early modern England. It is also no

---

3   Like all societies modern, democratic society creates its own basic understanding of life, for instance by naturalising freedom. In fact most societies throughout history have tended to understand censorship as natural – witness the hardly accidental wisdom in *Encyclopedia Britannica*, where 'freedom of expression' is aptly placed under the reference to 'censorship'.

strange coincidence that secularists today defend democracy by rigid condemnation of all and every real or imagined antagonist. In our so-called post-metaphysical times they cling to clear-cut principles in simplifying a more complex situation by confusing democracy as a political system with democracy as a cultural ethos.

The somewhat tragic history of democracy bears witness to the prevalence of this fallacy and its opposition in abandoning democracy altogether. To avoid derision we must nurture mutual recognition, moral courage and a real sense of justice, instead of opinionated doctrinarianism.

As outlined above, freedom of expression and freedom of speech are in themselves hardly natural, but this is not due to restrictions forced upon society for religious reasons. Almost certainly one can point out an intimate connection between the sacred and some kind of restrictions, including restrictions on expression, and also almost certainly one can maintain a corresponding connection between the early modern change of worldview, the new understanding of language, and the declining sense of the sacred.

Perhaps one can (roughly at least) indicate a clash of perceptions behind the cartoon crisis, with a thorough and persistent modern conception of language reducing everything to sheer objects and facts on the one hand, and on the other an ambiguous modernisation in very different Muslim societies with populations perceiving a condescending attitude while caught between the modern language of objectification and technology and the still active sense of language as participation in the sacred by creating its own reality.

Nevertheless, a meeting place might be possible. Of course violence, vandalism, and murder cannot be tolerated. But just as radical Muslims have to behave according to the law, other people – typically members of our modern 'Western' society – need to study our own history to come to terms with an understanding of the sacred and of our own modernity. If we could discover in this connection that the other side of objectifying language is a new sense of feelings and emotions needing expression, and often with an alleged right of their own, then we might also see that the Muslim reaction to the Mohammed cartoons may be more modern than we first realised. To perceive feelings as sacred is really a part of modernity, but as in Western societies we tend to see only one side at a time. When we use objectifying language, the language of emotions retreats into darkness, and vice versa.

To see language as Milton did as participating in truth and reality is one chance of coming to terms with both the power of critical engagement and respect for people without losing a sense of the sacred. Like democracy itself, freedom of expression is a weighty claim on citizens. The courage to distinguish is demanding because both freedom of expression and religion imply culture in its original sense of 'cultivating'. A critique of power as well of handling insults must be understood as a moral demand, and this demand cannot be managed with reference to the legal system alone.

Bibliography

Locke, John 1997 (1690). *An Essay Concerning Human Understanding.* London: Penguin.

Milton, John 2008 (1644). *Aeropagitica*, Maryland: Manor.

Montesquieu 1979 (1748). *De l'esprit des lois*, Paris: GF-Flammarion.

Taylor, Charles 1995. *Philosophical Arguments*, Harvard: Harvard University Press.

'STRONG PRINCIPAL EMOTIONS', 'FUNDAMENTAL ATTITUDES' AND 'ETHICAL PROBLEMS':

REPRESENTATIONS OF RELIGION IN THE DANISH PARLIAMENT

Henrik Reintoft Christensen

In the first months of 2006, Denmark was suddenly caught in the eye of a tornado. While the surrounding world erupted in chaotic swirls of demonstrations, flag burnings, death threats, boycotts and embassy infernos, no such things happened in Denmark, although the slightly panicky feeling of being caught in a tornado was evident. The Danish politicians were buffeted around by the events and demonstrated no coherent strategy for handling the crisis. They rode the storm slowly, but it left them bruised and battered (Sløk 2006). This was undoubtedly the most widely covered event in the Danish media with regard to religion in 2006. In fact, it actually surpassed the coverage of the September 11 attacks on the World Trade Center and Pentagon back in 2001. This chapter examines the representations of religion in the Danish parliament at the end of 2006, when the storm had all but quieted down and retrospective reflections became part of the public debate as they always do when a new year approaches.

Religion from a social problem perspective

The contemporary sociology of religion shows little interest in the relationship between religion and social problems. Most studies only focus on controversies related specifically to religion and fail to consider possible implications on a greater scale. James Beckford argues that there are several reasons why we should direct our attention to this relationship (Beckford 1990). First, because a shift from problems of material considerations to problems of self-determination, personal dignity and equality of rights has taken place as post-material values increasingly replace traditional material values (Inglehart 1977). This makes it easier for religious people or groups to contribute arguments to the public debates. Second, globalisation has facilitated the creation of global networks with specific agendas like the environment, peace and human rights, as well as a sense of interconnectedness between these problems. This has spurred a notion that only holistic measures can solve them, and for this purpose religion suits perfectly. Finally, the perceived urgency and complexity assigned to these problems emphasises action in contrast to lofty debates. All else being equal, actions performed by religious groups targeted at countering the effects of the perceived problems are more visible than any debate on what to do about the problems. However, "the factors that explain the growing relevance of religion to the new social problems of advanced industrial societies are the very same reasons why religion is also becoming more problematic" (Beckford 1990, 9).

The shift towards post-materialism raises issues not of distribution of wealth, but of how society sustains its immaterial values like democracy and freedom of speech. This may constitute a new problem as religious discourse has "a radical potential to turn societies upside down" (Beckford 1990, 10). Furthermore, globalisation has made it more difficult for any single nation state to monitor and control any discourse, including discourses, religious or not, that might have this radical potential. Finally, the pragmatism associated with action might have legal implications, as some religious activities might be indistinguishable from non-religious political or economic activities. The ensuing disputes consist of disagreement about the meaning and role of religion in the public sphere because "it calls in question the very distinction between public and private, religion and politics" (Beckford 1990, 11).

Representations of religion in the Danish parliament

The primary point of departure is threefold. First, it is a focus on what problems religion is related to generally. Second, a further qualification is the investigation into what kind of problems religion is represented as posing, or looking at the problems to which religion is a solution. Finally, I also look for instances where it is argued that we must show special consideration for religion (Bedi 2007). I assume that in debates on issues in which religion is only mentioned indirectly, less attention is paid to problems and solutions, which explains the first more general perspective. Furthermore, based on a notion of relevance and of political and cultural proximity (Galtung & Ruge 1965), I assume that religion is discussed more seriously and more clearly in problematisation terms when the context is domestic rather than foreign. Thus the article is divided into two sections on representations of religion in a foreign and a domestic context respectively.

The analysis is based on debates in the Danish parliament during the autumn of 2006.[1] The debates have been downloaded from the parliament's homepage using a list of preselected religion keywords, such as the terms for the world religions, their symbols, places of worship, religious specialists and members. In addition, the list also includes terms for atheism, secularisation, spirituality and New Age.

As a first introduction to or breakdown of the material, it is relevant to present the various debates. In the twelve debates on foreign issues, the discussions are centred on the global war on terror, the wars in Iraq and Afghanistan, the relationship between Turkey and the EU, and finally a single debate on the rejection of an EU agency on fundamental rights.

In the 26 debates on domestic issues, religion is not exclusively linked to conflict

---

1   References to quotations from parliamentary debates name the party, ideology or ministry to which the person belongs, the date of the debate, and that particular debate's place in the order of business. So a reference such as (Social Democrats, November 30, 4) means that this is a quotation by a Social Democrat from the fourth debate according to the order of business on November 30th.

and violence, but appears in many religion are more obvious than in others, most naturally the debates in which the different situations. In some cases references to heading of the debate and subject itself refer to religion.

Religion in a world of violence

In the Prime Minister's address at the official opening of the parliamentary year 2006/2007, the global war on terror is the single most important issue.[2] The very first sentence of his opening speech shows this. "On September 11th, 2001, 19 terrorists hijacked four planes in the United States" (Prime Minister October 3rd, 1). The speech begins at an abstract global level, before it turns to specific Danish foreign engagements and subsequently zooms in on Denmark with the following sentence: "The global value struggle also takes place in Denmark". The speech develops around two dominating themes, as can be seen in the following table of opposing keywords taken from the text.

TABLE 1: Structure and binaries in the prime ministerial address

Us	Them
'Freedom'	'Tyranny'
'Democracy'	'Dictatorship'
'Gender equality'	Inequality
'Freedom of speech'	Censorship
'Rational enlightenment'	'Fundamentalist darkening'[3]
'Separate religion and politics'	Confuse religion and politics

The Prime Minister himself does not mention censorship and confusion of religion and politics, but these characteristics follow logically from the rest of the text and the other keywords. It is not possible to identify either 'us' or 'them' any further, as the meaning of these concepts changes several times during the speech. 'Us' is used to denote both the West, Europe, Denmark, Denmark's Liberal Party, modern and secular people and so forth, whereas 'them' is primarily used as the negation or opposite of 'us'.

Apart from the global value struggle, the wars in Iraq and Afghanistan are the most frequently discussed issues that mention religion in a foreign context. In the foreign context, religion is always synonymous with Islam. In the debates on the situation in Iraq, all the politicians participating describe the conflict as one of sectarian violence

---

2   In the Danish context, commentators use a phrase that can be literally translated as 'the global value struggle' far more often than a phrase like 'war on terror', although this also exists.

3   The Prime Minister creates a metaphor drawing inspiration from the contrast between the Enlightenment and the medieval Dark Ages, when he refers to the darkened minds of the fundamentalists

among Sunni, Shiite and Kurdish groups. One of the discussions focuses on a possible withdrawal from Iraq. Here the Danish People's Party argue that further tension will arise if the troops are withdrawn, resulting in "power struggles among different religious groups" (Danish People's Party, December 5th, 10), and that this will leave "democracy [...] open to the terrorists and the fundamentalists" (Minister of Foreign Affairs, December 5th, 11). Furthermore, the Prime Minister and other members of parliament applaud several times that one of the successes of the war in Iraq is the establishment of a legal democratic parliament "where the central ethnic and religious groups are represented" (Prime Minister, December 5th, 10). It is interesting to note that the Prime Minister distinguished previously between them and us in terms of the ability to separate politics and religion, and now applauds the establishment of a parliament representing not only ethnic but also religious groups. He could have limited himself to applaud the inclusion of all political groups, and then implicitly let political mean both ethnic and religious – but he uses both ethnic and religious as terms to describe the situation. The debate is wrapped up by the leader of the Socialist People's Party, who concludes that all attempts to help the country have to involve "the political groups in Iraq that are not religious fanatics" (Socialist People's Party, December 5th, 10). The way religion in Iraq is represented in the Danish parliament is associated with violence and the usurpation of political power. Even though they have established a legal representative democracy, they are not like us because they still confuse religion and politics, and religion is antithetical to democracy, although it is the best they can do in Iraq.

The members of parliament refer not to Islam (whatever that is) but rather to a specific version of it, namely Islamism. Although Islamism is inspired by Islamic concepts and myths, Islamism is not tantamount to the Islamic religion, and is perhaps not even a religion at all. Rather, it is "a religious ideology with a holistic interpretation of Islam whose final aim is the conquest of the world by all means" (Mozaffari 2007, 21). Islamism is a particular form of Islam that is more political, violent, and critical of both the West and the established regimes in the Middle East. The notions involved when the politicians describe Islam refer more precisely to Islamism.

In a less violent conflict, this is also mirrored in the debates on Turkish membership of the EU. One of the problems with Turkey is "the restrictions on what you are allowed to express, especially in relation to religion" (Danish People's Party, November 15th, 7). It is the freedom of expression and freedom of religion that are the two problems with Turkey. "We cannot have a country that does not respect absolute freedom of expression and freedom of religion in the EU" (Minister of Foreign Affairs, November 15th, 7). To be a member of the EU implies "having that kind of freedom of religion that is the very precondition for Europe" (Minister of Foreign Affairs, November 15th, 7). Again, it is clear that they might have democracy, but as long as they confuse religion and politics by having Islamic legislation or showing special consideration of religious feelings they cannot become one of us.

In a later debate the Danish People's Party wants the parliament to reject an EU proposal for an agency for fundamental rights because they fear it will be a political agency disparaging scientists and politicians "who can see the problems with Islam" (Danish People's Party, November 30th, 9). They justify this fear with reference to "the instances where reports that have verified the way in which the increasing islamisation of Europe has led to further persecution of Jews have been shelved because they defile the political agenda" (Danish People's Party, November 30th, 9). Again, religion is Islam, and Islam is a problem from a Western democratic point of view because Islam is seen as incompatible with two of our most fundamental values, i.e. absolute freedom of expression and freedom of religion. The last debate also displays that Islam is not the only opponent. An elite exists that protects Muslims and thereby potentially undermines our fundamental values. This dual critique of both Muslims and the elite is what Rikke Egaa Sørensen and Vibeke Söderhamn Bülow call the culturalist and the systems critique respectively. Through a critique of the elite and the system it is possible to criticise Muslims and immigrants without risking charges of racism (1999, 85ff). The culturalist critique aims at showing how incommensurable the Christian and the Muslim cultures are, making integration between them impossible as well as explaining why Islam cannot democratise. That is a Christian/Western prerogative.[4]

In the following section, I will take a closer look at some of the debates on domestic issues because there is more depth and substance in the representations of religion in some of them than shown thus far.

Religion between system and lifeworld

Due to the openness and the inductive quality of the approach (Charmaz 2006), one of the main themes in one particular debate turned out to be a very useful analytical category in later readings of the material. In the debate on the taxation of deceased persons, the primary distinction when talking about death and religion was the distinction between the system and the individual. It was important for the politicians to show their respect for and understanding of the bereaved spouses in their difficult circumstances by making the tax system as simple and gentle as possible in order not to stress the surviving spouse unduly. As a result, the current system uses the surviving spouse's tax base to calculate the tax of the deceased person. The problem, according to those politicians who want to change this, occurs when the spouses have different relations to the state church. If the surviving spouse is a member of the church, then church tax becomes part of the tax base even if the deceased was not a member, and vice versa. The politicians who argue that nothing should be changed refer to the tax paid to the municipal authorities. If the spouses lived in different municipalities the tax would be based on the tax base in the surviving spouse's municipality. It should be no different with the church tax. The opposing politicians argue that there is a difference because 'strong principal emotions', 'fundamental attitudes', and 'conviction and faith'

---

4   The fact that the Danish People's Party manages to place the systems critique at a European level serves two of their primary political issues: curbing immigration and limiting EU influence on domestic politics.

make this an 'ethical problem'. Apart from the spokesman from the Danish People's Party who used the terms conviction and faith, nobody cloaked their argument for treating religion differently in religious terms.

Following the distinction between system and individual, most debates centred, not surprisingly, on the individual level, although some debates (especially those on the economy of the church) never focused on individuals at all. In these debates, the Church is a state institution on a par with other state institutions, which is also reflected in the fact that there is nothing particularly on religion per se in these debates. This should come as no surprise in a Western European democratic and secular nation state.

However, some cases deal with religion, and they are all based on lived lives and not on institutions, although their contexts are clearly institutional. It is interesting that the cases in which religion is perceived as a special case (claiming special consideration) are also the cases in which the present rules and regulations are found to be lacking. This applies to the debate on the religious service to prisoners, where it is pointed out that they are entitled to consult religious specialists (October 25, 1). It would have been just as plausible to mention a right to consult psychologists or other types of therapists, but this is not done.

In another debate on nursing homes for the elderly, one politician describes religion as a potentially important sorting characteristic when determining who can live at a given nursing home. She wants to give the elderly the possibility of choosing a nursing home that "resonates with their way of life and their values" (Danish People's Party, November 24th, 4). When elaborating on values and way of life there is one reference to dietary considerations and one reference to language, as some elderly immigrants do not speak Danish. All other clarifications stress that religion is an important reason for giving the elderly the choice of a nursing home. "It is sensible housing policy and sound practice that the elderly should have free choice. That they can choose to live in a home that is built on special values. It could be Christian values" (Danish People's Party, November 24th, 4). Later she elaborates on the idea of free choice, arguing that the provider of the home has the authority to refuse any elderly people. "If a particular religion is crucial for the operation of the home it would be unnatural for people with another religion to move into such a home" (Danish People's Party, November 24th, 4). "I cannot imagine a situation in which an atheist would want to live in a nursing home based on Christian values. They have to match" (Danish People's Party, November 24th, 4). A recent Gallup survey showed that the electorate of the Danish People's Party and people who vote communist are the least religious electorates in Denmark (Kristeligt Dagblad, October 29th). These are also the people who are the most critical of immigrants and Islam. As religion is the most important reason for giving the elderly the choice between different nursing homes, it is difficult to conceive of any other reason than making sure that nursing homes can be free of immigrants and Islam.[5] Finally, and

---

5   It is important to remember that Denmark is a social democratic welfare state with a universal welfare system that has provided the elderly with public nursing homes for many years.

as already mentioned in the debate on taxation of deceased persons, some politicians also claim that religion is a special case. As religiosity is not taken into account when calculating the tax base, they argue that the current rules must be changed.

On the other hand, there are also cases in which the current rules are not the problem. The problem is rather that the rules are not followed. This applies to the case of wearing a veil during security checks because it is impossible to identify people while they are wearing a veil (October 24th, 1). It also applies to the debate on the legal rights of priests charged with violating the teachings of the church (November 9th, 9). On the one hand, it is possible to argue that this case shows that religion is special since it does not deal with such violations within the common judicial system, but in a crossover institution employing theologians as well as judges and lay people. On the other hand, the pastoral courts do not take place in a church setting and are not based only on principles of teaching. Furthermore, they resemble the committees that try scientists for violations of scientific standards. As in the case of a pastoral court, scientists and judges in collaboration try such cases. In this respect religion is no more special than other social institutions like science.

Summing up, we can see that no changes in policy owes to religion at the level of administration. All the problems in which religious terms are involved at a systems level are articulated in terms that represent the Church (State Church Christianity being the only religion mentioned). In all instances, the politicians do not treat the religious institution differently than they would probably treat any other institution. In fact, several politicians stress that the parliament should only provide the framework of the church and leave it to the church itself to provide the content or the substance within this framework (Conservative People's Party & Social Liberal Party, October 24th, 12). On the individual level, where changes in policy affect individuals directly, religion is sometimes represented as a special case. When the current rules are perceived to be a problem, religion is represented as a special case and used as an argument for change. On the other hand, in some cases the problem is the failure to abide by the current rules. In these cases, representations of religion do not stress any particularity or claim a right to special considerations. This is illustrated in the following table.

TABLE 2: Relationship between religion and the current modus operandi of selected policies

		Religion is	
		special	not special
Current rules must be	changed	+	-
	upheld	-	+

At a systems level of effect religion is never articulated as a special case, so this level is not included in the table. In other words, religion is only represented as a special case at the individual level of effect when politicians want to change the current rules. Although this is phrased in relatively causal terms, with special consideration of religion seeming to determine whether the current rules are a problem or not, it is not possible to prove this causality. It is only possible to show the existence of a tendency and connection between the two, not whether considerations are taken in order to change the rules or whether insistence on the rules is due to an avoidance of any special considerations.

Religion and democracy

In the debates on foreign issues religion is not explicitly linked to easily identifiable problems or solutions. But Islam is generally represented as a problem with regard to insurgency, violence and democracy in Iraq, and with regard to freedom of expression, freedom of religion and democracy in Turkey and Europe.

In the debates on domestic issues there is much more variation in the use of religion as shown above. Let me in conclusion touch upon two paradoxes. The first paradox is that although several politicians want to take the specifically religious into account, most of them find it difficult to use religious terms and prefer non-religious terms like 'way of life', 'a sense of principle', 'fundamental attitudes', 'morality', and 'ethics' even though it is quite clear that what is also at stake is the special consideration applying to religious faith and conviction. The second paradox is that the current Danish Prime Minister has argued most vehemently for keeping religion in the private sphere – and yet he is the one who has talked most about religion in the public sphere. After having ridden the storm of the Cartoon Controversy, he wrote a feature for one of the largest newspapers in Denmark. He encouraged everybody to keep religion private with reference to the words of Jesus, "Render to Caesar the things that are Caesar's, and to God the things that are God's" (Mark 12:17), and to Martin Luther's doctrine of the two kingdoms. The debates in parliament also illustrate that his plea has been unsuccessful. Not only do many issues explicitly or implicitly mention religion, several members of parliament even argue that religion can claim affirmative action in some form or another. They hereby acknowledge that some laws and policies can be based on arguments that refer to religious claims, which in some respect blur the sharp distinction between religion and politics that is normally used when defining who we are. An alternative explanation focuses on the vicarious use of religion as a means to achieve something else, which could involve the exclusion of certain groups in society or showing concern for the individual facing an uncompromising system, making religion a functional argument without any real substance.

Bibliography

Beckford, James 1990. 'The Sociology of Religion and Social Problems'. *Sociological Analysis*, Vol. 51 (1), 1-14.

Bedi, Sonu 2007. 'What is so Special About Religion? The Dilemma of the Religious Exemption'. *Journal of Political Philosophy*, Vol. 15 (2), 235-249.

Charmaz, Kathy 2006. *Constructing Grounded Theory: A Practical Guide Through Qualitative Analysis*. Thousand Oaks: Sage.

Galtung, Johan & Mari Ruge 1965. 'The Structure of Foreign News – The Presentation of the Congo, Cuba and Cyprus Crises in Four Norwegian Newspapers'. *Journal of Peace Research*, Vol. 2 (1), 64-91.

Inglehart, Ronald 1977. *The Silent Revolution: Changing Values and Political Styles Among Western Publics*. New Jersey: Princeton University Press.

Mozaffari, Mehdi (2007). 'What is Islamism? History and Definition of a Concept'. *Totalitarian Movements and Political Religions*, Vol. 8 (1), 17-33.

Sløk, Camilla 2006. 'Defining the Core Values of the Danish Society in a Global World: The Danish Cartoon Crisis 2005/6'. Unpublished manuscript: Copenhagen Business School.

Sørensen, Rikke E. & Vibeke S. Bülow 1999. 'Ali og de fyrretyve k(r)oner. En analyse af Ekstra Bladets kampagne "De fremmede"'. In: Hervik, Peter (ed.), *Den generende forskellighed*. Copenhagen: Hans Reitzels Forlag.

IN THE NAME OF THE FATHER(S):
DIMENSIONS OF CIVIL RELIGION IN WAR ACCOUNTS[1]

Morten Brænder

In the closing scene of Steven Spielberg's fivefold Oscar winning World War II epos, *Saving Private Ryan*, the wounded Captain Miller (Tom Hanks) addresses the private (Matt Damon), whose life Miller's men were sent out to save in order to secure continuous support for the war effort on the home front. With his dying eyes glancing over the mutilated bodies of those who have fought and died under his command, Miller's last words are "James, earn this ... earn it!" Then the scene changes and we are back at the American Cemetery at Colleville-sur-Mer, where the aging James Ryan urges his wife to tell him that he has led a good life, that he has been a good man. By means of both style and content – the change of time, the Stars and Stripes waving over the white crosses behind the Ryans – is it clear that Miller's demand not only concerns the young 101st Airborne GI, who preferred to stay and fight instead of returning with the rescuing squad. First and foremost it addresses us, the moral descendents. Thus, this scene also highlights a central aspect of the sacrifice: that the value of death is defined not by the sacrificial act in itself, but rather by the subsequent interpretations and reaffirmations of this act. In this view, the strength of the sacrifice lies not in the divine references by which it is performed, but in its ability to become a rule of conduct. Spielberg uses the past to create a mirror in which we – posterity – can see our better selves.

Thus, on the one hand, such narratives of the nation seem like modern expressions of a social constant: Only through the myths revealed in such narratives, passed on from one generation to another, can we acknowledge our past and gain a notion of right and wrong; through them we become who we are (Anderson 1991, 6; Ricoeur 1980, 189). On the other hand, as Jürgen Habermas argued in the late 1980s, collective identity is not necessarily dependent on the existence of such cross-historical bonds. Patriotism can also be defined by the bonds of the constitution, by the rules defining mutual relationships recognised within a geographically confined space (Habermas 1997, 143). Hence, we have two ruling notions of national identity: One defined by bridging between past, present and future, and another characterised by the existence of a transcendent principle, by which human interaction can be measured. At face value, both these interpretations of national identity are secular (Anderson 1991, 36). Nevertheless, it is easy to see that the first of these (the notion that national unity is maintained by the reaffirmation of acts of sacrifice) can also be viewed as an expression of civil religion – that the

---
[1] I would like to thank Robert Wuthnow for enlightening comments and response on the idea and the study of the dimensionality of American Civil Religion.

cult of the national martyr can be seen as a cult proper, situated outside the domain of traditional religion. The question raised in this article, however, is whether the second of these interpretations (the notion that collective identity is established by principles transcending the collective) also has a civil religious equivalent.

I will not claim to be the first to address this question. With reference to Andrew Greeley, Gail Gehrig, who summoned up the civil religion debate in 1979, distinguished between Robert N. Bellah's 'transcendent' civil religion, and American 'folk religion' or 'religion in general' as analysed by Conrad Cherry and Martin E. Marty (Gehrig 1979, 11-18). Furthermore, in the 1970s as well as today, the distinction between these two dimensions of civil religion was deliberately used to politicise the question of national identity. Hence, Robert Jewett has juxtaposed 'prophetic realism' with 'zealous nationalism' and seen the latter as the dark side of American domestic and foreign policy (Jewett 1973; Jewett and Lawrence 2004).

Thus, my contribution in this respect is first and foremost empirical. From Bellah's pioneer article on 'Civil Religion in America' to the study of George W. Bush's post 9-11 rhetoric, the political speech has been considered as the archetypical media for expressing civil religion (Bellah 1991, Bostdorff 2003, Lincoln 2004). However, if civil religion is to be evaluated on the same footing as traditional religion, if it is to be seen as something else and more than tropes used by cunning politicians, then these tropes must have a resonator – someone must believe in them. Unlike the surveys in which this demand has been met with regard to the general public, my focus is on those who put their life at stake in the name of the nation – or to be more specific, the military personnel participating in the Global War on Terror.

The two dimensions: Transcendent and immanent civil religion

To sum up, following the distinction between transcendent and immanent national identity, my aim here is to show that we can also find two different ways of civil religious national identity, and that these two dimensions are both present in the justifications presented by servicemen deployed in Iraq.

TABLE 1: Dimensions of national identity

	Transcendent	Immanent
Religious	Vertical civil religion 'prophetic' civil religion (Bellah)	Horizontal civil religion 'priestly' civil religion, folk religion (Marty)
Non-religious	Patriotism Justice before loyalty, constitutionally bound (Habermas)	Nationalism Loyalty before justice, unity across history (Anderson)

'Vertical civil religion', placed in the upper left-hand corner, detaches the actual conduct of the nation from that of the national ideal. This is the reason why transcendent civil religion is often regarded in normative approaches as 'prophetic': By means of this detachment the actual deeds of the nation can be deemed just or unjust, in or not in accordance with an external ideal, or in Bellah's words with 'the covenant' (Bellah 1992, 179). The role of the prophecy – be it in the vision of an Old Testament prophet or in the discourse of prophetic civil religion – is to check the use and abuse of the privileges derived from this covenant.

But unlike patriotism, which exists 'etsi Deus non daretur', its civil religious equivalent specifically implies the existence of a divine being. In this regard it is, of course, similar to 'horizontal civil religion', which is placed in the upper right-hand corner. What sets the two apart is the relation between this divine being and the nation. Immanent civil religion does not detach the divine ideal from the conduct of the nation. Unlike vertical civil religion, in which the nation and the divinity are set apart, horizontal civil religion can only be mediated through the commemoration of the nation itself. To put it in another way: Whereas vertical civil religion emphasises a vertical relationship between temporal and eternal existence, horizontal civil religion focuses on the horizontal relation between past, present and future.

As reflected in the Old Testament vocabulary used in differentiating between 'prophetic' and 'priestly' civil religion, it is not new to distinguish between vertical and horizontal dimensions of religion. In fact, the distinction can be viewed as a core aspect of religion as such. The schism within Christianity which caused the breach between Rome and the Protestant Churches in the 16th century is – at least from the Protestant side – viewed as discord about the interpretation of the relationship between the vertical and the horizontal dimension of religious life. The distinction also transcends the boundaries of theology. In 1972, the sociologist James Davidson conducted a survey among Baptist and Methodist church members in which he showed the presence of both these dimensions, and demonstrated the way in which denominational affiliation, congregational affiliation and socio-economic status affected these dimensions differently (Davidson 1972).[2]

As for civil religion, the very idea that our affiliation with society is expressed and enacted religiously is – to certain extent – founded on the distinction between vertical and horizontal religion. In contrast to what is often called 'political religion', civil religion does not compete with traditionally institutionalised religion. Political religion, of which the most spectacular example is probably the abuse of religious-like symbols and rituals in totalitarian regimes like Nazi Germany or the Soviet Union, deliberately tries to take the place of church religion. It regards church religion as a threat, because the church offers the citizen a social locus beyond the reach of the state, and – as

---

2   Davidson's conclusions apply, of course, mainly to the Protestant denominations which he studies, and the possibility that the results would be different in e.g. a non-Prostestant setting cannot be excluded.

shown by modern history – rightly so.[3] Civil religion has an unexpressed but firmly institutionalised concordance with church religion. As the latter becomes privatised, the former offers a way of publicly expressing unity and community without leaving any breaches in the Jeffersonian 'Wall of Separation'. As a result of the ongoing process of differentiation, the functions of religion are split in two: Whereas church religion maintains the communication of individual salvation and individual rites of passage, the destiny of society and the observance of public rituals fall within the functional domain of civil religion.

This notion of functional differentiation easily leads to the assumption that church religion only concerns the vertical relation between individual and divine authority, and that the main purpose of civil religion is to maintain the social or horizontal dimension of religion. If this is true, it will render the distinction between immanent and transcendent civil religion implausible. However, before we reject the notion of a transcendent civil religion, two things should be taken into account. First, if the lines of demarcation drawn by social theory are not confirmed in practice, it is the theory that needs to be reconsidered and not the practice. Second, why should civil religion not entail the same complexity as that of church religion? As already noted above, all religion relates the individual both to the realm of transcendence and to the realm of the immanent. No church is an island. Even though the functional emphasis of church religion is on the personal salvation of the believer, it is forced to relate to the surrounding world, theologically as well as socially. Likewise, the main stance of civil religion may be on the establishment of social unity and coherence, but by implying the existence of a divine being it also implies the possibility of an external perspective on the nation itself – that is the possibility of a transcendent civil religion.

Thus, the question is whether our analysis reveals expressions which can be rendered as both civil religious and transcendent – i.e. expressions which relate the "citizens' role and (...) society's place (...) to the conditions of ultimate existence and meaning" (Coleman 1970, 70) without identifying this society with the divine cause itself.

Two final theoretical remarks are needed to build a bridge to the methodology. First, I do not imagine that the model proposed above by any means offers a satisfactory framework for interpreting the complex relationship between religion and nationalism. The model is a proposal, and like all proposals it should be subject to criticism and revision in order to meet the intention of the model, which is to offer a point of departure for empirical sensitive studies of civil religion.

Second, it is not my intention to contribute to the politicisation of the civil religion debate. The model is meant to be descriptive. We may with good reason assume that

---

3   I am referring, of course, to the fall of communism in Eastern Europe, which was in part facilitated and mediated by the churches. However, the relationship between state and religion in totalitarian regimes is not as unambiguous as expressed by this merely theoretical distinction between civil religion and political religion. In times of trial, the state – no matter how totalitarian it is – will need all the resources at its disposal, including the established churches.

the civil religious dimension one adheres to is connected to one's political background. Whereas conservatives will probably tend to find immanent civil religion appealing, liberals are more likely to make use of transcendent civil religion. However, bearing this insight in mind I will only use the terms 'conservative' and 'liberal' civil religion hesitantly. The insight that political preferences are connected to notions of the relationship between the national and the religious is interesting enough on its own terms, but politicising civil religion easily leads to normative misinterpretations. Claims about good and bad civil religion are more likely to fractionise the common pool of knowledge than to actually contribute to it. Furthermore, such claims also lead to the assumption that these two dimensions are mutually exclusive, which is probably not the case. As the two dimensions coexist in other religious contexts, we cannot allow ourselves the luxury of assuming that this is not the case with regard to civil religion. Ann Swidler has convincingly shown that justificatory accounts are extremely context-sensitive; and if that goes for civil religious justificatory accounts, too, we should only infer from discourse to firmly established meanings with great caution (Swidler 2001, 104).

Data: Milblogs

In order to illustrate the difference between immanent and transcendent civil religion, I will analyse two examples taken from my research into US military blogging in the Global War on Terror.

War stories have probably existed as long as socially organised violence, and to a certain extent the 'milblog' (an internet diary or web-log written by one or more servicemen in the field) is a modern version of the classical war letter or soldier diary. Unlike letters or diaries, however, milblogs are written and published shortly after the incidents described have actually taken place. It is therefore tempting to regard the milblog as a hitherto hidden source reflecting the thoughts and feelings of the serviceman – before the evaluation of the military, the development of the war and the concern of the surrounding world frame his view (Allison 2004, 78-79). This is, of course, only a qualified truth. Like letters and diaries, milblogs do not exist independently of the context in which they emerge. What makes the discourses expressed in the milblog interesting is the fact that they are created while the author is still deployed and without the advantage of hindsight. But they are (and should be) analysed as discourses and not as an unfiltered description of a sequence of events.

Furthermore, milblogs should not necessarily be regarded as a representative sample of the military as a whole. On the contrary, blogging has always been a haven for conservative pundits, and as far as milblogs are concerned this trait has probably only been reinforced by the fact that on April 17, 2007, a number of 'Operational Security' rules aimed at digital communication in general and blogging in particular came into effect (OPSEC 2007, 2-1g).

This point of concern is crucial with regard to the question of horizontal and vertical civil religion. If we regard conservatives as being more inclined to choose a horizontal justification for their participation in the war, will an analysis of milblogs reveal anything but horizontal justifications? No, probably not if we select our cases randomly. The two cases analysed in the following are therefore deliberately chosen because they differ with regard to a number of central points. Both cases have been chosen because they reflect on the legitimacy of the war, because I consider it most plausible to find expressions of civil religion in passages of justification. Both were published in 2005 at a time when the authors were corporals, and both bloggers use blogspot.com, one of the most popular domains among bloggers in general and milbloggers in particular. There, however, the similarity ceases: "Ma Deuce Gunner" is a man of Hispanic origin, serving in the army, and politically situated on the right. "Rachel the Great" is a white, female marine with a liberal stance.[4]

Ma Deuce Gunner: 'Happy Independence Day'[5]

Ma Deuce Gunner's blog is saturated with a martial aura. Not only do all his posts end with one or two commands, emphasised by the use of exclamation marks 'Scouts Out!!!... MDG... Out', a 'Ma Deuce Gun' is slang for the M2 machine cannon, usually placed on a HMMWV or in a helicopter, a weapon that has been in use since the Second World War. In this regard the subtitle of the header is interesting: "Protecting freedom ... half an inch at a time". Half an inch may, of course, refer to the line spacing, indicating the author's on-line fight for freedom *one line at a time*, but it also fits the 0.5 calibre size of the M2, thus referring to the notion that freedom should be defended *one bullet at a time*.

Style and grammar

Most blogs follow a fixed pattern. The header as well as general information about the author, along with gif-banners and links usually placed in the margin, indicates what sort of blog you are reading. Each post is marked by a title and a date, referring to the time it was *written*, and each ends with permanent links to the post as well as links to the comments made on it, marking the time when it was actually *published*.

As far as the post chosen for the present analyses is concerned, the fixed pattern regards not only the context but the text as a whole. The post was published on 4th July, 2005, and it is clearly Ma Deuce Gunner's intention to imitate an Independence Day speech, in style as well as in grammar. The language is grandiloquent. The three paragraphs of the post are composed as a classical logical judgment: Two premises, one general, and one specific, followed by a conclusion. And patterns of diathesis, mode and time are repeated and developed in the course of the text. By means of these patterns

---

4   In my analyses, I aim at using the pseudonym or 'nom de blog' of the author, even in the cases in which the real name is known. The only exception to this rule is when the information about the author specifically concerns his or her life apart from the blogosphere.

5   http://madeucegunners.blogspot.com/2005/07/happy-independence-day.html

the author establishes a bridge between past and present, between the founding fathers and the martyrs of the nation on the one hand, and himself and his fellow soldiers on the other. Thus, "We celebrate our freedoms gained and maintained by the blood of the men and women who *stood to defend* their countrymen, their republic, their liberty." He and his brothers-in-arms "proudly *stand to defend* the freedoms you [the readers] celebrate today." [my italics, MB].

This element of marking differences in time, and bridging between them, is also reflected in the use of pronouns. The solemn outlook of the text is supported by the dominant use of main clauses. Hence, there are only four relative pronouns in the text as a whole. Three of them, however, are used to establish some of its most central demarcation lines. In the first paragraph the use of 'who' serves twice to mark out the historical frame of interpretation; denoting the exemplary persons and acts of the past, and making them a measure of the present. In the second paragraph, the use of the relative pronoun in the sentence "Today, I write from the sands of Iraq, *in which we now* endeavour to secure a new democracy" [my italics, MB] serves both to underline the spatial reality of the present, the fact that the narrating subject is situated in the geographical periphery, and to establish a historical relation, this time by means of the implicit 'then', following from the explicit 'now'.

The importance of the historical and geographical framing of the text is underlined by the repetition of personal pronouns in the second and third person plural. The reference (in the first paragraph) to the martyrs of the past who "stood up to defend *their* countrymen, *their* republic, *their* liberty (…)" reflects the imperative demand of the third paragraph "Eat with *your* families, drink with *your* friends, play with *your* kids." [my italics, MB]. The spatial mirrors the temporal, and in between the two, literally in the second paragraph, the narrating subject, writing from Iraq, is situated. He is the one who has taken the burden of heritage on his shoulders, and he is the one who can thereby serve as the necessary means of realising the freedom of others.

Content

The fixed stylistic and grammatical structure of the text is also reflected in the content. Ma Deuce Gunner's 4th July speech presents a world in which everything has its proper place. This is probably most vivid in the notion of the sacrifice. It is noteworthy that in this respect the concrete mission in Iraq does not seem to play a significant role. The country, the purpose of the American presence in the Fertile Crescent and progress 'towards freedom', are all central elements in the second paragraph, but neither the insurgency nor the insurgents are mentioned. The sacrifice is not a question of living and dying, not a matter of friend or foe. It is a question of proper conduct. The concrete mission is only one in a long row of missions undertaken to fulfil the destiny of the nation, and in that respect both the adversary and the client are only steps on the way. What matters is – to follow the structure of the text – the relation between nation, soldier and civilian.

The soldier must serve; serve to make the world safe for democracy. The civilian must enjoy, and not abuse, his "freedoms (…), and pray for the prosperity of our nation, wisdom of our leaders, and safety of our soldiers." The connection between the two, between soldier and civilian, between periphery and centre, is secured by the notion of a unity existing across history; by the recognition of the present sacrifice as being in continuity with the sacrifices of the past. The sacrifice can only be recognised as a sacrifice proper by means of establishing this continuity between past and present. So the order of things comes at a price. The balance between the purpose of the sacrifice and the continuous recognition of this purposefulness is extremely delicate.

Next to the header of the blog is a drawing of a man on horseback, wearing a Stetson and carrying a Winchester rifle. Like many other conservative milbloggers, Ma Deuce Gunner depicts himself as a lone rider, living on the fringes of society. Like many other conservative milbloggers, he quotes George Orwell's famous statement that "[g]ood people sleep peaceably in their beds at night only because rough men stand ready to do violence on their behalf."[6] Their presence and their deeds may be unwelcome in the civilised world, but they, and their willingness to commit such deeds, are all that stands between civilisation and chaos. In the real world, people die to protect the freedom of others; so that others can maintain the illusion that such deeds are not necessary (Jewett, 90-98). Freedom is not free. Someone must defend it. The notion that this is the calling of America, a notion with which the author fully identifies, is commonly referred to as the idea of Manifest Destiny.

However, the idea that God has given the inhabitants of the New World a task to fulfil has always been connected with the warning that failure in following this call would lead to the loss of Divine Providence. This is the American Jeremiad, and this, the seamy side of belonging to the elect, is also present in the post – most importantly in the passage where Ma Deuce Gunner emphasises the conduct of those back home. This is the only time he uses capital letters in the text: "(…) on this day, feel NO pity for me and my men". Why? Probably because pitying would imply a differentiation between the mission and the soldiers, a differentiation with which the idea of the deeds of the soldiers as a sacrifice in continuity with the sacrifices of the past could not be maintained. In that perspective the phrase commonly used by Democratic politicians, that they are "against the war, not the soldiers", is an archetypical expression of such a patronising pity.[7]

According to Norman Fairclough, the final aim of critical discourse analysis (CDA) is to reveal the way in which discourses are structured or interwoven in a certain pattern. This pattern or 'texture' describes the internal relationship of the discourses, which in our analyses we assume represents, re-actualises and re-interprets a certain order of discourse, the linguistic expression of what sociologists name institutions (Chiapello

---

6   *Dadmanly*: July 29, 2005, *Fire and Ice*: November 24, 2005, *Madeucegunner*: June 10, 2005, *Snipereye*: January 6, 2007.

7   The Jeremiad is a very 'prophetic' or corrective element, and the use of this trait in this context points to the fact that contrary to the interpretation of Jewett, '*prophetic* civil religion' is not necessarily *tolerant* civil religion.

& Fairclough 2002, 189, 195). Following the observations made in the analysis of style and grammar, it is not surprising that the dominant discourses in Ma Deuce Gunner's Independence Day speech are America's universal call and the sacrificial vocabulary. As a speech made for a national holiday, instituted for the remembrance of the historical occurrences which led to the foundation of the collective, the natural grid of the statement is the connections between the past and the present, and between centre and periphery in the present. The rites of the national ritual, enacted in the centre of the present – apparently so crucial for maintaining the covenant – only make sense if they are properly connected to the past and to the periphery. As a whole, these discourses describe the pattern of a national cosmology, within which the past is made an exemplary model of sacrifice, and the sacrifices made in the periphery have the dual purpose of re-enacting the past (thereby proving it right), and of safeguarding the centre, the community, through which the continuity of the heritage can be secured.

Rachel the Great: "Pray that your loneliness may spur you into finding something to live for, great enough to die for."[8]

Style and grammar

The post chosen from Rachel the Great's blog is clearly not written with the intention of imitating an eloquent speech. On the contrary, as in Rachel's blog in general, the style here is very close to that of a diary proper. She often uses spoken forms like can't, isn't or ain't. The verbs are in the present, indicative, active, and the dominant grammatical subject is the first person personal pronoun.

Generally, personal pronouns are useful in drawing up social fields and in establishing social lines of demarcation. However, even though the pronouns used in this post do establish a set of different categories which are relevant for the justification of Rachel's deployment to Iraq, the way she depicts the relation between soldiers and civilians, periphery and centre, differs very much from what we saw in the above.

The 'I' faces a 'you', but 'you' is used only in its general sense to denote conditions shared by all men and women: "You can't pick and choose when you will or won't love your country. Either you do or you don't". The second person, singular personal pronoun is not the addressee of her remarks. The I/you-relation is not a face-to-face encounter, but a question of relating and submitting to a set of general conditions. Likewise, both 'those' and 'we' are used to denote categories in which Rachel herself is or may be included: "(…) I guess that *those* who do [love their country] are willing to pay the price for living in such a blessed place". "(…) it's the fact that *we* keep trying that matters most." The line of demarcation established by the pronouns is not a social boundary. It is a way of differentiating between the universal and the particular.

---

8   http://everydaygroundhogday.blogspot.com/2005/11/pray-that-your-loneliness-may-spur-you.html

Content

The title of Rachel's blog refers to the 1993 movie *Groundhog Day*, in which the main character, played by Bill Murray, is forced to live through the same day, experiencing the exact same series of events every time he wakes up. Neither this theme nor the reference to this movie is unusual in milblogs from Iraq. In fact, it is probably one of the most common ways in which these bloggers, regardless of rank, branch, gender and political values, describe the military experience.[9] Ironically, whereas the title of the blog thus emphasises the unchangeable nature of time in the service, it is exactly the opposite – the changes of time – which is the theme in this post. This notion of changeability contextualises Rachel's frustrations both as an inward effect, "*today* I am feeling so alone and trapped (…) [but] *tomorrow* I will wake up and feel much better", as a cause, i.e. as changes inflicted on her from the outside: "[t]here are such huge ups and downs and the roller coaster of it all is exhausting", and, most importantly, by contrasting the deployment to Iraq with the outer world.

As seen in the example above, reflections about the relationship between the world 'out here' and the world 'back home' is not an unusual theme in milblogs. It touches a number of core issues for those who are sent abroad: How strong are the bonds of the military brotherhood compared to one's family bonds? To whom do I owe loyalty? How should the people back home relate to us out here? And, of course, why am I here? Neither is it unusual to interpret this relationship in ontological terms. One of these worlds is real, while the other is based on an illusion. In Ma Deuce Gunner's blog, as in most conservative blogs, the world at home was revealed as the illusionary world. The civilian does not see that everything he takes for granted is being maintained only because, beyond the reach of his notions, others willingly sacrifice their lives for his rights and for his security. In Rachel's blog, however, this ontological scheme is reversed. Here, 'home' designates the real world, whereas the world and the people 'out here' are depicted as fake:

I think since I came back from R&R it's been harder on me. It made me realize how fake people can be out here and it made me miss the real world. Everyone leans on each other, so for the most part everyone acts like they are your friend, when in reality if you weren't trapped out here with them, you would never talk to them and you both know it. It makes you miss your real friends and real relationships.

By turning this scheme upside down, the answers to the questions of loyalty which follow from the experience of inhabiting two different worlds also change. Thus, the way Rachel distinguishes between the world at home and the world out here serves to amplify the way she justifies her participation in the war: The notion that the personal

---

9   See *Sergeant Lizzie*: October 20, 2004, *Si vis pacem para bellum*: February 13, 2005, *A soldier's thoughts*: April 10, 2005, *Ma Deuce Gunner*: May 10, 2005, *From my position ... on the way*: May 23, 2005, *Quiet Kidd*: September 13, 2005, *Semper Fidelis*: December 8, 2005, *Lumberjack in the desert*: July 10, 2006. *Sail Away Now*: January 16, 2007.

relationships in the world out here are superficial and momentary undermines the idea that the warrior enters the ranks of a community existing *across* history. Instead, life in Iraq, in 'Groundhog Day', is an artificial world, existing *apart from* history.

In Rachel's blog not the people but the place, and not the nation but the country are blessed. This becomes abundantly clear in the first lines of the post, in which she presents her answer to the question, "Why am I out here?" As in the Dag Hammarskjöld quotation in the title of the post, Rachel answers this question by defining what should be regarded as "great enough to die for". Just like Ma Deuce Gunner, she relates justification to sacrifice. Unlike Ma Deuce Gunner, however, Rachel does so by distinguishing between the cause and her love for her country:

I don't believe in this cause enough to die for it. I guess I believe i[n] my country though and support it and you can't just say something like that. You can't pick and choose when you will or won't love your country. Either you do or you don't and I guess those that do are willing to pay the price for living in such a blessed place. I really think America is the most beautiful country in the world and although it's not perfect, it's the fact that we keep trying that matters most. I wonder if those that have paid the price though would look back from where they are and say it was worth it.

The proper interpretation of the ambiguous last sentence of this statement could, of course, be the subject of a larger discussion. What is most interesting here, however, is the way Rachel emphasises the power of patriotism without establishing a trinity of interdependence between the serviceman, the civilian, and those who have paid the highest price.[10] In spite of the alleged meaninglessness of this concrete mission, and in spite of the lurking suspicion that even the sacrifices of the past may seem meaningless in the eyes of the martyrs, she still maintains that dying for one's country can be regarded as purposeful. The purpose is just not one which she can "pick and choose". Here, the justification of the sacrifice does not refer to the birthright of the nation or making the world safe for democracy. It is not modelled on the narratives of Manifest Destiny or the American Jeremiad. There is no call for civilians to recognise the value of the sacrifice by supporting the troops. Instead it is the serviceman herself who emphasises that "I believe in my country and *support* it". Here the justification is not horizontal but vertical, and therefore the function of the justified also becomes another. Instead of being a constitutive act in the continuous existence of the nation, it becomes a way of confirming a love which is bestowed on the individual independently of his or her will.

---

10   The word 'patriot' has changed its meaning over the years. Here I use it in a strictly descriptive sense to designate a person who loves his country and who is ready to defend it, regardless of political stance. In the conservatively biased sense, 'a true patriot'. I regard the word 'nationalist' as a more precise term.

Concluding remarks

The first post analysed above was written by a conservative, and the second by a liberal. The first expressed confidence in the cause, while the second doubted its legitimacy. Ma Deuce Gunner is a man, Rachel the Great a woman. He serves in the army, she in the Marine Corps. The differences between their ways of justifying their presence in Iraq may derive from one cause or a combination of several causes – or they may simply be accidental, and determining which is which would demand broader comparative analyses.

What is important in this context is that neither of the authors confines their justificatory accounts to mere this-worldly justice or ideology. On the contrary, they both clearly draw on civil religious discourses in so far as they both use 'symbolic system[s]' by which they relate "the citizen's role and American society's place in space, time and history, to the conditions of ultimate existence and meaning" (Coleman 1970, 70).

However, the symbolic systems they make use of, as well as their notions of society's place in space, time and history, differ radically. Ma Deuce Gunner emphasises how the right conduct follows from the cross-historical role of the community and the interplay between sacrifice and covenant. Rachel the Great describes how, in spite of all the good reasons against dying in this war, something greater than herself and greater than historically determined bonds still determines her will to sacrifice. In *Everyday is Groundhog Day in Iraq* there is no mention of the nation or of the maintenance of interdependence between servicemen and civilians. Instead, Rachel the Great consistently uses the word 'country', and the relationship in focus is univocally vertical: Love of one's country is predestined. It is from this love and not from the proper conduct of those at home or from one's participation in a brotherhood of warriors existing across time that the willingness to fulfil one's duties flows.

Bibliography

Army Regulation 530-1, Operations Security (OPSEC), April 19, 2007.

Allison, Fred H. 2004. 'Remembering a Vietnam War Firefight: Changing Perspectives over Time'. *The Oral History Review* 31, 2, 69-83.

Anderson, Benedict 1991 [1983]. *Imagined communities: reflections on the origin and spread of nationalism*. London: Verso.

Bellah, Robert N. 1991 [1967]. 'Civil Religion in America'. In: *Beyond Belief, Essays on Religion in a Post-Traditional World*. Berkeley: University of California Press, 168-189.

Bellah, Robert N. 1992 [1978]. 'Religion and the Legitimation of the American Republic'. In: *The Broken Covenant, American Civil Religion in a Time of Trial*. Berkeley: University of California Press, 164-188.

Bostdorff, Denise M. 2003. 'George W. Bush's Post-September 11 Rhetoric of CovenantRenewal: Upholding the Faith of the Greatest Generation'. *Quarterly Journal of Speech* 89, 4, 293-319.

Chiapello, Eve & Norman Fairclough 2002. 'Understanding the new management ideology: a transdisciplinary contribution from critical discourse analysis and new sociology of capitalism'. *Discourse and Society* 13, 2, 185-208.

Calhoun, Craig 1994. 'Social Theory and the Politics of Identity'. In: Craig Calhoun (ed.) *Social Theory and the Politics of Identity*. Massachusetts: Blackwell, 9-36.

Coleman, John A. 1970. 'Civil Religion'. *Sociological Analysis* 31, 67-77.

Davidson, James D. 1972. 'Religious Belief as a Dependent Variable'. *Sociological Analysis* 33, 81-94.

Gehrig, Gail 1979. *American Civil Religion – An Assessment*. Connecticut: Society for the Scientific Study of Religion.

Griffin, Christopher 2006. 'Driven to print'. *Armed Forces Journal* August 2006. (http://www. armedforcesjournal.com/2006/08/1936101)

Habermas, Jürgen 1997. 'Der europäische Nationalstaat – Zu Vergangenheit und Zukunft von Suveränität und Staatsbürgerschaft'. In: *Die Einbeziehung des Anderen, Studien zur Politischen Theorie*. Frankfurt /M.: Suhrkamp, 128-153.

Jewett, Robert 1973. *The Captain America Complex: the dilemma of Zealous Nationalism*. Philadelphia: The Westminster Press.

Jewett, Robert and John S. Lawrence 2004. *Captain America and the Crusade Against Evil: the dilemma of Zealous Nationalism*. Michigan: Wm. B. Eerdmans Publishing Co.

Lincoln, Bruce 2004. 'Bush's "God Talk"'. *Christian Century* 121, 20, 22-29.

Ricoeur, Paul 1980. 'Narrative Time'. *Critical Inquiry* 7, 1, 169-190.

Swidler, Ann 2001. *Talk of Love*. Chicago: Chicago University Press.

Blogs cited: All available on http://www.milblogging.com/

Ma Deuce Gunner
Everyday is Groundhog Day in Iraq
A soldier's thoughts
Dadmanly
Fire and Ice
From my position ... on the way
Lumberjack in the desert
Quiet Kidd
Sail Away Now
Semper Fidelis
Sergeant Lizzie
Si vis pacem para bellum
Snipereye

THE LABYRINTH SOLVED?

SAYYID QUṬB'S RADICAL ISLAMIST VIEW OF DEMOCRACY

John Møller Larsen

"Leave them, that you do not trouble yourself with these people who will die, who have gone astray in a labyrinth[1] of deceptive hope (…)" (Quṭb 2003, 2126). In this manner Sayyid Quṭb, the Egyptian teacher and *litterateur*, turned Islamist ideologue, paraphrased sura 15:3 of the Qur'ān referring to the unbelievers. In Quṭb's view modern man had indeed gone astray in self-deceit and self-aggrandisement, but what did he offer to remedy this condition?

Quṭb has remained a major source of inspiration for Islamist radicals and for modern Islamism in a broader sense right up to the present day. While the criticism waged against the overall realities of the modern world is prominent in his Islamist works, and is in some sense even constitutive of them, the more specific purpose of this article is a brief presentation of Quṭb's view of democracy and public participation in the governing of society as evinced in his major opus, the Qur'ānic commentary *Fī Zilāl al-Qur'ān* (*In the Shade of the Qur'ān*).[2] Quṭb only makes a few explicit references to 'democracy' (*dimuqrāṭiyya*), but his views on the matter are made sufficiently clear by his comments on matters pertinent to democracy, by his views on *shūrā* (an Islamic term usually translated 'consultation' and equated with an Islamic form of democracy by Muslim modernists), and first and foremost by the central ideas constituting his view on the relationship between God and man. It is to two of these ideas that we should first direct our attention.

By way of introduction, however, a few words on Quṭb's life seem appropriate.[3] Quṭb (b. 1906) was educated as a teacher in Cairo and worked as such until he was employed by the Ministry of Education in 1940. Since his student years he had been a very active participant in contemporary literary and cultural debates, and apart from works of literary criticism he also published both poetry and novels. During the 1940s he became increasingly preoccupied with social questions, and his former secular views gave way to an increased Islamist orientation. A study tour to the United States (1948-50) nourished his anti-Western sentiments, and after his return to Egypt he became involved with the Muslim Brotherhood. In 1952 the Brotherhood supported the revolution of Nasser and the Free Officers; but relations with Nasser soon went sour as he was not prepared to share the power of the military regime, and in 1954 there was

---

1 *Matāha*, which also carries the sense of 'a trackless wilderness'.
2 An English translation which at present covers the suras up to and including sura 47 and suras 78-114 is currently being published (Quṭb 1999-2008). The translations presented here are my own.
3 Accounts of Quṭb's biography can be found in Carré 2003, 1-8, and Damir-Geilsdorf 2003, 19-55.

a crack-down on the Brotherhood. Quṭb was sentenced to 15 years of imprisonment, and during the next ten years – witnessing torture and killings of imprisoned Muslim brothers – his views on religion and politics were steadily radicalised. In 1964 he was released, only to be arrested again the following year. Accused of conspiring against the state, he was sentenced to death by a military court and executed in August 1966.

Axial notions

Quṭb's Islamist discourse revolved around a range of notions inseparably imbued with religious and political meaning, some of them describing his view of the *ideal*, some the *actual* relationship between God and man. The dichotomy between ideal and reality, between utopian vision and scorching polemic, is at its most conspicuous in the two widely discussed terms *ḥākimiyya* (sovereignty) and *jāhiliyya* (barbaric ignorance), terms with far-reaching consequences in Quṭb's thought. In their specific sense both words were borrowed from the Indo-Pakistani Islamist ideologue Abū l-Aʿlā al-Mawdūdī (d. 1979), but *jāhiliyya* would – as we will see – undergo an important change in Quṭb's understanding.

Ḥākimiyya is the sole prerogative of God, and accordingly the true meaning of Islam, in Quṭb's view, involves submitting to the absolute sovereign of the universe whose will has found its final expression in the Qurʾān and the *sunna* of the prophet Muhammad. Rejection of this basic principle and attempts to devise human legislation in disregard of the two sources amount to revolt and secession. When the Qurʾān was revealed, Quṭb explains, its verses were meant

to be 'the daily commands' which the Muslims received in order to act upon them immediately after receiving them, as the soldier in his barracks or on the battlefield receives 'the daily command' with agitation, understanding and a desire to carry it out (…) (Quṭb 2003, 2563).

So, to put it bluntly, it is not for man to question but to obey. While God's ultimate sovereignty over creation is of course a central Islamic tenet, its actual political consequences have varied greatly throughout Islamic history. For Quṭb it became an operative principle in his rejection of a world steeped in *jāhiliyya*.

In the Qurʾān *jāhiliyya* had been used polemically against the ethos of the pre-Islamic Arabs. Later, it would primarily designate the pre-Islamic period in the Arabian Peninsula, but from time to time authors would still employ it to characterise supposedly un-Islamic behaviour in their own time.[4] Al-Mawdūdī used the term extensively in his polemics, and considered most of Islamic history to have been "a mixture of *jāhiliyya* and Islam" (Shepard 2003, 523). Quṭb's use of the term in his early Islamist period was already characterised by a strongly polemical proclivity, but in his late writings he came to consider virtually the entire world to be in a state of *jāhiliyya*, a

---

4   For the use of the term in the Qurʾān and subsequently, see Shepard 2001.

state of rebellion against God, the 'Muslim' world included (Shepard 2003, 534). In his commentary on sura 5 he gives a succinct definition:

Jāhiliyya (…) is the rule of some humans over others, because it involves some humans being in servitude (or: worship, *'ubūdiyya*) of others and involves leaving the servitude of God, rejecting the divinity of God and – in accordance with this rejection – recognizing the divinity of some humans and the servitude to them to the exception of God (…) the one who rejects the *sharī'a* of God accepts the *sharī'a* of *jāhiliyya* and lives in *jāhiliyya* (Quṭb 2003, 904).

While Quṭb considered *jāhiliyya* to be a transhistorical reality, Islam had been present in varying degrees of purity since the days of Muhammad (Quṭb 2003, 209). There had been a steady decline, though, and eventually Islam had practically been wiped out of existence. According to W. Shepard, "Most of his statements (…) indicate that he saw this as happening only with the full onslaught of Western imperialism in the 19th century" (2003, 529).

So, even with this brief description of two central tenets it is clear that Quṭb's religio-political vision went directly counter to any idea of democracy based on popular sovereignty. How, then, did these basic views translate into a more detailed discourse?

At grips with democracy

By the time Quṭb wrote his Qur'ānic commentary (the publication of which started in 1952), the Egyptian experience with parliamentary bodies of Western inspiration had lasted for the better part of a century, beginning with khedive Ismā'īl's Assembly of Delegates in 1866. The years of British domination (1882-1952) presented a mixed picture. Under the consul-general Evelyn Baring (Lord Cromer; in office until 1907) the free press thrived and the nationalist movement was able to regain its momentum after Colonel 'Urābī's failed uprising that had led to the British occupation. Meanwhile, public influence on policy was curbed by the institutional framework giving the khedive (the king from 1922) extensive power, and by the British *de facto* having the last word on important issues. The political situation thus remained volatile as the parties concerned vied for power, and it was further exacerbated by the strains of the two World Wars. By 1942 Quṭb left Egypt's major nationalist party, the Wafd, to join the breakaway Sa'dist party. He had, however, lost faith in the politics of the old parties and felt that the West had betrayed Egypt, so he soon declared himself independent (Damir-Geilsdorf 2003, 33-35). When we consider Quṭb's approach to the perceived fallacies of democracy, it is helpful to distinguish between his dogmatic and his 'pragmatic' lines of argument.[5] His dogmatic approach is ultimately based on the notion of *ḥākimiyya*, divine sovereignty,

---

5   For an exposition of Quṭb's views on Western democracy, see Choueiri 1997, 106-15 (including a comparison with the views al-Mawdūdī).

and the challenge to it from *jāhilī* forces. This basic conflict is then illustrated in specific polemics against social ideas seen to be human constructs:

When 'nationalism' raises its banner or the 'fatherland', the 'people' or the 'class' raise their banners... and people are bent on worshipping these banners to the exclusion of God (...) then this is a worship of idols (*'ibādat al-aṣnām*)... For an idol need not take the form of a stone or a piece of wood; an idol may be a doctrine or a banner![6]

It might of course be argued that democracy as a framework does not necessarily entail nationalism or even marked class conflicts, as the democratic experience of at least the recent decades have shown (e.g. value-based politics). Such an argument would not have had much effect on Quṭb, for the applicability of the charges of idolatry is ascertained when he states that human life "does not thrive through feudalism or capitalism", "through communism or scientific socialism", "theocracy", nor "through dictatorship or democracy" (Quṭb 2003, 2075) and elsewhere tells us that "In every earthly system some people take others as their lords to the exclusion of God... This happens in the most advanced of democracies just as it happens in the basest of dictatorships..." (Quṭb 2003, 407). For Quṭb, democracy is an unacceptable idea *per se*. While there may be varying degrees of sophistication in the different systems of government, the bottom line is that democracy belongs squarely in the category of *jāhiliyya* and polytheism (*shirk*) or idolatry. But though Quṭb certainly insisted on the primacy of dogmatic argument, he did also employ arguments of an altogether different kind, which I have termed 'pragmatic'.

Quṭb, who maintained a negative view of most historical forms of Christianity (which had distorted the original teachings of Jesus, the non-divine prophet and messenger of God), identified 'the church' as a main culprit in the rise and development of democracy in Europe:

Europe fled from God – having fled from the tyrannical church which committed outrages in the name of the false religion! – and it rebelled against God (praised be He) – having rebelled against the church which at the peak of its oppressive power ruined all human values![7]

After the defection from the church, Quṭb explains that

people there thought they would find their humanity, freedom and honour – as well as their welfare – under the aegis of the individualistic (and democratic) systems, and they set all their hopes on the freedoms and guarantees which man-made[8] constitutions ensure them, the principles of parliamentary representation, the free press, judicial and legal guarantees, and the rule of the

---

6   Quṭb 2003, 2115, just as the idol "may be a value, [or] an outlook", 1801. The frequent use of "..." belongs to Quṭb's text and should not be mistaken for signs of omission, which are given as "(...)".

7   Quṭb 2003, 1754; similarly 1942.

8   Arabic *waḍ'ī*, which may also be rendered 'positivist' or 'conventional'.

elected majority... till the last of the halos by which these systems are surrounded... What is the result? The result is the tyranny of 'capitalism', the tyranny which transforms all these guarantees and all these creations into mere slogans[9] or mere phantasms! The overwhelming majority fell into abject servitude to the tyrannical minority owning the capital, thereby dominating the parliamentary majority as well! And the man-made constitutions! And the free press! And the rest of the guarantees which people there [i.e. in Europe] thought to be a guarantee of their humanity, freedom and honour, detached from God, praised be He!!![10]

This passage addresses several issues, but the main problem identified is "the tyranny of capitalism", which would appear to be an inevitable outcome of democracy. Throughout his commentary Quṭb deals with different aspects of capitalism, always denouncing it. If there were any doubts about the merits of capitalism when it arose four centuries ago, he explains, "the experience of these centuries does not leave any room for doubt" (Quṭb 2003, 326). One of the problems was the concentration of capital, and with Hjalmar Schacht (a former leader of the German Reichsbank) as his authority, Quṭb explains that in an economic system based on *ribā* (interest or usury) eventually "all the capital on earth will end up in the hands of a very small number of usurers" (Quṭb 2003, 321). Nothing positive could be attributed to it – it "burdens industry with usurious interest which is added to the basic expenditure and burdens commerce and consumption", and "it steers industry and all investment in a direction in which there is no regard for the [actual] interests of industry or the consumers" (Quṭb 2003, 639). The attempt by some Islamic modernists (e.g. Muḥammad 'Abduh) to distinguish between usury and taking other types of interest, which from this perspective seemed acceptable, was anathema to Quṭb. Capitalism, Quṭb believed, was also detrimental to a peaceful relationship between nations, because "armed war between nations, armies and states" was caused by the "usurers possessing the global capital [who] ignite these wars directly or indirectly" (Quṭb 2003, 331). So none of the institutions accompanying democracy could protect the "humanity, freedom and honour" of the Europeans against the greed and warmongering of the capitalists.

It was not that non-Islamic systems were incapable of certain positive results. Quṭb explained that "'Socialism' is a social and economic school of human making, susceptible to good or bad. And 'democracy' is a system for living or ruling (*ḥukm*) of human making, too, its human making susceptible to good or bad..." (Quṭb 2003, 1083). Parts of life in the ideal Islamic society might well resemble parts in a *jāhilī* society, but this did not mean that any part of Islam is *jāhilī*. The branches may have a resemblance, but the roots of the societies are totally different. Whereas societal systems engendered by men were of a transient nature, the Islamic system was endowed with permanence

9   Arabic *lāfita*, 'sign'.
10   Quṭb 2003, 1754; similarly 1942-43.

and with sufficient flexibility to meet the needs of society at all times and in all places. Quṭb addressed those

who care little about their religion and do not esteem God as He should be... When today you present Islam to people in the name of socialism and the name of democracy it is because these two belong to the fashions of contemporary orientations. Capitalism was for a certain period the favorite fashion with people who thereby left the feudal system! Just as absolute authority for a certain period was the coveted fashion, [i.e.] in the period of the national unification of scattered states, like in Germany and Italy in the days of Bismarck and Mazzini for instance! And tomorrow, who knows what will be the common fashion among the social and earthly systems and the systems of authority which one slave imposes on another (Quṭb 2003, 1083-84).

For Quṭb, the economic prosperity and technical prowess of the West mattered little. Quṭb considered it a world without direction and purpose, and he would often catalogue its vices and predicaments such as the disorder in sexual relations, the 'craze' for sports, cinema, dancing and fashion, the trivialities of pop culture, drug addiction and alcoholism, spiritual emptiness, anxiety, fear and mental illness.

The Islamic utopia

Against the scourges of modern day *jāhiliyya* and rebellious democracies, Quṭb posed his vision of the Islamic state, the kingdom of God. This would be a supremely just and pious society, wholly submitted to the *ḥākimiyya* of God, dedicated to the implementation the *sharīʿa* and continuously expanding its realm by the necessary and divinely sanctioned means (i.e. missionary activity and jihad).

Generally speaking, Quṭb was reluctant to be specific about a range of central issues in the Islamic state of the future. The devil is in the detail, and specifics would have laid open the road to controversy. While this vagueness may sound like a stratagem, he used it deliberately, undoubtedly in good faith, and he was clear on his reasons: "The Islamic method is a realistic method that does not occupy itself with issues that have not arisen in reality, and hence it does not at all occupy itself with legal rulings connected with these issues which have no existence in reality!" (Quṭb 2003, 1519). Once it has materialised, "that special society may need (...) banks and insurance companies and birth control... and so on, or it may not need it! That is because we cannot estimate its basic needs in advance, nor its size or its form, so that we can legislate for it in advance!" (Quṭb 2003, 2010). Quṭb despised the endless theoretical discussions in *fiqh* ('jurisprudence'), which he termed "a *fiqh* derived from cold pages" (Quṭb 2003, 1735), and instead spoke of a *dynamic fiqh* (*fiqh ḥarakī*), an understanding of the law arising among the believers in the midst of the battle for an Islamic state and capable of meeting the challenges from shifting realities.

While Quṭb did not elaborate on the technical procedures of election, government and administration, he did offer a description of some basic characteristics. The ideal state would be governed by a just *imām* (leader) or caliph. Like Muslim reformers and modernists, Quṭb embraced the concept of *shūrā* (consultation), which had a limited Qurʾānic basis but some precedent in the traditions of Muhammad and the early Caliphate.[11] In classical treatises it had expressed the idea that the caliph should consult with leading men in society, though there was no unanimity as to who these men were. In the modern period the term was influenced by the European idea of parliament, and among the Islamic modernists there was a tendency to equate the two,[12] all the while insisting on the eminently Islamic character of *shūrā*. In his commentary on sura 3:159, Quṭb explained that

> *shūrā* is a fundamental principle and (…) an Islamic system cannot be built on any other fundament… As for the [specific] form of the *shūrā* and the means by which it is realised, these are matters susceptible to change and development according to the conditions of the *umma* [i.e. the Islamic ʿcommunityʾ or ʿsocietyʾ] and the concomitants of its life (Quṭb 2003, 501).

While again this is somewhat vague, elsewhere Quṭb explains that in the ideal Islamic state

> the ranks of people become distinct and their positions in society are established, based on credal scales and values which everybody know, such as bravery in jihad, piety, righteousness, worship, morals, strength and competence (Quṭb 2003, 2008).

More specifically, the mechanisms required to recognise personal merit are grounded in the societal structure:

> In the Muslim society people of every city quarter know each other, have mutual relations and are responsible for each other (…). Therefore people of every city quarter know those who have the abilities and talents, weighed on credal scales and values, so it is not difficult for them to charge those among them who possess bravery, piety and ability [with the necessary tasks]… whether it is for the consultative council (*majlis al-shūrā*) or for local matters. As for the general positions of authority (*al-imārāt al-ʿāmma*), the *imām* – whom the *umma* has chosen following a nomination by the people of loosing and binding (*ahl al-ḥall wa-l-ʿaqd*, i.e., the traditional Islamic term for those responsible for the election of a caliph) or those giving consultation (*ahl al-shūrā*)… he will choose from among the group of selected men, whom the dynamic movement has specified. The dynamic movement (…) is persistent in Muslim society, and jihad continues until the Day of Resurrection (Quṭb 2003, 2008-9).

---

11   For expositions of Quṭbʾs views on *shūrā*, see Choueiri 1997, 115-17; Carré 2003, 179-81, 196-7; Damir-Geilsdorf 2003, 153-57.
12   See for instance Hourani 1983, 144.

However, this all raises more questions than it answers. For instance, who has the final word, the *imām* or the consultative council? If the *imām* decides, as would seem to be the case elsewhere in Quṭb's writings, what separates this from dictatorship?[13] He can be deposed if he strays from the *sharīʿa* – but who is to decide if he has done so? Is this conundrum solvable at all? It is difficult to see how. Quṭb would not acknowledge the problems inherent in his societal vision. He firmly believed that a truly faithful society would overcome all obstacles through divine guidance and intervention.

A final quotation from his commentary illustrates the difference between Islam and democracy. Commenting on sura 49:12, a verse which commands believers to avoid loose assumptions about each other and not to pry into each other's business or slander each other, he says:

> So what a degree of protection of the dignity of people, their freedoms, their rights and their esteem this text reaches! And how remote is not that at which the best land marvels, such as democracy, freedom and protection of human rights therein, [how remote is it not] from the degree which the noble Qurʾān extols for those who believe (…)? (Quṭb 2003, 3345).

The same duality of argument as Quṭb employed in his polemics against Western democracy is clear in his depiction of the Islamic state in the quoted passages and elsewhere. On the one hand the Islamic state should be established and maintained with a mindset of unquestioning faith; on the other hand it is not only a virtuous but also a perfect society providing social justice, cultural authenticity, traditional patriarchal family structures, dignity and power. The demands of dogmatics blend with the allure of solutions to profoundly this-worldly concerns.

Concluding remarks

Quṭb's writings have had a complex reception history. The militant Islamist groups that became active from the 1970s were influenced by his thinking, though this often remained unacknowledged by the groups themselves (Damir-Geilsdorf, 249). In some regards these groups interpreted his ideas in ways he would probably not have condoned. Quṭb left key questions open to interpretation: When, for instance, would the use of violence in the struggle against *jāhiliyya* be allowed, and against whom could it be used? Difficulties such as this have left his work open for followers, apologetes and critics. But even if certain central issues are difficult to settle, and even though any text needs an interpreter, Quṭb's commentary is not a foundational text separated from its readers by centuries or millennia. It takes an unambiguous stand on numerous issues which are just as relevant today as they were in the mid-twentieth century. Quṭb, it is true, was in some regards an original exegete who lived 'in the shade of the Qurʾān' and gained an intensely personal relationship with the sacred

13 For this question specifically, see Damir-Geilsdorf 2003, 156-57.

text during long years of incarceration under Nasser. From his years as a writer and critic he brought with him an aesthetic perspective that he employed on the Qurʾān to great effect. None of this, however, changes the fact that his commentary establishes a discourse with clear limits and stresses its religio-political key points with such forcefulness (and repetitiveness!) that it would require a herculean interpretative effort to do away with them.

Like any phenomenon of some scope, Islamist thought and praxis vary, even to the point of violent internal confrontation; and so it is reasonable to ask if Quṭb was merely a peripheral figure inspiring militant groups on the radical fringe, or if his work has had a wider influence. Answering such a question is difficult for many reasons (e.g. the fact that Quṭb's radical writings are banned in many Muslim countries, while at the same time numerous illegal printings have been made). At the beginning of the 1980s one scholar believed that Quṭb's commentary had "become the standard by which the Qurʾān's message is interpreted in many mosques and homes" (Haddad 1983, 68), while in the 1990s it was estimated that it "may actually be the most widely translated and distributed Islamic book of all time" (Jansen 1997, 51). The Islamic Foundation based in Leicester in the United Kingdom currently publishes the English translation of the commentary. This institution, which was founded in 1973, is hardly an obscure, marginal enterprise – at the inauguration of a new building in 2003, for instance, the Prince of Wales lauded its efforts in scholarship and inter-faith dialogue. Yet, for all the accolade, the publishers have not deemed it necessary to demand any significant caveats in the translators' introductory prefaces to Quṭb's commentary in spite of its totalitarian bent and equally troubling traits such as a virulent anti-semitism. Instead, the text on the back covers of the volumes states that "Now that it is available in English, it will continue to enlighten and inspire millions more."

When Quṭb emphasised *shūrā* (however limited the authority associated with it may actually have been), it was probably due to the same unavowedly modern ideal of public participation in the governing of society that prompted al-Mawdūdī to speak of 'theo-democracy' in his writings on the Islamic state – truly a contradiction in terms. As for al-Mawdūdī, C.J. Adams rightly remarked that "The rationale reflects a desire to have things both ways: to reject the very foundation of the concept of democracy as it is normally understood while at the same time claiming for oneself its appeal and its advantages" (1983, 119). Throughout his writings on the workings of the future state, Quṭb's descriptions evince an outright Orwellian logic. He would emphasise the basically peaceful nature of Islam and contrast it with the belligerence of the capitalist states, yet at the same time be adamant that the ultimate objective of Islam was global supremacy and that jihad could never be reduced to a defensive principle – war, indeed, is peace! Similarly, he would describe the Islamic revolution as a liberation of humanity from the tyranny of man-made systems, yet limit this freedom to laws and principles derivable from the Qurʾān and the *sunna*. Jews and Christians would be allowed to practise their religions under Islamic rule – and so religious freedom was another characteristic of Islamic society. But of course this would only be true as long as it in no way conflicted with the Islamic framework of society, and a Muslim converting to another religion would be liable to capital punishment for apostasy.

Utopian thinking can have dangerous consequences – very dangerous consequences, as testified by twentieth-century history. Quṭb certainly did not solve the labyrinth of modernity in which he and like-minded Muslims believed modern man had been trapped. The best he could offer in societal terms was visions of past greatness and dreams of a future utopia. While the most dire consequences of his thought *might* have taken considerably longer to materialise if Quṭb had lived longer and been able to serve as an exegete of his own works, struggle and bloodshed would at some point be an inevitable outcome of his dream of a pure society.

Bibliography

Adams, Charles J. 1983. 'Mawdudi and the Islamic State'. In: John L. Esposito (ed.), *Voices of Resurgent Islam*. New York & Oxford: Oxford University Press, 99-133.

Carré, Olivier 2003. *Mysticism and politics: a critical reading of Fi Zilal al-Qurʾan by Sayyid Quṭb (1906-1966).* (Transl. from the French by Carol Artigues and revised by W. Shepard). Leiden: Brill.

Choueiri, Youssef M. 1997. *Islamic Fundamentalism*. Revised edition. London & Washington: Pinter.

Damir-Geilsdorf, Sabine 2003. *Herrschaft und Gesellschaft: der islamistische Wegbereiter Sayyid Quṭb und seine Rezeption*. Würzburg: Ergon-Verlag.

Haddad, Yvonne Y. 1983. 'Sayyid Qutb: Ideologue of Islamic Revival'. In: John L. Esposito (ed.), *Voices of Resurgent Islam*. New York & Oxford: Oxford University Press, 67-98.

Hourani, Albert 1983. *Arabic Thought in the Liberal Age 1798-1939*. Cambridge: Cambridge University Press.

Jansen, Johannes J.G. 1997. *The Dual Nature of Islamic Fundamentalism*. London: Hurst & Company.

Quṭb, Sayyid 1999-2008. *In the Shade of the Qurʾān*, vol. 1-15 & 18. (Transl. M.A. Salahi and A.A. Shamis). Leicester: The Islamic Foundation.

Quṭb, Sayyid 2003. *Fī Zilāl al-Qurʾān*, 6 vols. 32. legal printing. Cairo & Beirut: Dār al-Shurūq.

Shepard, William E. 2001. 'Age of Ignorance'. In: Jane D. McAuliffe (ed.), *Encyclopaedia of the Qurʾān*, vol. 1. Leiden & Boston: Brill, 37-40.

Shepard, William E. 2003. 'Sayyid Qutb's Doctrine of Jahiliyya'. *International Journal of Middle Eastern Studies*, 35.4, 525-545.

ISLAMIC LAW IN EUROPE

THE CHALLENGE OF LEGAL PLURALISM

Karen-Lise Johansen Karman

The demands for mosques, Muslim cemetery requirements and the recognition of Islamic diet regulations illustrate the fact that the fulfilment of Muslim traditions and Islamic rules is important for a growing proportion of the population in Western Europe. It is crucial for many amongst Muslim minorities to maintain their Muslim identity, respecting religious rules while remaining within the framework of Western legal systems. Islamic jurists have not yet developed clear guidelines or a specific jurisprudence (*fiqh*) for Muslim minorities, but in the last decade a number of Muslim *fiqh* councils have appeared in the West. These councils attempt to clarify possible conflicts between the legal system and Islamic rules, seeking practical solutions enabling Muslim minorities to conform to the non-Muslim setting and still organise their lives in accordance with Islam.

This paper aims to demonstrate how the European Council for Fatwa and Research (a Western Islamic judicial institution) both contributes to legal pluralism and assists Muslim minorities to manoeuvre in multiple systems of legal order. Examining the Council's fatwas (pronouncements of the application of Sharīʿa to particular moral or public issues, embodying an interpretation of religious law), the paper surveys how the Council guides Muslim minorities in navigating a public sphere with diverse social and legal norms.

Legal pluralism

In 2003, the Islamic Institute of Civil Justice based in Toronto proposed arbitration tribunals using Muslim Personal Law. In fact, the idea of private parties voluntarily agreeing to have their disputes resolved by an arbitrator using foreign legal principles, including religious principles, was not new. Ontario's 1991 Arbitration Act allowed civil disputes to be resolved outside the courts, as long as the results were not in breach of the law. Other religious groups, including several Jewish communities, had created religious arbitration tribunals to resolve civil matters (Bakht 2004, 2). However, concerns about resolving family and inheritance disputes in accordance with *Sharīʿa* prompted heated discussion and led to a significant amendment of the Act. The government argued that religious arbitration had become a threat to the common ground of society, and that a unified system in family matters should be applied to all regardless of creeds. Consequently, the legal enforceability for any family arbitration conducted in accordance with religious law was abolished. In the 1970s, the Union of Muslim Organizations of

UK and Eire (UMO) went a step further than the Canadian Muslim community and submitted a proposal for official recognition of a separate system of Islamic family law which would automatically be applicable to all British Muslims (Poulter 1990, 147). The proposal was reiterated publicly in 1996, but again rejected. September 2008 it was announced that a network of five Sharī'a courts were given full powers of the judicial system to rule on Muslim civil cases, ranging from divorce and financial disputes to those involving domestic violence. Classifying the Sharī'a courts as arbitration tribunals Muslim jurists have taken advantage of a clause in the Arbitration Act 1996 that makes arbitration tribunals' ruling binding in law providing that both parties in the dispute agree to give it the power to rule on their case.

The opponents of an official recognition of religious court are concerned with social cohesion, and they argue that a uniform system of law is needed to maintain a cohesive society with an increasing number of religious and ethnic minorities. Furthermore, several aspects of Islamic law – in its various existing forms – would not be acceptable within the European legal-political context. For example, polygynous marriages, the husband's unilateral rights to divorce (ṭalāq), and the relatively strict assignment of custody of minor children to the father or the mother according to the child's age (Rohe 2007, 21). Despite the lack of recognition of a separate system of Muslim personal law, the Muslim minorities have identified several avenues facilitating the application of Muslim customary and legal traditions. They resort, for instance, to mediation rather than courts in civil disputes; they make wills that take account of Islamic inheritance law; and they marry twice, once through the official channels and again according to Islamic rules.[1] It may be argued that although modern states seek control by requiring uniform adherence to a single official structure of law, one can speak of *legal pluralism*, since local communities insist on preserving their own legal values alongside the official system (cf. Yilmaz 2005).

Legal pluralism is an attribute of a social field and not of 'law' or of a 'legal system', and is generally defined as the presence in a social field of more than one legal order. It does not require the presence of more than one entire legal system; multiple legal 'mechanisms' are enough to say that a field exhibits legal pluralism (Griffiths 1986, 38). The most commonly used concept to describe multiple systems of orderings in complex societies is Moore's notion of a 'semiautonomous social field', which is one that

can generate rules and customs and symbols internally, but that … is also vulnerable to rules and decisions and other forces emanating from the larger world by which it is surrounded. […] it has rule-making capacities, and the means to induce and coerce compliance; but it is simultaneously set in a larger social matrix which can, and does, affect and invade it, sometimes… (Moore 1973, 720).

---

1   Personal interview with Suhaib Hassan, secretary of the Islamic Sharī'a Council in London and member of the European Council for Fatwa and Research (ECFR), London, 16 February 2006. The interviews with members of the ECFR cited in this article were part of my doctoral research on contemporary fatwa councils and their rulings for Muslim minorities.

In the past, the studies of legal pluralism focused mainly on colonised societies, and on the intersections of indigenous and European law. Beginning in the late 1970s, the concept of legal pluralism has been applied to the study of non-colonised urbanised societies and refers to relations between majority groups and religious, ethnic or cultural minorities, and unofficial forms of ordering located in social networks or institutions (Merry 1988, 872). Legal pluralism confronts *legal centralism*'s idea that law is a single, unified and exclusive hierarchical normative ordering by drawing attention to the social fields' normative heterogeneity. Most of the legal systems of modern Western nation states are understood as a legally uniform and centralist system applicable to everybody without exception. However, the different attendant perceptions of legal practices within different social fields, as well as local law and ethnic minority laws and customs, defy the idea of an easily identifiable unified legal order. Although the states formally have monopolies on law and some forms of orderings have coercive state power behind them, alternative legal and non-legal normative orderings exist in modern societies. The existence of alternative legal normative orderings demonstrates that the coercive power of the state is not sufficient to justify people's obedience to law.

When studying legal practices among religious minorities, it has often been advanced that their acceptance of legal norms lies in the law's alleged divine nature. Contemporary Muslim jurists' attempts to adapt religious-grounded legal norms to Western society by engaging in dialogue with Muslim minorities living in the West indicate, however, that the divine character is not sufficient. In order for legal norms to be justified they also need to be in line with the concerns, social norms and customs of people; or as Habermas argues, the production of legitimate law requires citizens' communicative freedom to participate in public discussion and freedom to voice concerns that are taken in consideration by policy makers (1992, 492).[2]

Shari'a stands for the normative order that Muslims have developed as an Islamic way of life. Its translation as 'Islamic law' is not fully adequate, because Shari'a refers to both legal and social norms, and covers a wider range of meanings than those attributed to 'Western law'.[3] Muslim jurists in the past were quite aware of the need to reconcile contradictions between social and legal norms (Masud 2001, 3), but the tendency to assimilate social norms into Shari'a and portray them as divine and immutable has led to the impression of a stagnated Islamic jurisprudence (ibid.). In the following, we discuss the way in which Muslim scholars concerned with Muslim

---

2   Some criticise the legal pluralists' use of labelling normative ordering 'law' and argue that it is more accurate to use the term 'normative pluralism' than 'legal pluralism', given that normative orderings may not be legal, but include non-legal elements as moral and political norms, and customs and habits (Tamanaha 1993, 193). Since social and legal issues are dealt with by the same authorities in the same fashion in Islamic scholarship, it follows that the term 'legal pluralism' is not strictly correct. However, using this term may be the only realistic way of summarising the debate in a fashion comprehensible to Western audiences, since legal authorities are not ordinarily consulted in the West for guidance in social and religious matters.

3   Islamic law covers many aspects of religious, political and civil life, usually divided into '*ibādāt* (ritual) and *mu'āmalāt* (social relations). The law thus includes matters such as worship, personal morality, family relations and public welfare.

minorities' balancing act between Western legal systems and an Islamic normative ordering are negotiating the adaptation of Sharī'a to the circumstances of the Muslim diaspora.

Fiqh al-aqalliyyāt – A legal theory for Muslim minorities

Fiqh al-aqalliyyāt – minority jurisprudence is a legal discipline that endeavours to adapt Sharī'a to local circumstances. The idea of developing a legal doctrine for Muslim minorities was first introduced by Taha Jabir al-Alwani,[4] the former president of the Fiqh Council of North America, and later adopted by Yousuf al-Qaradawi, the present president of the European Council for Fatwa and Research (ECFR).[5] The aim is to apply Islamic values and law in a modern non-Muslim Western society by transcending an historical contextual interpretation of Sharī'a and making allowance for the conditions of the non-Muslim society. In order to identify Islamic solutions to contemporary problems and fulfil the essential purposes of Islam, advocates of the fiqh al-aqalliyyāt argue that it is necessary to develop a new dynamic legal methodology. A method that pays attention to both religious science and modern knowledge, and facilitates an interpretation of Islamic teaching that is consistent with both the higher Sharī'atic principles and non-Muslim circumstances (Al-Alwani 2003).

In the introduction to the ECFR's first fatwa collection, al-Qaradawi refers to the concept of a fiqh al-aqalliyyāt and describes it as a legal theory that deals with the "legal critical issues related to the Muslims living outside the Islamic world." Al-Qaradawi emphasises the universality of Islamic laws and underlines that Sharī'a is consistent with all Muslims' circumstances and therefore all Muslims are obliged, regardless of their place of residence, to apply the 'customised' Islamic commands (Al-Qaradawi 2003, 7). Al-Qaradawi is representative of the newer Islamic awakening/ revivalist reform (al-ṣaḥwa al-islāmiyya), which does not make him a 'legal reformist' calling for a general abatement of Islamic legal norms and instead stresses the spiritual and ethical norms of Islam. By contrast, the revivalists are committed to revitalising Sharī'a and to the reintroduction of Islamic law in relevant forms (Salvatore 1997, 197-217).

---

4   Al-Alwani is an Iraqi-born graduate of the Faculty of Sharī'a and Law at al-Azhar University in Cairo. In the mid eighties, he emigrated to the United States and helped to establish the International Institute of Islamic Thought (IIIT). He now serves as President of the Graduate School of Islamic and Social Sciences – Cordoba University, http://www.cordobauniversity.org/gsiss/faculty/Alalwani.asp.

5   Al-Qaradawi is an Egyptian scholar who studied Islamic theology at al-Azhar University. His links to the Muslim Brotherhood led to imprisonment in 1954; he is now based in Qatar, where he is Dean of the Sharī'a Faculty at Qatar University. His appearance on al-Jazeera's religious talk-show Sharī'a and Life and his independence from the state-run Egyptian religious institutions has made him one of the most respected scholars in the Arab world and beyond (Skovgaard-Petersen 2004, 115).

European Council for Fatwa and Research

This vision led, on the initiative of the Federation of Islamic Organizations in Europe (FIOE), to the establishment of the European Council for Fatwa and Research in 1997. One of the objectives of the ECFR, as stated in its constitution, is "to issue collective fatwas that meet the need of Muslims in Europe, solve their problems and regulate their interaction with the European communities all within the regulations and objectives of Shari'a."

The formation of a specific Muslim minority jurisprudence is not included as one of the Council's aims. Generally speaking, the members support the idea of developing a *fiqh al-aqalliyyāt* that outlines how Muslim minorities can best fulfil the Islamic precepts, and confine themselves to the Shari'a in daily life. However, some scholars are reluctant to accept the concept; some argue that the terminology wrongly gives the impression that Muslim minorities are obligated to a different set of Islamic duties than other Muslims. These scholars maintain that Islamic duties remain invariably the same for all Muslims, acknowledging only that the practice of the Islamic obligations may differ. Certain duties may be temporarily abrogated and the implementation of some rules might be suspended. The opponents argue, however, that this does not entail the permanent abolition of some duties, and also that Islamic rules for minorities need to be redefined in a new jurisprudence of minorities.[6] To overcome the confusion and disagreement, the topic became the main research subject at the Council's twelfth ordinary session held in Dublin, 2004. Based on research presented by various Muslim scholars, the Council formulated a resolution stating that the Council ultimately agrees that the use of the term '*fiqh* of minorities', meaning the legal rulings concerning Muslim minorities, is correct. This final resolution comments on the use of the term *fiqh al-aqalliyyāt*, but the development of such a legal doctrine is not included as an objective of the Council.

One definite objective of the Council is to further the institutionalisation of Islam in Europe. For instance, it has developed a set of recommendations advising how Muslims can best promote and ensure the establishment of Islam in Europe. Muslims are advised to raise their children in an Islamic environment by establishing Islamic schools. The Council encourages the Muslim community to exercise every possible effort to secure the recognition of Islam, and to seek the right of the community to arrange its affairs in compliance with the Muslim faith. Furthermore, it urges Muslims to establish judicial bodies to preside over their personal status and religious affairs.[7] By the members' common consent, the establishment of Islamic arbitration courts is an important means of easing Muslims' religious lives in Europe.

The philosophy of the Council is that the Muslim minorities have no right to struggle for the implementation of Shari'a as a general legal system. However, it is legitimate to strive for an implementation of Shari'a in personal affairs and for the es-

---

6   Interview with Abdullah al-Judai (member of the ECFR), Leeds, 15 February 2006.
7   *Fatwas of European Council for Fatwa and Research* (2002). Islamic INC. Publishing and Distribution, Cairo.

tablishment of Islamic courts.[8] The Council has issued a couple of resolutions regarding legal arbitration according to Islamic law in the West, in which it recommends that Muslims in Europe refer to Islamic law in personal affairs and financial dealings. It states that the fundamental principle must be that a Muslim chooses arbitrators or an arbitration establishment committed to the rulings of Islamic law. It adds that it will be permissible to resort to non-Muslim arbitration bodies for the sake of achieving what is required according to Sharī'a, i.e. it is permissible to include conditions in contracts, and have them confirmed by a non-Muslim attorney or other official authorities.

The legal opinions of the Council

Since its establishment, the ECFR has received numerous questions dealing with points of Islamic law. By giving fatwas (non-legally binding advisory rulings), the Council clarifies Islamic rules and directs the Muslim minority to live according to the principles of Sharī'a. The customs of the minorities are taken into consideration; if it is found that there is nothing un-Islamic about minorities' new behaviour in terms of Islamic practices, such behaviour will be declared legally accepted. In 2002, the Council published its first (and so far only) collection of fatwas. It consists of 43 legal opinions, and the nine headings (under which they are subsumed for ease of reference) demonstrate the wide range of matters that the Council deals with: invitation/mission to Islam (da'wa); ritual purity (ṭahāra) and prayer; finance; earnings and work; marriage and divorce; family and Muslim households; nourishment; manners and behaviour; and finally miscellaneous topics.

Many of the fatwas concern family and household topics, the majority of which concern relations between men and women and relations between Muslims and non-Muslims. Following the Qur'ānic verse (60:8-9), the Council distinguishes between non-Muslims that fight and treat Muslims as enemies and those who deal with Muslims kindly and "do not fight them due to religion and did not actively seek to expel Muslims from their homes and lands."[9] 'Allegiance' to the first group is forbidden, while the Council encourages good relations with the latter group. In particular, the Council urges Muslim converts to maintain close relations with non-Muslim relatives. One fatwa rules, for example, that it is unlawful for a Muslim husband to prevent his converted wife from visiting her Christian parents.[10] Nor does the Council have any objections to the attendance of religious ceremonies in synagogues or churches (for instance a non-Muslim relative's funeral), although Muslims should refrain from participating in the religious ceremonies and prayers.

The Council receives many questions relating to ritual behaviour ('ibādāt), which is traditionally presented as a restricted area excluded from interpretation (ijtihād).

---

8   Interview with Rashid Ghannoushi (member of the ECFR), London, 6 February 2006.
9   Fatwa 33, First Collection of Fatwas, second part.
10   Fatwa 31, First Collection of Fatwas, first part.

However, new developments raise questions regarding religious practice and scholars do not refrain from dealing with the area that constitutes the 'rituals of Islamic law'. The Council has issued a ruling permitting the combination of two of the five daily prayers (*zuhr* and *'aṣr*) during the winter in Europe, when the days are short.[11] It also finds it legally permissible to hire churches for the purpose of prayer, and argues that Christian symbols in the Church have no effect on 'the soundness of the prayer'.[12] The ECFR has issued several fatwas on the requirements of burial and prayers over the dead. It encourages Muslim minorities in the West to establish their own cemeteries; however, it adds that it is not harmful to be buried in a non-Muslim cemetery if other alternatives are not available.[13] The Council permits female converts living in the West to refrain from wearing the headscarf (*ḥijāb*), since this obligation is not one of Islam's pillars, but a secondary duty. Nevertheless, the Muslim community is obliged to support the Muslim woman and to encourage her to cover her head, since it is regarded as a sinful act not to wear the veil.[14] It is also possible to link the provisions relating to food and drink with *'ibādāt,* which seems to be a topic of great concern among the petitioners. The Council forbids Muslims to sell alcohol and pork, and in one ruling a young man working at McDonalds is encouraged to find a new job. The ruling says that if he cannot be excused from selling pork, he should "find alternative means of making a living that does not involve sales of *ḥarām* products."[15]

Most of the questions that deal with Islamic legal norms concern Muslim personal law. In a legal opinion about the guardianship powers of male legal representatives of the bride, the required approval of the guardian of an underage girl is commented upon, but no attention is paid to the illegality of marrying underage persons in most Western countries.[16] Complete ignorance of Western legal norms is also found in a ruling on polygamous marriages. It describes in detail the Islamic permission of a man marrying up to four women. It strongly defends this Islamic principle and takes no notice of the Western legislation that prohibits polygamy.[17] The same thing appears in a decision on women's right to divorce. It summarises the Islamic principles of divorce, but ignores European laws.[18] In a few rulings, it is acknowledged that some matters lie in the hands of the Western legal systems. In answering a question regarding a divorce issued by a non-Muslim judge, the Council rules that the principle is that a Muslim resorts only to a Muslim judge, but due to the absence of an Islamic judicial system in non-Muslim countries, it is imperative to comply with the rulings of the non-Muslim judge in the event of a divorce.[19]

---

11   Fatwa 4, First Collection of Fatwas, second part.
12   Resolution 9/3, Ninth Ordinary Session, July 2002.
13   Fatwa 21, First Collection of Fatwas, second part.
14   Fatwa 6, First Collection of Fatwas, first part.
15   Fatwa 14, First Collection of Fatwas, second part.
16   Fatwa 12, First Collection of Fatwas, first part.
17   Fatwa 13, First Collection of Fatwas, second part.
18   Fatwa 16, First Collection of Fatwas, second part.
19   Fatwa 17, First Collection of Fatwas, second part.

Several petitioners have expressed interest in knowing the Council's legal stance on Muslims' permanent residence in non-Muslim societies and Muslims' participation in political democratic processes. In 2006, the Council dedicated its Sixteenth Ordinary Session to a discussion of these topics. The Council argues that it is not permitted to live amongst non-Muslims if doing so compromises your Islamic identity, but that it is lawful to migrate outside the Muslim majority world, provided the right to practise Islam exists there. As stated in a resolution adopted at the meeting, contributions to social, political and economic activities in non-Muslim countries are legal, as long they do not contradict Islamic rules with regard to creed, practice and morals. All Muslims should abide by Muslim morals, including the rules of *ḥalāl* and *ḥarām*, as well as by the laws and regulations of the host countries.

To the best of my knowledge, the question of political participation was raised for the first time in 1998, but at that time the Council hesitated to issue an authoritative ruling on this topic. The ECFR claimed that this matter was a context-dependent issue for which a general ruling was not possible. The argumentation was that if the interests of Muslims could only be served by political participation, then such participation was permissible as long as it did not have any negative consequences for Muslims. Whether political participation served this purpose or not was to be decided locally. It may be concluded that, basically, the Council found participation in a non-Islamic political system contrary to Islamic legal norms. However, provided that it benefited the social conditions of Muslims it was considered legitimate to compromise the Islamic rules. Almost ten years later, in April 2007, a fatwa issued by the Council on the same topic was published at the website 'Islamonline' run by al-Qaradawi. The question was as follows:

Is it permissible for Muslims living in non-Muslim countries to take part in elections held in those countries? Keeping in mind that such elections may make Muslims be[come] members of the legislative organs in countries where there is not any consideration for the Shari'ah, is that permissible?

The Council issued a detailed fatwa and inter alia answered,

Thus, Muslims' participation in elections is a national duty. [...] Besides, it is a kind of mutual cooperation with those whom Muslims think as potential candidates who, if they win the elections, will bring benefits for the society in general and Muslims in particular.

In the lengthy ruling, the scholars try to come to terms with a new situation by working it into recognised classifications and known traditions. The rationality of the Prophet's way of acting is transferred to the Muslim minorities' present situation and is used as the argumentation for legalising their political participation. It is noteworthy that the ruling does not define political participation as a religious duty, but merely as a national duty. The ECFR is selective in its way of answering the question. As is normal in legal decisions, it treats matters which it finds relevant for the discussion and ignores that part of the question which has a more controversial character, namely the issue of participating in legislative organs that overrule the Islamic legal norms. In fact, the question alludes to an objection often advanced by Islamist groups. These groups argue that involvement in Western democratic political processes involves ignoring the Sharīʿa in favour of man-made laws, which is contradictory to Islamic law principles. The failure to discuss this reflects the fact that the Council members had to choose which aspects to include in their answer, and the fact that they were compelled to avoid legal matters of a more contentious character.

Conclusion

Modern societies are currently witnessing a growing diversity of social fields with their own distinct traditions, values and worldviews, challenging the idea of a unified legal and normative system which is accepted by all citizens. The findings in this paper demonstrate that the Muslim minority communities in the West tend to preserve religious legal traditions and confirm the existence of different legal norm orders within modern society, the state legal system being but one of them.

By means of its fatwas, the European Council for Fatwa and Research adds to this legal plurality. The Council strongly encourages Muslim minorities to arrange civil matters in accordance with Sharīʿa by securing legal recognition of Islamic customs and by establishing judicial arbitration bodies that rule according to Islamic law. As the presentation of its rulings shows, the Council occasionally ignores the European legal context and elaborates on Islamic rules that are in direct opposition to and irreconcilable with the Western legal system. In other rulings, the Council seeks to accommodate Islamic legal rules to Muslim minorities' living conditions by studying their new customs and legalising an already widespread practice. In this context, the Council contributes to the development of a minority Islamic jurisprudence that involves a new reading of the Islamic legal heritage and a receptivity to the social norms and concerns of Muslim minorities, something which is required in order to ensure the legitimacy of Islamic legal norms in a non-Muslim setting.

While emphasising the necessity of abiding by Islamic legal norms regardless of place of residence, the Council also encourages the adherence of Muslims to the non-Muslim legal system by permitting participation in elections and public debates. Modern legal norms require only outward compliance regardless of individual motivation, but they should have a rational basis that makes it possible for people to accept that they deserve obedience. Thus, the basis of modern law is no longer exclusively a sacred foundation, but rather 'reason', which explains why modern legislation depends on citizens' involvement in public discussion and political participation (Habermas 1992, 181-182). The legitimacy and the democratic procedure of modern legal order rely on citizens making use of their participatory right and understanding themselves as authors of the law (ibid., 230). In line with this legal theory, Muslim scholars allow participation not only in order to influence lawmaking, but also to serve the social 'common good'. Although these scholars give occasionally rulings ignoring Western legal norms, they maintain that there is no inherent discontinuity in participating in Western democracy and respecting Western legislation while abiding by Sharīʿa in personal affairs. Accordingly, they advise Muslim minorities to fulfil their duties as citizens and respect Western legal norms as well as to uphold Islamic legal and moral rules.

The idea of applying a Muslim minority jurisprudence in Europe may raise questions such as, "Will corporal punishment like stoning to death or amputation associated with Islamic law be introduced in the European legal system?" The answer is that the application of Islamic legal norms must comply with the rules of public policy. If the application of legislation influenced by Islamic law would lead to a result that is incompatible with constitutional civil rights in various European countries, for instance, the provision cannot be applied. Although European standards of human rights, democracy and the rule of law are untouchable, this does not mean that Islamic law cannot be applied. As Rohe points out, a great number of Islamic laws do not contradict the standards mentioned. They may also enjoy protection by virtue of the freedom of religion, and are therefore applicable (Rohe 2007, 139). In other cases, the regulation of Islamic legal norms may operate in the shadows, without the knowledge of the official legal system.

Bibliography

Al-Alwani, Taha Jabir 2003. *Towards a fiqh for Minorities. Some Basic Reflections*. Washington: The International Institute for Islamic Thinking.

Al-Qaradawi, Yousuf 2003. *Fiqh for Muslim Minorities*. Cairo: Al-Falah Foundation.

Bakht, Natasha 2004. 'Family Arbitration Using Sharia Law: Examining Ontario's Arbitration Act and its Impact on Women'. *Muslim World Journal of Human Rights*, 1, 1-24.

Fatwas of European Council for Fatwa and Research 2002. Islamic INC. Publishing and Distribution, Cairo.

Habermas, Jürgen 1992. *Faktizität und Geltung. Beiträge zur Diskurstheorie des Rechts und des demokratischen Rechtsstaats*. Frankfurt/Main: Suhrkamp.

Griffiths, John 1986. 'What is Legal Pluralism?' *Journal of Legal Pluralism*, 24 (1-2), 1-56.

Merry, Sally Engle 1988. 'Legal Pluralism'. *Law & Society Review*, 22 (5), 869-894.

Masud, Muhammad Khalid 2001. *Muslim Jurists' Quest for the Normative Basis of Sharīʿa*. Inaugural Lecture at ISIM, Leiden.

Moore, Sally Falk. 1973. 'Law and Social Change: the Semi-autonomous Social Field as an Appropriate Subject of Study'. *Law and Society Review*, 7 (4), 719-746.

Poulter, Sebastian 1990. 'The Claim to a Separate System of Personal Law for British Muslims'. In: Mallat, Chibli & Jane Connors (eds.), *Islamic Family Law*. London: Graham & Trotman, 147-166.

Rohe, Mathias 2007. *Muslim Minorities and the Law in Europe. Chances and Challenges*. New Delhi: Global Media Publication.

Salvatore, Armando 1997. *Islam and the Political Discourse of Modernity*. Reading: Ithaca Press.

Skovgaard-Petersen, Jakob 2004. 'The Global Mufti'. In: Schaebler, Birgit & Leif Stenberg (eds.), *Globalization and the Muslim World. Culture, Religion and Modernity*. New York: Syracuse University Press, 153-165.

Tamanaha, Brian Z. 1993. 'The Folly of the "Social Scientific" Concept of Legal Pluralims'. *Journal of Law and Society*, 20 (2), 192-217.

Yilmaz, Ihsam 2005. *Muslim Laws, Politics and Society in Modern Nation States: Dynamic Legal Pluralisms in England, Turkey and Pakistan*. London: Ashgate Publishing.

PART II

Democracy, church, and ethics

THE AUTHORITY OF THE BIBLE IN PRIVATE AND PUBLIC LIFE

Johannes Nissen

Introduction

The concepts of 'private' and 'public' are usually seen as opposites. Many Christians would like to limit the authority of the Bible to their private lives, but denounce its authority in public life. Hence, the church is welcomed when it supports traditional 'family values'; but criticised when it speaks on economic and political matters, when it opposes oppression and speaks for the poor and exploited. However, there are deep divisions within the churches on some moral issues which are usually conceived of as belonging to the private sphere, e.g. homosexuality, contraception and abortion (Forrester 1997, 1).

In Western culture many forms of Bible reading tend towards what has been called the "hermeneutics of privatism" (Gorringe 1998, 74). Congregations read the Bible to deepen their devotions to Christ as the Saviour, and they resolutely avoid political questions. The commentaries of the academy, on the other hand, have raised historical-critical questions which aim to reconstruct the text of the Bible and situate it within the history of ideas. Though their tenor is very different from the devotional works, they too avoid political questions.

While 'private' and 'public' are regarded as alternatives, this need not apply to the terms 'personal' and 'public'. Nevertheless, it is common to distinguish between personal ethics and social ethics. The former represents a focus upon those aspects of moral life which involve direct interpersonal relationships, whereas the latter focuses on the larger and more complex aspects of human life in society. This is a useful distinction so long as it is not assumed that personal ethics are in any way separable from wider social structures and processes, or that moral judgments and behaviour or important ethical questions are private or merely individual maters (Allen 1986, 469). In fact, any effort to establish boundary lines between social ethics and personal ethics is artificial. Sexual ethics, for example, might appear to be interpersonal rather than social, yet sexual life is strongly influenced by its socio-cultural context and in turn has a significant impact upon that context (Allen 1986, 592).

The authority of the Bible is disputed in both personal ethics and social ethics. However, the main focus of this article will be on the public sphere, since it is in this area that most people would question the authority of the Bible. Hence, there will be an emphasis on concrete issues such as the church-state relationship, peace and violence, and justice.[1]

---

1   For a more detailed analysis of various issues within social ethics as well as personal ethics, see Nissen 2003a.

The use of the Bible in ethics

To begin with, it might be useful to present a brief survey of the most important ways of using the Bible in ethics. I suggest that the various approaches can be classified in four major groups (see also Nissen 2003a, 227-277).

The first category covers theories according to which the moral teaching of Scripture is of no or very little relevance for ethics. A few examples must suffice. The first theory is that of interim ethics. According to this theory, Jesus taught a heroic and rigorous obedience applicable only to the brief time before the cosmic crisis associated with the dawn of the apocalyptic kingdom. Two other theories are existential ethics and situations ethics. According to these theories, Jesus taught no ethics at all in the sense of offering guidance about what actions ought to be taken. What he taught is reduced to the love command in a formal shape.

The second category consists of *prescriptive* approaches. Here the focus is on individual biblical 'commands'. The Bible is seen as a collection of commandments, rules and advice that can speak to every possible contingency in the modern world. Examples of this approach are biblicism and casuistry.

The third category suggests that the Bible offers basic criteria, perspectives or paradigms. One example is the *moral law model* that takes Scripture to be the revelation of a moral law of certain rules and principles to be obeyed. The *moral ideal model* takes Scripture to be the source of moral ideals, of certain goals to be striven for (e.g. neighbour love; justice; freedom; the imitation of Jesus). The *analogical model* takes Scripture to be the source of moral precedents. One can discern God's judgment for a contemporary situation in the precedent provided by his recorded judgment in some similar biblical situations.

The fourth category emphasises *theo*-logy as a source of moral action. These are theories which focus on the *indicative* (what the Bible tells us God is like and what it tells us about how God acts) and take this as a point of departure for recommending how the Christian, in freedom and responsibility before God, should best respond to God in the present situation (the basic ethical *imperative*). Examples of this category are various models such as 'ethics as a response to God's action', 'narrativity and ethics', and 'moral formation of the identity'.

The first two categories are open to criticism. In the first category (interim ethics, existential ethics etc.) the authority of the Bible is limited to the private sphere. One of the arguments against the normative claims by Jesus has always been that his radical personalism is not relevant to problems of power and structure. Furthermore, it is argued that eschatology means the abandonment of social ethics. However, in the New Testament, eschatology also has an intrinsic link with creation and the fulfilment of the creator's purpose (McDonald 1993, 143).

The second category (biblicism, fundamentalism) does not limit the authority of the Bible to personal ethics. However, the problem with this approach is that it reduces moral life to Christian legalism. And with regard to the diversity of the Bible in particular, the advocates of this position are faced with great difficulties.

Instead of the first two categories, I would suggest a multi-dimensional approach based on the third and fourth categories. One might speak of the *great variety* model. This model takes Scripture to be a witness to a great variety of values and norms through a great variety of literary forms. It refuses to reduce the forms of moral instruction in the Bible to a single form, or to reduce the moral themes in the Bible to a single theme. The Bible 'informs' the agent or 'illuminates' the situation, but it is not sufficient to authorise any particular judgment.

Several of the models which can be classified as belonging to the third and fourth categories insist on seeing the Bible as having authority in both personal and public/social life (e.g. ethics of discipleship, formation of moral identity, liberation ethics). Later on in this article we shall return to some of these models.

The hermeneutical challenge: From a position without power to a powerful position

During most of its first three hundred years, the church remained a minority group within the Roman Empire. This fact has raised the question of the relevance of a biblical ethos. The solution for many has been to maintain the split between private and public.

Towards the end of the first century, emperor worship became increasingly common. The Christians and other minority groups had to show their basic loyalty to assure the state that its lordship would not be diluted or compromised by any competing loyalties. It goes without saying that the early Christians rather consistently failed this test because they had taken an oath to One who they believed stood above Rome (Lee 1976, 64).

The Roman state had what we would call totalitarian traits. Like most totalitarian states, Rome viewed religion as having two distinct dimensions or 'faces'. There was the private face of religion, which involved what we might call 'faith' or beliefs. This operated in a purely interior way, in the mind of heart, and had as its major concern the question of eternal destiny. In addition to this private face, there was a public dimension to religion which could be seen any time a religion translated its interior commitments into public or social action.

In general, Rome was not interested in the private face of religion. If Christians wanted to believe in the madness about a crucified carpenter being the saviour of their souls, then that was their private misfortune. They could even style him 'Lord' if they chose – that is, a lord of a purely spiritual, interior realm. When this acknowledgment of Christ as Lord began to spill over into their public lives, however, the Roman state became nervous. For Rome, the public face of religion had to be coordinated with the organism that *is* public, namely the state. In this organism, there was no room for a lordship that superseded or in any way criticised the lordship of the state (Lee 1976, 65-66).

Conditions changed radically when the church was granted legal standing and Christians gained positions of power and influence. When Constantine became the first Christian emperor, the church downplayed whatever might suggest criticism of Constantine's way of ruling. This is in contradiction with Jesus' reaction to the power structures in society.[2] After the Constantinian shift, the central question was how did the church cope when its members were suddenly vitally involved in the power of sophisticated political and social institutions (Duchrow & Liedke 1989, 164).

The doctrine of the two kingdoms

The Protestant reformation reacted strongly against the medieval church because it had degenerated into papal power politics. However, the churches of the Reformation themselves ultimately became institutional churches with power. An alliance between throne and altar dominated many regional churches for several centuries. According to the Lutheran doctrine of the two kingdoms, church and state occupy two quite different spheres of responsibility, and this has paved the way for the privatisation of religion, especially in pietism (Gorringe 1998, 67).

Luther himself is often considered to be a conservative ethicist who separated public and private morality and advocated an 'ethic of disposition', a conception which is strongly influenced by outstanding scholars such as E. Troeltsch and R. Niebuhr. However, the idea that Luther's reform did not affect social structures has been criticised in an analysis of Luther's writings about economics. Scholars like C. Lindberg have demonstrated that Luther's point of departure by no means excludes but rather demands social analysis from the midst of life. It was precisely Luther's theology which enabled him to develop a radical ethic that clearly went beyond mere charity.

Moreover, careful studies within the Lutheran World Federation have pointed out that a clear distinction should be made between Luther's understanding of the two kingdoms and later Lutheran tradition (Hertz 1976). In Luther's argumentation of this doctrine, the eschatological dimension plays a dominant role. This element has been lost in later generations. As a result, the doctrine of the two kingdoms has led to church-centredness and dualism. Now it is argued that God rules the world in two ways. There is an important difference between his rule of power and his rule of grace through the gospel. The purpose of the power is to serve as a dike against sin, to preserve law and order and prevent human beings from destroying each other by taking the law into their own hands. By means of power the state was supposed to provide justice. Its function was seen as anti-chaotic. Conservative Lutheranism developed a theology of 'order' rooted in cosmic design (Nissen 2000, 243).

There is a tendency to consider love as something operating in the individual sphere, and to let power and violence be active in the structure of society. But is this

---

2   Mark 10:42-43: "You know that among the Gentiles those whom they recognise as their rulers lord it over them, and their great ones are tyrants over them. But it is not so among you...". On this passage, see Nissen 2003b, 145-146.

distinction possible? One might ask why the passage on non-violent resistance from the Sermon on the Mount has been applied only to personal life, whereas the instruction concerning submission to the state in Romans 13 has been turned into an abstract principle with eternal value. Both texts should be seen in their historical contexts before asking about their meaning for us today (Nissen 2003b, 141-142).

Romans 13 and the Sermon on the Mount

Rom 13:1-7 has often been seen as *the* biblical view on the church-state issue. Unfortunately, it has often been wrenched from its historical and literary context and read as requiring uncritical obedience to the state, no matter how unjust and pernicious the regime. The link between Rom 13:1-7 and its literary context highlights three points that have theological importance: the emphasis on doing what is good, the conscience, and the balance between conformity (Rom 13:2) and non-conformity (Rom 12:2).

Paul's statement in Rom 13 is an example of a strategy of conformity. Similar strategies can be found in other texts, e.g. 1 Tim 2:2. This strategy is based on the idea that the state promotes what is good. The situation of a conflict between demands made by the Roman magistrates and the Christian conscience is not taken into consideration in Rom 13, simply because it had not arisen. A conflict between conformity and non-conformity might arise in other circumstances. In such cases Paul would have been more critical of the state. His basic conviction is similar to the statement in Acts 5:29: "we ought to obey God rather than men".

In other New Testament texts relating to the issue of governing authorities, the perspective is more critical. 1 Pet 2:13-17 has many items in common with Rom 13, but its orientation is different. The letter is characterised by a balance between loyalty and critical distance. Several scholars have pointed out that the paradigm for the role of Christians in society can be found in the exhortation of Jeremiah 29:7: "Seek the welfare of the city". Revelation 13 is quite different from Rom 13. In Revelation there is a passionate protest against the totalitarian type of political rule. The book implies both a theology of liberation and a theology of martyrdom. Like the rest of the New Testament, God's justice should be comprehended in the context of the cross.

The Sermon on the Mount was interpreted by the medieval church as a form of dualism – its teachings were commands for monks and clergy. This splitting of humankind into two classes was criticised by Luther. In his view the teachings are for all Christians. The Sermon is for every Christian in his or her inner attitudes, but the outer self that has responsibilities to other persons should obey the authorities in the world and not the commands of the Sermon. This interpretation can be characterised as two-realm dualism (Stassen & Gushee 2003, 130).

Interpreters usually consider the antitheses to be hard teachings and high ideals. They compartmentalise Jesus' teachings as being intended for attitudes but not actions, or for another future dispensation but not for the present time, or merely as illustrations of general principles like love but not meant to be followed in particular. When people encounter these words, they usually ignore them or interpret them to mean something else. The result is what Bonhoeffer calls "cheap grace".

Instead of operating with a perfectionistic ethic based on twofold antitheses, this part of the Sermon should be seen as *a transforming initiative* (Stassen & Gushee 2003, 133-135). As exemplified by the first antithesis (Matth 5:21-26), there are three aspects of this transforming initiative: It transforms the person who was angry into an active peacemaker; it transforms the relationship from one of anger into a peacemaking process; and it hopes to transform the enemy into a friend.

Serving one God

In the Sermon on the Mount Jesus proclaims that there is only one God who is Lord of all of life. No-one can serve two masters (Matth 6:24). In several of his writings Luther made a similar point. One example of this is the exposition of the Ten Commandments in the Large Catechism. On the First Commandment, and particularly on the admonition "You shall have no other gods", Luther writes:

A god is that to which we look for all good and in which we find refuge in every time of need. To have a god is nothing else than to trust and believe in him with our whole heart... For these two things belong together, faith and God. That to which your heart clings and entrusts itself is, I say, really your God.

These phrases are usually understood in individual terms, and this is certainly one possible meaning. But Luther continues by adding examples of idols. Top to the list is Mammon. By this he means the early capitalist system (for further documentation, see Duchrow 1995, 218).

Despite this emphasis on serving only one God, many Protestant theologians in the twentieth century operated with some kind of two-realm dualism. To exemplify this position we can refer to Emil Brunner, who in discussing the Christian relationship to the economic order writes:

It is unfair and absurd to require a Christian business man to conduct his business 'according to the laws of the Sermon on the Mount'. No-one has ever conducted business on these lines or ever will; it is against all the rules of business itself. The 'office' of a business man belongs to a specific order which is not that of the relation between one person and another.[3]

McDonald rightly notes that here is a frank recognition that the business world has its own symbolic system which the business man must follow or perish. The Christian, like any other, is at the mercy of this ruthless, impersonal system. But any opportunity

---

3 E. Brunner, *The Divine Imperative*. London 1937, 434. Here quoted from McDonald 1993, 151. The German original: *Das Gebot und die Ordnungen.* Tübingen: J.C.B.Mohr/Paul Siebeck, 420.

to express human value should be gratefully accepted. Brunner continues with the following remarks about Christian business:

But ... the seriousness of his Christian life must manifest itself in the fact that he fights with all his power against the evil autonomy of his official work, and that he tries again and again to break through it, which means that he treats the people with whom he has to do in business as his neighbours, to whom he owes love, and that he conducts his business as a service to the community.

According to McDonald, this observation that one does not act *merely* as a member of an institution, but always as a person who can find room for love not in the work of the institution itself but 'between the lines', sounds like relegating the gospel to the coffee break! (McDonald 1993, 150-151).

A good number of our modern problems have come about because the whole of life is not kept in view; instead, it is carved up into components, each of which can then be held in the manipulative grip of expertise and technology (Duchrow 1995, 123). Liberation theology criticises this tendency to split life into a private and a public realm.[4] It is argued that the Christian gospel contains both an individual and a social dimension, and that the two are inseparable. 'Liberation' conveys the fact that salvation applies to both persons and their communities. It is impossible for the Kingdom of God to come on earth within the hearts of individuals unless it is expressed in the social relations that govern their lives as individuals (Rowland and Corner 1990, 162).

The quest for a just society

The distinction between justice and justification is parallel to the distinction between the two kingdoms. While the former concept indicates a social relationship, the latter points at a sort of private transaction between God and the believer. However, a number of biblical scholars have argued recently that the Lutheran reading of the Pauline doctrine of justification is far too dominated by Luther's characteristically late-medieval concern for the salvation of his soul. They argue that Paul's teaching on justification and on justice is set entirely within the context of the dispute about whether Jews and Gentiles could be reconciled to one another within one community of faith, with the breaking

---

4   There is a risk that modern man will return to the idolatry and polytheism characteristic of the religion criticised by Old Testament prophecy. Cf. also Boesak (1980, 35): "Viele Christen leben so: Gott ist für den Gottesdienst zuständig, ein anderer Gott für die Politik, einer für die Wirtschaft und einer für das persönliche Leben. Solche Menschen erwarten natürlich, dass die Predigt dieses heidnische Lebensmuster respektiert, und wehe dem Prediger, der dieses heilige, selbstgebaute Gartenhäuschen abbrechen will. Wir kennen das ja gut: Das Argument 'Geschäft ist Geschäft' und 'Politik ist Politik' wird mit biblischen Zitaten unterlegt, um Gott nur noch in der religiösen Ecke zu tolerieren. Auf dem übrigen Terrain werden eigene 'Gottesreiche' mit eigenen Gesetzen und eigenen Geschäftsgebaren eingerichtet – schallisoliert gegen das Wort Gottes und ohne Gehör für die Thora und die Propheten".

down of barriers and the establishment of a community in which ancient hostilities are overcome. Justification and justice are relational terms; it is social justice which is at issue here, not a private transaction between God and the believer. God's justice is experienced as pure grace, and this justice is expressed in inclusive community, in which there is a special care for the weak, the poor, the stranger, the orphan and the widow (Forrester 2001, 200).

The biblical view of justice is that of bringing harmony to the community through the establishment of right relationships; it is summed up in the legislation concerning the year of the jubilee (e.g. Lev 25). Justice means the removal of barriers which prevent human beings from participating fully in the benefits and responsibilities of the community. According to Luke 4:16-30, Jesus made a public declaration that the time had come for the fulfilment of the jubilee laws. Most commentators think it unlikely that Jesus intended a literal year of jubilee with a strict adherence to all the laws. Rather, he was using jubilee language metaphorically to indicate the purpose of his own mission. However, there is a consensus that jubilee points to the kind of society that will be manifest when God fully reigns among his people. The new community called into being by Jesus Christ was to be a jubilee community not every 49 years, but in its daily practice; cf. Acts 2:44-45; 4:32-37 (Kirk 1999, 105-106).

It is often asserted that the early Christians showed little or no interest in changing society as such. This assertion is based on the question: to what degree did Christians perform actions outside the community – actions that could change the social situation or even the structures of society? However, to present the problem in this way is problematic. The search for a just society was a central concern for the first Christians, but they did not try to achieve this goal by acting outside the community. Instead they aimed at constructing a community which in itself is an example of a just society. As J.H. Yoder has put it, "the primary social structure through which the gospel works to change other structures is that of the Christian community." (Yoder 1972, 157). In other words, the early Christians aimed to construct a community which in itself was an example of a just society.

The message contained in the biblical vision of society is a message concerning the individual worth and dignity of all people *realised in community with others*. More specifically, it is a heritage grounded in the story of a people who are the focus of God's special care, despite their lowly and despised status in the world – whether they be slaves in Egypt, the poor of Israel, widows, orphans, the sick or the oppressed of society. The people of God must be a righteous people with a special concern for all those who are lowly and oppressed, for all the 'nobodies' of this world, for the 'discarded people' (Nissen 2000, 257).

In the Bible, justice appears again and again as the vindication of the poor and the oppressed. The justice of God's reign has an objective reality; it is something that we seek; we do not construct it or make it. It is a gift, not a prize to be earned. But the gift carries with it a call. Those who seek God's righteousness are called to walk in the ways of justice, to anticipate in their practice the justice of the coming Kingdom.

Justice is pervasively relational. It has to do with the proper structure of relationships between God and people and among people.[5]

Bible, church and politics

Ulrich Duchrow and Gerhard Liedke (1989, 155-174) have made a useful distinction between four different ways of being the church:

a) *The peace church*, which refuses to participate in the violent power at the cost of suffering; it aims to build an alternative community (e.g. the Mennonites, Quakers, Brethren).

b) *The liturgical-eucharistic-contemplative church*. This way of being the church demonstrates symbolic community life in God's love (e.g. the Orthodox churches).

c) *The institutional or mainstream church*, which has to face the crucial question of taming power or being tamed by power (e.g. the Lutheran churches).

d) *The liberation church*, which aims to transform the systems of power in solidarity with the parts of humanity and creation oppressed by violence (e.g. liberation churches, especially in Latin America).

The tendency of the institutional church is to assimilate itself to the existing power and to be tamed by it rather than taming it.[6] This has prompted exponents of the liberation church to call on the church to rid itself of the positions of the Constantinian era. The point of departure for this way of being the church is not the refusal to participate in an unjust system, which was true of the peace church position.

It is important to notice the difference between the position of the peace church and that of the liberation church. The peace church approach takes up the insight running through the whole Bible that God takes the side of the poor and that just peace and the minimisation of violence in creation are his will. It emphasises, however, that Jesus seeks to do this through renunciation and alternative communities, and by suffering conflict with the powers-that-be – in the hope of the coming of the kingdom. The liberation church also begins with the rejection of injustice and the development of an alternative community, but emphasises that Jesus acted for the empowerment of the poor. Unlike Jesus, it goes so far as to demand and support the disciple's involvement in the process of shaping power. In so doing, the liberation church takes up the

---

5   Cf. Forrester 2001, 199. Christian theological ethics would suggest that more than fairness is necessary at the heart of a decent society. "If Rawls is right that justice is 'the first virtue of social institutions', it must surely be a justice which is informed by love, by the *agape* of the Christian story, a justice which is more than fairness, a justice which is sometimes generous and sometimes is capable of eliciting sacrifice for others." (Forrester 2001, 205).

6   For further reflections on the tension between pacifism (cf. the peace churches) and the theory of just war (cf. the institutional church), see Nissen 2009. This article also discusses the relationship between four sources of authority for theology: Bible, tradition, reason and experience.

experience of the church *after* Constantine and interprets Jesus and the kingdom of God in the light of this. The liberation church is interested not only in taming and reforming structures, but also in their transformation.

Duchrow and Liedke argue convincingly for the point that the institutional church should develop in the direction of the liberation church.

After the experiences of the Constantinian period, it is fully clear that assimilation to power simply cannot be defended biblically any more, which means that the minimum to be expected from the institution church is prophetic criticism and rejection of the misuse of power....The decisive step on the way from being an institutional church tobecoming a liberation church is the step from taming to transformation of power (Duchrow & Liedke 1989, 170).

The institutional church must at least take the first step to becoming the church of the poor and a church in solidarity with the poor (p. 171).

The peace church and the liberation church approaches are two different forms of ethics of discipleship. The peace church approach represents a more literal understanding of the Bible. As already indicated, it is not possible to show a direct involvement by Jesus and his first followers in the shaping of the socio-political power structures. On the other hand, in the light of the entire biblical witness, we cannot dismiss the question as to whether the followers of Jesus could refuse, if offered the opportunity to shape the power structures in favour of the poor and in the spirit of shalom (Duchrow & Liedke 1989, 172).[7]

The church as an inclusive community of hospitality

The traditional division between personal ethics and social ethics does not comprise that which is characteristic of biblical ethics, i.e. a communitarian ethics (Nissen 2003a, 284-285). This aspect is underlined by the model of 'moral formation of identity'.[8] The church is a hermeneutic of the gospel. The message and the ethics are inseparable from the life of the church (Forrester 1997, 4). This point can be illustrated by a concrete issue: the role of the church in relation to foreigners.

Recent decades have witnessed the emergence of a stigmatisation of foreigners in Europe. In Denmark and other welfare states public care for the nation legitimises the exclusion of groups that are different from what is considered to be a national fellowship. The reverse of care in the welfare society is a wall of protection *against* foreigners.

Exclusion can be identified as a fundamental challenge for European societies today, first of all because of the suffering of the victims, but also because it lays bare the inhuman logic of a system that values money over people and thus brings with it the

---

7   The life story of Dietrich Bonhoeffer shows that the peace church and the liberation church approaches are not contradictory (Duchrow & Liedke 1989, 172).

8   Cf. Hauerwas 1984, 99: "The church does not have a social ethic; the church is a social ethic."

seeds of social breakdown and potentially disastrous political consequences. Churches and other religious and moral authorities have an essential role to play in recalling the equal value of human beings.

To confront the rising tide of racism, ethnocentrism and xenophobia, firm action is necessary. This includes: information, tolerance (mutual understanding), opposition to racist actions and ethnocentric ideology, and a positive counter-offensive. The wider issues are how to handle difference, respond to the 'other' and negotiate plurality. This is a challenge for both the church and the state.

According to the WCC document *Religious plurality and Christian self-under-standing*, religious plurality challenges us to acknowledge 'others' in their difference, to welcome strangers even if their 'strangeness' sometimes threatens us, and to seek reconciliation even with those who have declared themselves our enemies (p. 2). Our theological understanding of religious plurality begins with our faith in the one God who created all things, the living God present and active from the beginning. The Bible testifies to God as the God of all nations and peoples, whose love and compassion includes all humankind.

The Bible speaks of hospitality primarily as a radical openness to others based on the affirmation of the dignity of all (p. 5). The Christian community is fundamentally an inclusive community of hospitality. The grace of God manifested in Jesus Christ calls Christians to an attitude of hospitality in our relation to others. Our hospitality is not limited to those in our community: the gospel commands us to love even our enemies and to call for blessings upon them (Matth 5:43-48; Rom 12:14).

The willingness to accept others in their 'otherness', then, is the hallmark of true hospitality. In some cases this may create a conflict between church and state; for instance when the welfare state demonstrates a public care which excludes foreigners and other minority groups.

Christians have an imperative to serve as the voice of the voiceless. Refugees have no voice in the governments of their countries of exile. Thus the church has a special and unique role to play in ensuring that refugee voices are heard (Ferris 1993). The message from the gospel is clear: strangers, refugees, outcasts are to be treated as brothers and sisters. In seeking to live in accordance with this, conflicts with state authorities are at time perhaps inevitable. Governments which limit benefits to one particular group or refuse protection to those fleeing for their lives are not acting in accordance with the values of the kingdom.

In a situation like this Christians might practise civil disobedience following the example of Jesus. His concern for people in need made him a transgressor of the sabbatical laws. Having cured the man with the withered hand he asked: "Is it lawful to do good or to do harm on the Sabbath, to save life or kill." (Mark 3:4). For him the most important thing was the law of love. In fact, Paul said something similar: submission to the state is motivated by the taxation issue (Rom 13:6-7). This leads directly to the following statement: "owe no-one anything except to love one another, for the one who loves another has fulfilled the law." (Rom 13:8).

Both formation and malformation may be the result of the encounter of the churches with the public world.

Instead of being agents of just social transformation, churches too often uncritically conform to unjust social and economic patterns within their cultural and national context. The result is moral malformation of the membership of the churches, which inevitably has a similar influence on the wider society (Best & Robra 1997, 62).

Such malformation was notably the case in South Africa during the Apartheid regime. The *Kairos Document* of 1986 examines three ways of relating to the state. The first form, 'State Theology', is defined as the theological justification of the status quo. It blesses injustice, canonises the will of the powerful and reduces the poor to passivity, obedience and apathy (*Kairos Document* 1986, 17). The second form, 'Church Theology', is described as a theology of 'peace' and 'reconciliation' in a situation marked by injustice and strife. This theology is about passive conformism to the ruling powers; it suppresses necessary conflict with them, or at least avoids it. The document calls for a third form, 'Prophetic Theology'. Its first task must be "an attempt at social analysis or what Jesus would call 'reading the signs of the times'" (p. 37). In contrast to 'State Theology', 'Prophetic Theology' insists that "a church that takes its responsibilities seriously in the circumstances will sometimes have to confront and disobey the State in order to obey God" (p. 50).

Prophetic theology is always a message of hope and encouragement for the oppressed. It is a challenge not simply to the forces of oppression and injustice, but also to the church (Forrester 1997, 19). It calls on the church to *be* the church, showing in its life the justice, reconciliation and unity that it proclaims and seeks in the world.

Bibliography

Allen, Joseph L. 1986. 'Personal ethics', and 'Social ethics'. In: J. Macquarrie & J. Childress (eds.), *A New Dictionary of Christian Ethics*. London: SCM, 468-489 and 592-593.

Best, Thomas F. & Martin Robra (eds.) 1997. *Ecclesiology and Ethics. Ecumenical Ethical Engagement, Moral Formation and the Nature of the Church*. Geneva: WCC.

Boesak, Allan A. 1980. *Ein Fingerzeig Gottes. 12 Südafrikanische Predigten*. Hamburg: Lutherisches Verlagshaus.

Duchrow 1995. *Alternatives to Global Capitalism. Drawn from Biblical History, Designed for Political Action*. Utrecht: International Books and Kairos Europe.

Duchrow, Ulrich & Gerhard Liedke 1987. *Shalom. Biblical Perspectives on Creation, Justice and Peace*. Geneva: WCC Publications.

Ferris, E.G. 1993. *Beyond Borders. Refugees, Migrants and Human Rights*. Geneva: WCC.

Forrester, Duncan. 1997. *The Church and Morality. Reflections on Ecclesiology and Ethics*. Geneva: WCC.

Forrester, Duncan 2001. 'Social Justice and Welfare'. In: R. Gill (ed.), *The Cambridge Companion to Christian Ethics*. Cambridge: Cambridge University Press, 195-208.

Gorringe, Tim. 1998. 'Political readings of Scripture'. In: J. Barton (ed.), *The Cambridge Companion to Biblical Interpretation*. Cambridge: Cambridge University Press, 67-80.

Hauerwas, Stanley. 1984. *The Peaceable Kingdom. A Primer in Christian Ethics*. London: SCM.

Hertz, Karl H. (ed.) 1976. *Two Kingdoms and One World*. Minneapolis: Augsburg Publ. House.

Kairos Document 1986. *The Kairos Document. Challenge to the Church. A Theological Comment on the Political Crisis in South Africa*. Introduced by J.W. de Gruchy. Grand Rapids MI: Eerdmans.

Kirk, J. Andrew. 1999. *What is Mission? Theological Explorations*. London: Darton, Longman and Todd.

Lee, Clarence L. 1976. 'Church and State in Tension'. In: W.H. Lazareth (ed.), *The Left Hand of God. Essays on Discipleship and Patriotism*. Philadelphia: Fortress Press, 31-70.

McDonald, J.I.H. 1993. *Biblical Interpretation and Christian Ethics*. Cambridge: Cambridge University Press.

Nissen, Johannes 2000. 'Conformity, Nonconformity, and Critical Solidarity. The Church-State Issue and the Use of the Bible'. *Mission Studies* 16, 1-2, 240-262.

Nissen, Johannes 2003a. *Bibel og etik. Konkrete og principielle problemstillinger*. Aarhus: Aarhus University Press.

Nissen, Johannes 2003b. 'Prophetic Diakonia. Biblical Perspectives and Present Challenges'. In: V. Mortensen (ed.), *The Role of Mission in the Future of Lutheran Theology*. Aarhus: Centre for Multireligious Studies, 139-151.

Nissen, Johannes 2009. 'Between Conformity and Nonconformity: The Issue of Non-violent Resistance in Early Christianity and in Christian Tradition'. In: S. Doserode (ed.), *Christianity and Resistance in the 20th Century. From Kaj Munk and Dietrich Bonhoeffer to Desmond Tutu*. Leiden and Boston: Brill, 29-53.

'*Religious plurality and Christian self-understanding*'. 2006. WCC document, Geneva, 5 pages.

Rowland, Christopher & Max Corner 1990. *Liberating Exegesis. The Challenge of Liberation Theology to Biblical Studies*. London: SPCK.

Stassen, Glen H. & David P. Gushee 2003. *Kingdom Ethics. Following Jesus in Contemporary Context*. Downers Grove Ill.: IVP Academic.

Yoder, John H. 1972. *The Politics of Jesus*. Grand Rapids MI: Eerdmans.

CHURCH BETWEEN NATION AND EMPIRE

Peter Lodberg

In the dying days of 2005 and the beginning of 2006, Denmark experienced its worst international crisis since World War II as a consequence of the Mohammed Cartoon Crisis. Danish embassies in the Middle East were attacked by angry people protesting against the defamation of the prophet in a Danish newspaper. The Danish flag and pictures of the Danish prime minister were burned by angry people in the West Bank and Gaza. A boycott of Danish products was organised by some Arab states, and international diplomacy tried to limit and control the outburst of anger in the streets of cities like Beirut, Teheran and Ramallah. The Danish government argued that it would not and could not try to limit the freedom of expression and prohibit the publication of the cartoons in an independent newspaper. If people were offended by the cartoons, the government advised them to take their case to the Danish courts. According to the government, freedom of expression is a matter of law and not of politics.

But as the crisis developed it was clear to many Danes that the crisis was becoming increasingly political, and that it was linked both to social tensions in many Middle East states and to the fact that Denmark was part of the invasion forces in Iraq. The popular and state-controlled protests against Denmark expressed a deep dissatisfaction among people in the Middle East about the role of the US-led invasion of Iraq, but instead of attacking the US directly, the Mohammed Cartoon Crisis was used to attack one of its allies, Denmark, a country which most people in the Middle East had never heard of before. So Denmark served as a perfect scapegoat in the international power game and the competition between Saudi Arabia and Egypt to be the leader of the Moslem Middle East.

But why did such a small nation state of five million people become part of an international crisis? My observation is that Denmark was caught between nationalism and imperialism – nation and empire – a relationship which has developed since 1989 and especially since September 11, 2001. It is a fluid situation, where nation and empire in a globalised world blend some of their characteristics in ways that change all aspects of society – including the life of the churches. In this chapter I will try to describe and evaluate some of these changes from the perspective of the Lutheran Church in Denmark, which is also located somewhere between nation and empire.

Empire lite

Many different empires have existed throughout history. At some point they all collapse like the Persian, Egyptian, Roman and British empires. So far China is an exception. The Chinese Empire has existed in different forms throughout history, and is an exception to the rule that empires always collapse. In the northern hemisphere the British Empire was followed by the impressive growth of the American economy and cultural influence. According to Michael Ignatief, former Director of the Carr Center for Human Rights Policy at Harvard University, the American dominance is captured by the phrase *empire lite* (Ignatief 2003). By this he means that the essential paradox of nation-building is that temporary imperialism – empire lite – has become the necessary condition for democracy in countries torn apart by civil war. According to Ignatief, Americans have had an empire since Teddy Roosevelt. The irony is that the Americans persist in believing that this is not the case.

This is a new kind of empire compared with the ones known from history. It is *empire lite* because it is American hegemony without colonies, a global sphere of influence without the burden of direct administration and the risks of daily policing. It is an empire without a consciousness of itself as such, because it is a country that thinks of itself as the home of liberty and freedom and the friend of anti-imperial struggle everywhere. According to Ignatief, America is the new Rome, and empire lite is the new face of empire. Just like the old empire (Rome), the new Rome (the US) is learning the lesson of history: overwhelming military superiority does not translate into security, and the challenge to the United States lies in escaping Rome's ultimate fate: decline and fall. Part of the answer is hidden in the observation that empires endure only so long as their rulers take care not to extend their borders, as formulated by Edward Gibbon in his first volume from 1776 *The Decline and Fall of the Roman Empire*. Ignatief maintains that nobody likes empires, but that there are some problems for which there are only imperial solutions. And that it is a problem that Europeans do not understand this connection, because European states have reduced the martial and military elements in their national identity in the process of continental integration. In Europe national identity has become post-military and post-national after 1945, but the problem is that the Americans cannot operate a global empire without European diplomatic and economic cooperation.

Ignatief's analysis also refers to *empire lite* as *the humanitarian empire*, or the new face of an old figure: the democratic free world, the Christian West. This is a situation in which the Americans dictate Europe's place in this new grand design, and US policy is:

multilateral when it wants to be, unilateral when it must, and it uses its power to enforce a new international division of labour in which America does the fighting, the Canadians, French, British, and Germans do the police patrols in the border zones and the Dutch, Swiss and Scandinavians provide the humanitarian aid (Ignatief 2003,6).

There is a certain sense of 'the white man's burden' in Ignatief's analysis. To my mind he is too optimistic and triumphalistic about the possibility of what he calls 'the Christian West' to establish freedom, a social market economy and democracy in 'the Global South'. Even though Ignatief has regretted his support for the war in Iraq, his analysis and its practical political consequences are still an important part of the political discussions in many countries – including my own.

Ignatief talks about *the Christian West* as a political, cultural and religious entity. But is it not actually an imperial construction that does not cover our present situation in Europe? Separation between state and church, secularisation and multi-religiosity make it very difficult – if not impossible – to speak about the Christian West as a reality. On a more theoretical level the concept of the Christian West is also problematic, because it indicates that the Christian faith is a political tool that should be used against political and religious opponents. But despite these ambiguities, Ignatief's use of the concept of the Christian West is a good example of the fact that theologically and biblically inspired metaphors still play an important role in public life.

Biblical metaphors in the Christian West

Biblical metaphors are used and misused in political discourse by presidents and prime ministers in the US, Britain, Denmark and elsewhere. For instance, the Prime Minister of Denmark, Anders Fogh Rasmussen, has used the biblical story about sheep and goats (Matth 25) to distinguish enemies from friends during the Mohammed Cartoon Crisis in 2006. And in particular, President George W. Bush has become known as a highly prominent moralist who often speaks about good and evil, right and wrong. His speech on June 1, 2002 at the United States Military Academy, West Point, is very important in understanding the basic idea of the empire: "*We are in a conflict between good and evil, and America will call evil by its name*" (Singer 2004, 1). According to Peter Singer, President George W. Bush thinks of evil in terms of deeds, people, and things/forces, which raises for Singer the question of what this meaning of evil may have in a secular modern world.

We will not follow Peter Singer's argument, but only challenge his view that we are living in a secular modern world. The very fact that some of the most influential political leaders today publicly acknowledge their religious interest shows that the picture is much more complicated, and that religion plays an important part in the public arena. My claim will be that such leaders play an important role in the public discourse in the midst of a fluid global situation, where the issue of identity and violence has become one of the most challenging questions to answer after the collapse of the stable but dangerous bi-polar world system during the Cold War. Their ability to address the issue of identity and violence is partly the reason why so many people elected them to office in the first place. This does not answer the question of how they use biblical metaphors (responsibly or irresponsibly), but it does show that politics and secularity are much more complicated than Peter Singer and others tend to think.

The nation as God's chosen people

In our empire lite, as a culture shaped by Christianity – for worse and for good, political discourse is influenced by biblical metaphors and theological concepts. This can and should not be avoided. It is part of the public role of Christianity, the Christian Church, and Christian theology. The challenge is to define and describe the right use of biblical metaphors and theological concepts in an empire lite – the same challenge as that faced by the Christian church throughout history, with the relationship between state and church assuming a number of different forms.

One of the basic biblical metaphors that unites the US and Europe in a way that links theology with politics is the concept of *God's chosen people*. This should only be interpreted as an ecclesiological concept, but unfortunately it is often used politically to define the foundation and mission of the nation state. *God's chosen people* has a long history of political importance, and it is the big idea that shapes Britain and the US as Clifford Longley has shown (Longley 2002). His thesis is that the secret behind the feeling of American and British national identity is the powerful, transforming analogy between their own situation and that of the ancient Israelites. They were selected as *God's chosen people* with the same purpose and destiny as the Jewish people: to save the world. Among many other things, this explains the deep sense of relationship and fellowship between Britain, the US and Israel today. The so-called Chosen People Syndrome (or paradigm) was a common factor in British and American history, and explains some of the ideological background of the British Empire, its mission and many wars – an ideology that reached its zenith in David Livingstone's 'three Cs': Commerce, Christianity, and Civilisation. In Thomas Pakenham's words, the divine mission was accentuated in the Scramble for Africa that took place after Lingstone's death in 1873:

In Britain, the Scramble was taken calmly – at first. Then there was growing resentment towards the intruders. Britain had pioneered the exploration and evangelisation of Central Africa, and she felt a proprietary right to most of the continent. Besides, there was a vital interest at stake for Britain. As the only great maritime Empire, she needed to prevent her rivals obstructing the steamer routes to the East, via Suez and the Cape. That meant digging in at both ends of Africa.

And it was in Protestant Britain, where God and Mammon seemed made for each other, that Livingstone's words struck the deepest chord. The three Cs would redeem Africa (Pakenham 1991, xxv).

Pakenham is realistic enough to note that this was not the way Africans perceived the Scramble. To them there was a fourth 'C' – Conquest – and this was the one that eventually dominated. It shows that the Chosen People paradigm is more than just a metaphor: it is a policy that prescribes how people and nations should behave in the future without any considerations about the consequences for the local people. A Chosen People is blind to the sufferings of other peoples, because in its own thinking it embarks on war with a view to benefiting the people it is conquering. The irony is that sufferings can be excused because they are to the benefit of the people suffering. The more the better – which leads to a circle of violence.

Today, the Scramble is for the Middle East after the British Empire has given up and left the Islamic world with the structure and idea of the *nation* that is unfamiliar to Islam and Middle East politics. So far, it seems that Marxism and Arabic nationalism have lost the race to the last two contenders: Islamism and American empire lite. Islamism is engaged in building the umma, and the Americans are struggling with nation-building in Iraq, Afghanistan, Lebanon, Israel/Palestine and Somalia. The US is trying to include the remaining Moslem nation states like Egypt or Saudi Arabia in its empire lite. While the Christian West is fighting the Islamistic East – and vice versa – the price is paid by the Christians in the Middle East who are fleeing to safe places in the old Christian West: the US, Britain, Australia and New Zealand.

The nation as a Christian invention

It was through British imperialism that the notion of *nation* was exported to the rest of the world including the Middle East, because *nation* and nationalism were 'invented' in Europe. Adrian Hastings links the idea of the nation to the use of the Bible in the European churches (Hastings 1997). Ethnicity makes a nation when language changes from oral to written language. People become a nation when they have literature in their own language. It happens in Christianity when the Bible is translated and gains its place in a living tradition, in casu the Christian church. So according to Hastings, the nation and biblical Christianity are interrelated. There are several factors which play an important role in linking European peoples to the idea of the nation:

– The idea of a *people/nation*: the Old Testament talks about Israel/the Jewish people; the New Testament talks about New Israel/the congregation. This is a people that is different from other peoples;
– The people has been chosen. It is God's people, and its destiny and history are in God's hands leading to fulfilment and salvation;
– God's chosen people has well-defined institutions that unite the people politically and religiously. There is a king, a temple, and a hierarchy of ministries in a well-organised church with a clear power structure;
– A tension between the local and the universal (the church) that is transformed into tension between the local and the centre (the state).

According to Hastings, reading the Bible and proclaiming the Christian message in a well established institution like the church lies behind the dominant role that Europe and the US play in the world today, because it makes the principle of peaceful competition among nation states possible.

On the one hand I am not suggesting that we can avoid tensions in the Middle East or elsewhere by being aware of the Christian dimension of the *nation*, even though doing so may enable us to avoid the false self-image that Europeans or Americans are free from their own cultural and religious background when they enter into war in countries with a predominantly Moslem population. On the other hand, the conflicts should not be understood as a self-fulfilling prophecy of Huntington's Clashes of Civilizations theory, because there are also dominant economic and political reasons behind the wars in the Middle East (Huntington 1997). However, in Clifford Longley's words the problem involved in understanding a people, nation or empire as God's chosen people is that

(t)he effects of a powerful nation convinced it has God on its side are not self-limiting. It can often act, rightly or wrongly, with impunity. Indeed, in the extreme case, the Chosen People status can grow into a condition of zealous religious nationalism that is potentially Fascistic (Longley 2002, 281).

I also agree with Longley when he states that the best way of ensuring that this potential is not realised is to be aware of it, and to take steps to correct or resist it.

That is as necessary for Americans themselves as it is for the rest of the world. But whether America and the world have the courage and wisdom equal to this daunting task is another matter (Longley 2002, 281-82).

Thus, it is an important theological task to deconstruct the political use of concepts like *God's chosen people* and *the Christian West* in order to ensure a free space for political discussion and decision making. This does not leave out theological reflection and engagement with political issues, but ensures a fruitful division of labour between theology and politics. In a multi-religious global world, the issue of political theology and political religiosity becomes very important.

Political theology is the challenge

After the Mohammed Cartoon Crisis a good number of people in Denmark said that religion and religious people should stay out of politics. The old liberal and communist saying that religion is a private matter united secularists on all sides. In particular, Lutheran theology and the Lutheran Church were praised by many because Lutheranism ensures the inner privacy of religion, separation between faith and politics, state and church as a consequence of Luther's teaching of the two regimes. A great number of people – including the Prime Minister – said that Islam should become like the Lutheran Church of Denmark: silent, powerless and invisible.

But Christianity and Lutheranism are public and work with ideas, concepts and persuasions that claim a universal importance. The very connectedness to Judaism makes Christianity a public religion with consequences for religion and politics. According to Jan Assmann, the public and political dimension of Christianity is linked to the change from polytheism to monotheism that took place in Judaism (Assmann 2003). It changed the traditional religious question about clean and unclean to a question about justice and injustice. Monotheism becomes political theology with consequences for ethics, law and politics. The Jewish law is not so much about the cleanness of priests, the correctness of rites or the fullness of sacrifice, but about doing justice to God and to the Jewish people. The God of the Old Testament is served not through sacrifice but by doing right. And when the people failed to do justice prophets came forward to call the people back to the way of justice. The God of the Old Testament is a God of justice and freedom, who calls his people from Egypt and challenges them to live according to the law and moral responsibility. The biblical themes of freedom, law and justice make monotheism a political theology. For the first time in history political issues are made central to religion, and they become yardsticks to distinguish between good and bad religion, true and false religion. False religion shows its true political face when it allows suppression, injustice, lack of law and arbitrariness. When God liberates his people from Egypt he acts in a political way that challenges the political and religious power of the Egyptian Pharaoh. The instrument of liberation is the law, and Egypt becomes the antithesis of the political and religious culture of the Israelites. False politics is what happens in Egypt, and the Israelites are free to establish an alternative society and an alternative lifestyle in which people are free from bondage and free to serve one another. By serving in this manner they fulfil the commandments of the law.

In the New Testament the political and religious interconnectedness is continued. The message is that Jesus continues the prophetic tradition of the Old Testament in a new way. Just like the Israelites, Jesus was also in Egypt and was called back to bring salvation to God's people. The central idea in Matthew is that God's justice and faithfulness to his Covenant is now fulfilled through the Son of the people, who identifies with the story of Exodus. The New Testament, then, tells the story about how the Son of the people is challenged to understand his ministry in a universal perspective that begins at the margins: the down-trodden, the sinner, the prostitute, the children, the pagan, the poor and the woman. Doing justice is still the central point that links history to eschatology, religion to politics: "(A)nything you _did_ for one of my brothers here, however humble, you _did_ for me." (Matth 25:40). To act lawfully and in accordance with the covenant is to meet the basic needs of a person: to give food, to give drink, to welcome the stranger, to cloth the naked, to help the ill, and to visit people in prison. Martin Luther addresses this basic duty of everybody in a political manner in his interpretation of the fourth prayer of the Lord's Prayer: "_Give us today our daily bread_". According to Luther, it is the duty of the prince to ensure peace in the land to allow the farmers to cultivate their fields and people to trade in the market place. Luther's basic point is that the prince is responsible for the welfare of the people, for ensuring that their basic needs are met. He suggests that the prince should replace the Saxon shields with a loaf of bread on all Saxon coins so that the prince and everybody else will remember what the purpose of politics is: not war, but peace; not weapons, but bread. The challenge is that sometimes you need weapons to ensure peace and a sufficient supply of bread. Luther and Melanchton knew about this dilemma from their own experience and tradition. In the Augsburg Confession Art. 16 they formulated the idea of the Just War theory, but it should be underlined that the perspective used is important. What is often called the Just War theory should rightly be called a Just Peace theory in order to stress that it is a theory that should restrain the use of force and not encourage it, because the aim of the theory is the establishment of the welfare of everybody.

The inverted Messiah as a criterion

Of course we are living today under very different political and religious conditions than those applying in the time of New Testament or the Reformation. Churches have accommodated a variety of different political systems during the course of history, but the challenge to meet the basic needs of ordinary people is still the same. It is also a challenge to combine religion and politics in the right way under new political circumstances. One of the big theological and political challenges in Europe after World War II was to combine Christianity and democracy. It is debatable whether churches have succeeded in this, but there is no doubt that mainline Christian theology in most churches around the world today includes favouring the liberal democratic state based on law and order for everybody irrespective of religion, political view or race. I would also argue that sound theology does not identify a political system (e.g. democracy) with the will of God, but that there is a dialectical tension between actual politics and theological ideas. Christian theology and churches were taught this lesson the hard way before and during World War II, because they failed to speak out against Fascism, Communism and Nazism.

The theological reason why Christianity must avoid any identification with a certain political project or system is linked to what Michel Gauchet has called *the inverted Messiah* (Gauchet 1997:188). According to Gauchet, Jesus is unique in the history of religion because he inverts the concept of God in his own person. Jesus was heading not for victory but for defeat. He was not heading toward the glorious attestation of his truth; he was heading for abandonment and the uncertainty of an ignominious death. He did not mobilise his people in a worldly mission; he sacrificed himself, alone and unrecognised, to save everyone else. Gauchet continues: "Reversing the reversal through the resurrection, triumphing over death after death's victory, took place as to confirm the exemplary necessity of passing through extreme abandonment and humiliation" (Gauchet 1997, 188). Jesus' genius was to use the memory of the chosen people, of Moses and his founding actions, as the source for a god that breaks free from terrestrial domination. Jesus urged a removal not only from the world's empire, but from the world itself. The God of Jesus is the truly universal god, directly accessible to all. Moses freed his people from Pharaoh's hand. Jesus extracted his followers from Caesar's hands, not by leading them toward a terrestrial promised land, but by removing them from the world while remaining in it. His empire (kingdom) is not of this world, but it is already at work when people's basic needs are met. History and eschatology relate to each other like the Chalcedon formula: without confusion, without change, without division, without separation. According to Gauchet, this was the first and most important step towards the western deconstruction of the hierarchical principle, paving the way for the western 'miracle' that is the tension of two orders of necessity, each so firmly entrenched that it could resist the other (below-above, human-God, earthly-godly, state-church, spiritual-secular). The West's dynamic arose from the confrontation between two equally comprehensive and equally Christian legitimating systems, which could not be made hierarchical. The critique of power (Machtkritik) became a child of the Christian West and was used against both church and state to the benefit of a secularisation process – especially after the Enlightenment. The sharing of power became a way of taming the absolute power executed by one person, and the churches lost their political power to the state and to the people. In Europe state and church often include the same people, but they represent different organisational forms, with different aims and styles of work.

Conclusion

Christian theology in an empire is not a new thing. Christian theology was born in an empire (Roman) interpreting the Jewish theology, established in opposition to Pharaoh's empire in Egypt. Jesus was understood as the second Moses, and the Church as the new Israel, as God's chosen people. Theology became political theology, because the relation to God and one another was formulated in accordance with justice, freedom and peace, which is basic to the fulfilment of the old and new Covenant. Jesus adds at least three elements to the old understanding of the law: incarnation, universality, and the perspective of the outcast with whom he identifies. This introduces a totally new way of thinking: the tension between godly and human and the process of deconstruction of the hierarchical principle. Power sharing and the critique of power become an important element in this process, which eventually also includes the secularisation of religious life. Whenever theology, churches or political parties try to eliminate the in-built tension in concepts that combine political and religious elements, serious problems will arise. Political leaders can misuse the church and theology in two ways: either by abandoning Christianity in the public sphere, or by identifying their politics as Christian politics.

Bibliography

Assmann, Jan 2003. *Die Mosaische Unterscheidung – Oder der Preis des Monotheismus.* München: Carl Hanser Verlag.

Gauchet, Michel 1997. *The Disenchantment of the World. A Political History of Religion.* Princeton: Princeton University Press.

Hastings, Adrian 1997. *The Construction of Nationhood. Ethnicity, Religion and Nationalism.* Cambridge: Cambridge University Press.

Huntington, Samuel P. 1997. *The Clash of Civilization and the Remaking of World Order.* London: Touchstone Books.

Ignatief, Michael 2003. *Empire Lite. Nation-Building in Bosnia, Kosovo and Afghanistan.* London: Vintage.

Longley, Peter 2002. *Chosen People – The big idea that shapes England and America.* London: Hodder and Stoughton.

Pakenham, Thomas 1991. *The Scramble for Africa 1876-1912.* London: Abacus.

Singer, Peter 2004. *The President of Good and Evil. Taking George W. Bush Seriously.* London: Granta Books.

SIN AND CRIME, PENANCE AND PUNISHMENT
ECCLESIASTICAL DISCIPLINE IN THE MIDDLE AGES

Per Ingesman

Introduction

The timespan from 1050 to 1250 was the great reform period of the medieval Church. Headed by the popes in Rome, the Church first set out to create a new clergy of a higher moral standard than before, a clergy living in celibacy and free from any dependence on kin and secular authorities. Having succeeded in this enterprise, the Church also tried to reform its lay members. Towards the laity the intention of the Reform Papacy was to create, by means of cathecising instruction and clerical control, true Christians who lived up to the requirements of the Church in both thought and deed. As part of this so-called 'pastoral revolution', in 1215 the Fourth Lateran Council made yearly confession mandatory for all Christians (Morris 1989, especially 489-496).

New ecclesiastical legislation was an important instrument in the reform policy of the Papacy, and in the period from the eleventh to the thirteenth century the legal apparatus of the Church developed into a highly sophisticated system. Together with the old law of the Church, stretching back to Antiquity, the new papal laws were collected in a monumental law book, the *Corpus Juris Canonici*, or Canon Law. And in every corner of Western Europe ecclesiastical courts, presided over by judges with a university training in Canon Law, were set up to enforce the new rules and regulations of the Church (Brundage 1995, especially 44-69).

The efforts of the Reform Papacy can be seen as a large-scale 'project' that could be called 'the making of Christian society'. The project implied that certain fields of society should be handed over totally to the Church and its legal regulation. As a result, three large fields in medieval society came to be regarded as belonging to the ecclesiastical domain: education, poor relief, and marriage. In particular, the fact that marriage (including family relations and sexuality) became regulated by Canon Law and church courts was of decisive importance to the lives of ordinary people in the Middle Ages (Brundage 1995, especially 70-97; Brundage 1987).

The legal regulation of lay people's marital and sexual life was, however, only one aspect of the way in which the new reform policy of the Church came to affect ordinary people's lives. The mandatory confession of 1215 was also an important instrument of ecclesiastical discipline. Here it was through the confession of sins and the imposing of penitential acts in the sacrament of penance that the regulation took place (Tentler 1977).

The lawyers and theologians of the medieval Church were clearly aware that the jurisdictional and sacramental way of regulating people's lives were two sides of the same coin. They talked about the *forum internum* and the *forum externum* of the Church – also called *forum poenitentiale* and *forum iudiciale*. You could say that they applied a distinction between sin and crime – with sin being something to be confessed to your priest and settled by the sacrament of penance, while crime was something to be handled by the law courts and punished by either fines or corporal punishment. It is, however, important not to think that this distinction was based on an assumption that the two kinds of condemnable acts were different by nature. In principle the difference was between secret and public offences: 'crimes' that were punished by the ecclesiastical law courts were for the most part the more serious or more notorious cases of 'sins', which would have been dealt with by confession and sacrament of penance if they had been kept secret. It was not until after the Protestant Reformation, when the State took over crimes and left the Church to deal with sins, that a more clear-cut distinction between sin and crime was drawn on the assumption that the two acts were different by nature – crimes being 'secular' and sins 'spiritual' (Trusen 1990; Schilling 2002).

I hope to be able to elucidate the prehistory of this fundamental change following the Reformation in a current research project on ecclesiastical discipline and social control in the Middle Ages. It is my hypothesis that a development took place during the medieval period which transferred the most serious sins from the system of penance to the system of the ecclesiastical law courts, thus transforming them into 'crimes'. And I think that this could be seen as a first step towards the situation after the Reformation, when the State took over crimes fully from the Church. This article intends to give a preliminary presentation of my line of argumentation. I will first show how the penitential system of the Christian Church developed in the period from Antiquity to the High Middle Ages, underlining especially that it underwent a 'legalistic turn' in the thirteenth century. This gave the penitential system, like the jurisdictional system, an element of social control – in other words, it intended not only to console the spirits, but also to regulate the behaviour of people. Then I will demonstrate that the jurisdictional side of ecclesiastical discipline during the medieval period in a way 'grew out' of the penitential system. It developed and expanded partly by taking over more and more 'sins' from the penitential system. The result of these developments taken together was the creation of the two-sided system of ecclesiastical discipline, with both an 'inner' and an 'outer' *forum*.

I will underline the close connection between the penitential and the jurisdictional disciplinary systems by concentrating on their treatment of sins and crimes within the same field, namely the sexual field. This will also enable me to throw light on one of the most important ways in which the medieval Church affected the daily lives of its members. I will end the article by using attitudes to sexuality as an example of the importance of the medieval system of ecclesiastical discipline for the general evolution of Western culture.

The penitential system

In the period between the third and the fifth century, the Ancient Church introduced the practice that although grave sins such as idolatry, adultery and murder led to exclusion from the Church, it was possible to be readmitted after an appropriate period of penance, albeit only once. And detailed rules had been fixed concerning how 'fallen' sinners should behave in their period of penance, and what kind of rituals they had to go through to be admitted as full members of their congregations again (Karpp 1969).

In the Early Middle Ages between 500 and 1000, the public penance from Antiquity was supplemented by the so-called 'private penance', which gradually gained so much importance that a new penitential regime came into being. The public penance for which the bishop was responsible continued to exist, but came to be reserved for the most serious offences. Most sins were dealt with in private penance: You confessed them to your parish priest in secret, and he gave you absolution and imposed a penance like fasting or refraining from sex during a certain period. In contrast to the old public penance, this private penance could be repeated as often as necessary. The penance to be imposed for every possible sin was to be found in so-called penitentials, handbooks to guide parish priests in their confessional practice (McNeill and Gamer 1990; Hamilton 2001).

Analyses of sexual sins in the early medieval penitentials have been carried out by a number of scholars, but I shall concentrate on the treatment by the American legal historian James A. Brundage (Brundage 1987, 152-169, cf. Payer 1984; Lutterbach 1999).

Of course you had to be married to have sex; but even if you were married sex was prohibited during menstruation, pregnancy and child nursing. The background to these prohibitions connected with *the woman's biological cycle* involved very ancient ideas that sexual contact with the woman during such periods made a man ritually impure – unable to take part in religious services.

Sex on the day before and on the various feast days of the Church, as well as sex during Lent and on the two fast days every week (Wednesday and Friday), was also prohibited. The background to these prohibitions, related to *the Church's liturgical cycle*, was partly that during fasting you had to be abstinent in every respect, including sexually, and partly that sexual intercourse created a kind of ritual impurity.

Apart from these extensive demands for sexual abstinence, the penitentials contain many other restrictions on marital sexuality. It was important that intercourse only took place with the sole purpose of producing children. So oral sex and anal sex and intercourse in strange positions (for instance from behind 'in the manner of dogs') were not allowed.

In 1215 the use of private penance, developed during the Early Middle Ages, was made mandatory. But another important change took place as a consequence of the pastoral revolution. Whereas in the Early Middle Ages there was a fixed penance for every sin, the decision of 1215 commanded the confessor to act as a doctor, *medicus*, assessing in each individual case what treatment to apply, taking into account both the personal situation of the sinner and the circumstances of the sin. Thus, a new penitential regime was introduced which has been called the 'arbitrary system' of penance in opposition to the 'tariff system' of the Early Middle Ages (Tentler 1977, especially 16-27).

The new system made hearing confession and imposing penance a far more complicated task than before, and in the wake of the 1215 decision new types of handbooks with guidance for parish priests in their role as confessors were produced. They were either large, alphabetically arranged handbooks on topics of moral theology (so-called *summae*), or shorter manuals with step-by-step instructions on how to proceed when questioning a penitent and assessing the penance to be imposed on him (Tentler 1974; Tentler 1977, especially 28-53).

In particular, the new *summa* genre shows that profound changes had occurred since the time of the penitentials. Firstly, handling sin had become a science. From the eleventh to the thirteenth century theology had become an academic discipline to be studied in the scholastic tradition of the new universities. What the *summae* and manuals gave to confessors was an application of academic scholastic theology to practical moral questions. It was in this way that what the university theologians taught about usury being a grave sin (for instance) was transformed into a moral requirement that every merchant would meet when he came to his priest to confess (Tentler 1977, especially 28-53, cf. Biller and Minnis 1998; Langholm 2003).

Secondly, the *summae* show that from the middle of the thirteenth century there was a clear tendency for legal elements and ways of thinking to be involved in the institution of penance, now one of the seven sacraments of the Church. Instead of being seen only as a *medicus*, as stated in the 1215 decision, the confessor was now regarded as a *iudex* or judge as well. It was this "Verrechtlichung der Bußpraxis", as a German legal historian has called it, that opened up for talking about a double *forum* in the Church: the penitential *forum* and the judicial *forum* (Trusen 1990, especially 257-264).

An analysis of the late medieval *summae* and confessional manuals has been carried out by the American historian Thomas N. Tentler. What is different from the penitentials is the detailed discussion of moral questions and how to handle them. As an example Tentler, like Brundage, concentrates on the treatment of marital sexuality. He has reached some of the same conclusions as Brundage regarding the penitentials: in the High and Late Middle Ages the ecclesiastical regulation of sexuality also reveals the same old attitude of the Church that sexuality is an evil which might be necessary to continue the human race, but which should otherwise be confined as much as possible, and should only take place with the sole purpose of producing offspring and continuing the human race (Tentler 1977, 162-232).

The conclusion in Tentler's book is important in our connection. Taking his point of departure in the new notion of the confessor as a doctor and a judge at the same time, Tentler underlines that it was a leading principle of the medieval institution of confession to balance between two functions, between giving consolation to troubled souls on the one hand, and condemning sin and thereby enacting social discipline on the other (Tentler 1977, especially 345-349).

The jurisdictional system

The sacrament of penance was an instrument used to handle sin, and from 1215 all Christians were forced to make use of it at least once a year. The parish priest was able to give absolution for most sins, but some were so serious that a sinner was forced to make a public confession and do public penance. This would normally take place in a cathedral church supervised by the local bishop or his so-called penitentiary (Mansfield 1995). The difference between such 'public sins' and ecclesiastical crimes – be it adultery or usury, heresy or witchcraft – was a question of contrition and confession: When you felt sorrow over an offence and confessed it, either in private to your parish priest or in public to your bishop, then it was a sin that could be forgiven, only requiring that you accepted an appropriate penance. A crime, on the other hand, was a misdeed you tried to hide. So crimes had to be uncovered by the ecclesiastical authorities, perhaps with the help of neighbours of the person involved. Ecclesiastical crimes were normally punished with fines, but more serious punishments could also be applied, such as imprisonment or even burning at the stake.

The way in which the external or jurisdictional *forum* of the high and late medieval Church largely grew out of the older penitential system is only just beginning to be studied in international research. One important foundation for future studies has been laid in a comprehensive book by the German legal historian Lotte Kéry. Her theme is the contribution of medieval Canon Law to the development of a public criminal justice within the Church which was also important for the secular legal system of the State. Kéry clearly shows how a public prosecution of crimes grew out of the old system of penance in the early medieval period (c. 800-1050). Thereafter, the development of Canon Law into a scientific discipline at the new universities of the High Middle Ages made it possible for the learned jurists to work out a theoretical distinction between sin and crime, penance and punishment. The result was the theory of the two parallel sides of ecclesiastical discipline, the penitential and the jurisdictional (Kéry 2006, cf. Trusen 1990).

Kéry starts her description with the situation in the Carolingian Empire of Charlemagne around 800. Ecclesiastical law courts at the episcopal sees had been established from the time of Constantine the Great in the fourth century, but in the centuries immediately after the fall of the Roman Empire not very much is heard about them. However, from around 800 it is clear that the legal system of the Church was growing stronger. Besides the episcopal law courts in the cathedral cities, local ecclesiastical law courts were developed which were known in German as 'sendgerichte'. They were not permanent law courts, but court sessions which the bishop held when he visited a local community. These 'sendgerichte' took care of all legal cases, including – or perhaps especially – crimes among the laity. This is the first medieval evidence that 'sins' were removed from the penitential system and handled by a legal body, thus being transformed into 'crimes' (Kéry 2006, 65-118).

During the High Middle Ages local ecclesiastical courts at the level below the diocese became permanent. They are best known from central Western Europe and

England, but they existed everywhere within the Roman Church. They were normally presided over by archdeacons, and gradually they came to specialise in criminal cases. That has to do with the fact that during the High and Late Middle Ages a jurisdictional struggle took place between the bishops at the centre of the diocese and the archdeacons in the local districts. The bishops won, and the courts of the archdeacons either disappeared or were restricted to handling only a reduced spectrum of more uncomplicated cases, among them especially criminal cases (Schwab 2001, especially 363-418, cf. Poos 2001, xii-xx and xlv-lii).

A fine insight into the jurisdictional activity at the level below the diocese can be found in a recent edition (by the American historian L.R. Poos) of the act books of two lower ecclesiastical jurisdictions in late medieval England (Poos 2001).

His edition contains a great number of examples of how an ecclesiastical court at the lowest level treated fornication and adultery, breaches of ecclesiastical incest, and cases in which married couples refused to live together or in other ways did not show each other the appropriate marital affection. So-called *inquisitores*, local lay people who were appointed to oversee the moral situation in the various parishes, would report the names of such persons to the court, which would then cite them to free themselves from the accusations. If they were unable to do so they would be punished according to their misdeed. Whippings around the parish church a certain number of times (for instance three or six), and possibly also around the local market square are the most common form of punishment. In many cases it is specified that the offender shall be dressed in a bare shirt and have a naked head and feet. Especially when members of the clergy have committed fornication, a reading of the psalter in church can be added. Apart from the whippings, fasting on water and bread or pilgrimages (for instance to Lincoln or Canterbury) on bare feet could also be imposed. However, in many cases offenders paid a small amount of money that was used as alms instead of enduring physical punishment.

This activity of local English church courts in the fourteenth and fifteenth centuries resembles a system of public penance. The punishments are clearly acts of penance, although they could perhaps be commuted to small amounts of money. It is also clear that the humiliation of sinners, which played such an important role in public penance, was an important ingredient here too. We must, however, still regard public whippings, pilgrimages etc. as punishments, since they were – as far as we can see – imposed on people and not accepted by them freely like acts of penance in a private confession were.

The English evidence presented in Poos' edition seems to be an old-fashioned way for ecclesiastical legal courts to act. When we consider more modern forms, those represented by the episcopal courts that were the winners in the struggle for jurisdiction with the archdeacons, the picture is different. The courts of the bishops had university-trained judges (normally called 'officials'); their prosecution of criminal cases as public offences was clearer; and last but not least their imposition of fines (often very large fines) was consistent for the crimes in question (Schwab 2001). In an attempt not to prove but simply to illustrate the development that I think took place when the episcopal courts took over from the courts of the archdeacons, I will give a concrete example, namely the handling of adultery (1) by the local court of the chapter of Lincoln in England around the middle of the fourteenth century, and (2) by the official of the archbishop of Lund in Denmark more than a century and a half later, around 1520. While people who had committed adultery were sentenced to whippings, a sentence which could perhaps be commuted to small amounts like 3 or 6 pence by the English court, the Danish official collected fines of one or two cows or the equivalent thereof in money for the same crime (Poos 2001, passim; Ingesman 2007, 373-374). This was not unusual, since everywhere in Western Europe on the eve of the Reformation complaints were raised against the bishops because of the enormous fines that their officials and courts exacted (cf. Albert 1998, 216-218 and 297-299).

Final remarks

During the High and Late Middle Ages a process of differentiation took place within the Church's system of discipline. Sin and crime, penance and punishment, were separated from each other into two specific disciplinary systems: the 'inner' or penitential system and the 'outer' or jurisdictional system. Both were *fora*, legal courts presided over by judges. In the penitential system the priest was the judge, although he was also a doctor 'curing' sins; while the jurisdictional system was presided over by a judge proper, a clergyman with a university training in Canon Law. During the Reformation the two sides of this disciplinary system were separated, with the State taking over the jurisdictional system and the Church keeping the penitential system. Many historians of early modern Europe have argued that after the Reformation the State initiated a new disciplinary offensive towards the population, but in my opinion it is more correct to say that it continued what the Church had started in the Middle Ages. Of course the State reinforced existing disciplinary efforts, but the ultimate goal remained the same: 'the making of Christian society'.

The disciplinary system of the medieval Church determined how people actually behaved, but of course it also shaped popular values and perceptions, especially concerning sexuality. Let me end this article by mentioning some of the points of view in existing research on the long-term effects of the medieval Church's disciplinary system in this respect.

When Thomas N. Tentler first put forward his thesis that the medieval confessional *summa* was an "instrument of social control", he was fiercely reproached by a Catholic specialist on the topic (Tentler 1974; Boyle 1974). However, his point of view received substantial support a few years later when the great French historian of ideas Michel Foucault, in the first volume of his *History of Sexuality*, pointed out that the medieval system of confession and penance was a factor of extreme importance for the shaping of sexuality (cf. Payer 1985). Since then a number of scholars have followed in the footsteps of Foucault and further explored the importance of the medieval penitential system, and especially the mandatory confession, in shaping human attitudes (Little 2006). Almost echoing Foucault's characterisation of post-1215 man as "a confessing animal", some have even said that confession was an important factor in the shaping of modern man, since it created a self-identity with a strong individual consciousness, not seen before in the kin-based society of the Early Middle Ages (Dinzelbacher 2001, cf. Morris 1972, especially 70-75). Along the same lines, a French historian called Jean Delumeau has argued that the introduction of the mandatory confession was an important element in the Church's successful attempt to transform Western European culture from a medieval 'shame culture' into a modern 'guilt culture' (Delumeau 1990).

Future research, exploring these connections in more detail, will undoubtedly provide many corrections. I think, however, that it is clear by now that the disciplinary efforts of the medieval Church contributed distinctively to the making of both modern man and modern culture in the Western world.

Bibliography

Albert, Thomas D. 1998. *Der gemeine Mann vor dem geistlichen Richter. Kirchliche Rechtsprechung in den Diözesen Basel, Chur und Konstanz vor der Reformation.* Stuttgart: Lucius & Lucius.

Biller, Peter and A.J. Minnis (eds.) 1998. *Handling sin: confession in the Middle Ages.* York: York Medieval.

Boyle, Leonard E. 1974. 'The Summa for Confessors as a Genre and Its Religious Intent'. In: Charles Trinkaus and Heiko A. Oberman (eds.), *The Pursuit of Holiness in Late Medieval and Renaissance Religion.* Leiden: Brill, 126-130.

Brundage, James A. 1987. *Law, Sex, and Christian Society in Medieval Europe.* Chicago: University of Chicago Press.

Brundage, James A. 1995. *Medieval Canon Law.* London: Longman.

Delumeau, Jean 1990. *Sin and Fear. The Emergence of a Western Guilt Culture 13th-18th Centuries.* New York: St. Martin's (French 1983).

Dinzelbacher, Peter 2001. 'Das erzwungene Individuum. Sündenbewusstsein und Pflichtbeichte'. In: Richard van Dülmen (ed.), *Entdeckung des Ich. Die Geschichte der Individualisierung vom Mittelalter bis zur Gegenwart.* Darmstadt: Wissenschaftliche Buchgesellschaft, 41-60.

Hamilton, Sarah 2001. *The Practice of Penance 900-1050.* Woodbridge: Boydell.

Ingesman, Per 2007. 'Kirkelig disciplin og social kontrol i senmiddelalderens danske bondesamfund. En casestudy af det ærkebiskoppelige gods under Lundegård 1519-1522 og Hammershus 1525-1540'. In: Agnes S. Arnórsdóttir, Per Ingesman and Bjørn Poulsen (eds.), *Konge, kirke og samfund. De to øvrighedsmagter i dansk senmiddelalder.* Århus: Aarhus University Press, 329-380.

Karpp, Heinrich (ed.) 1969. *Die Busse. Quellen zur Entstehung des altkirchlichen Busswesens.* Zürich: EVZ-Verlag.

Kéry, Lotte 2006: *Gottesfurcht und irdische Strafe. Der Beitrag des mittelalterlichen Kirchenrechts zur Entstehung des öffentlichen Strafrechts.* Köln: Böhlau.

Langholm, Odd 2003. *The Merchant in the Confessional. Trade and Price in the Pre-Reformation Penitential Handbooks*. Leiden: Brill.

Little, Katherine C. 2006. *Confession and Resistance. Defining the Self in Late Medieval England*. Notre Dame (Ind.): University of Notre Dame Press.

Lutterbach, Hubertus 1999. *Sexualität im Mittelalter. Eine Kulturstudie anhand von Bußbüchern des 6. bis 12. Jahrhunderts*. Köln: Böhlau.

McNeill, John T. and Helena M. Gamer 1990. *Medieval Handbooks of Penance. A translation of the principal libri poenitentiales and selections from related documents*. New York: Columbia University Press.

Mansfield, Mary C. 1995. *The Humiliation of Sinners. Public Penance in Thirteenth-Century France*. Ithaca: Cornell University Press.

Morris, Colin 1972. *The Discovery of the Individual, 1050-1200*. London: Harper & Row.

Morris, Colin 1989. *The Papal Monarchy. The Western Church from 1050 to 1250*. Oxford: Clarendon Press.

Payer, Pierre J. 1984. *Sex and the Penitentials. The Development of a Sexual Code 550-1150*. Toronto: University of Toronto Press.

Payer, Pierre J. 1985. 'Foucault on penance and the shaping of sexuality'. *Studies in Religion/Sciences religieuses*, 14,3, 313-320.

Poos, L.R. (ed.) 2001. *Lower Ecclesiastical Jurisdiction in Late Medieval England. The courts of the Dean and Chapter of Lincoln, 1336-1349, and the Deanery of Wisbech, 1458-1484*. Oxford: British Academy/Oxford University Press.

Schilling, Heinz 2002. '"Geschichte der Sünde" oder "Geschichte des Verbrechens"? Überlegungen zur Gesellschaftsgeschichte der frühneuzeitlichen Kirchenzucht'. In: Heinz Schilling, *Ausgewählte Abhandlungen zur europäischen Reformations- und Konfessionsgeschichte*. Berlin: Duncker & Humblot, 483-503.

Schwab, Christian 2001: *Das Augsburger Offizialatsregister (1348-1352). Ein Dokument geistlicher Diözesangerichtsbarkeit. Edition und Untersuchung*. Köln: Böhlau.

Tentler, Thomas N. 1974. 'The Summa for Confessors as an Instrument of Social Control'. In: Charles Trinkaus and Heiko A. Oberman (eds.), *The Pursuit of Holiness in Late Medieval and Renaissance Religion*. Leiden: Brill, 103-125.

Tentler, Thomas N. 1977. *Sin and Confession on the Eve of the Reformation*. Princeton: Princeton University Press.

Trusen, Winfried 1990. 'Zur Bedeutung des geistlichen Forum internum und externum für die spätmittelalterliche Gesellschaft'. *Zeitschrift der Savigny-Stiftung für Rechtsgeschichte. Kanonistische Abteilung*, 76, 254-285.

SAVING THE WORLD

SHAPING EUROPE: THE RELATION BETWEEN CHURCH AND POLITICS IN THE THEOLOGY OF BERNARD OF CLAIRVAUX

Else Marie Wiberg Pedersen

Introduction

A few years ago, the term 'crusade' unexpectedly and curiously came into use as an active noun and not only as a reference to historical events, when the president of the Unites States, George Bush, on September 16th, 2001 (seven days after 9/11) employed it to designate the fight against terrorism.[1] Ringing the bells of the medieval crusades with all their negative connotations in a 21st century setting, the term 'crusade' sent a bad signal to the Muslim world. But it was also more than unsuitable in a modern western world whose aim is to promote democracy and freedom.

For many people, the term 'crusade' signals controversy between Muslims and Christians, forced conversion and the subjection of one culture and political system to another, or even 'holy war'. So when on September 12th, 2006 (five years after 9/11), in a lecture on 'faith and reason' focusing on an inner-Christian discussion, Pope Benedict XVI also introduced the subject of Christianity and Islam plus holy war (or *jihad*), he immediately set the world, especially the Muslim world, on fire.[2] The pope referred to an argument made by Emperor Manuel II Paleologus in a 1391 dialogue with an 'educated Persian' in which Manuel II pointed to an irrationality in Islam: "Show me just what Muhammad brought that was new and there you will find things only bad and inhuman, such as his command to spread by the sword the faith he preached." The aim was that of contrasting a forceful spread of faith through violence with a religious conversion through the use of reason, promoting the view that both Islam and Christianity, when based on reason, state that there is 'no compulsion in religion' (*sura* 2, 256). But the Muslim world saw the pope's lecture as yet another attack on Islam, a reaction which in many ways stood in direct continuation of the request by Al-Azhar (the highest ranking religious authority in Egypt and most respected Sunni Muslim authority in the world) that the Vatican should apologise for the crusades.

However, it is reasonable to ask what the medieval crusades were about and why they were conducted. Were they primarily due to political or theological reasons, or were they simply unreasonable? Was the forced conversion of Muslims at stake, or were the crusades about something else? Let me immediately state that there is no one simple

---

1   On the lawn outside the White House, Bush used the unwise words: "This crusade, this war against terrorism, is going to take a while." See http://www.whitehouse.gov/news/releases/2001/09/20010916-2.html
2   http://www.vatican.va/holy_father/benedict_xvi/speeches/2006/september/documents/ hf_ben-xvi_spe_20060912_university-regensburg_en.html

answer to these questions. Many different so-called crusades took place between 1096 and 1444, comprising not only the eight major crusades that took place between 1096 (beginning of First Crusade) and 1270 (end of Eighth Crusade), but also the Albegensian (1209-29) and the Baltic (1147-48) crusades. And each had its own different cause and purpose, oscillating between the political and the religious. It is a highly complex story, the details of which I shall not even try to do justice in this short article.

In this article I will focus on the Second Crusade (1146-1148) and the Cistercian abbot and prominent 'church politician' Bernard of Clairvaux (1090-1153), who has been most closely linked with this crusade and its defeat. I shall deal with the causes of the crusade(s) and its aftermath with specific reference to Bernard's part in it and the politics surrounding him, since both Bernard and the Second Crusade are of central importance in the history of the 12th century and in European history as a whole. The connection between the spiritual leader of the Cistercians and the warlike campaigns against the enemies of Christendom remains a question of endless fascination, and many questions are still unsolved. This is due to the existence of seemingly inconsistent or contradictory sources, but perhaps even more to the negligence of some sources such as Bernard's letters to the pope in 1146 and 1149, which could shed light on the origin of the Second Crusade (Ferzoco 1992, 95-97). The study of these sources provides a more comprehensive picture of the relationship between religion and politics in Europe in one of its important formative periods, as well as indicating how religion and politics can be understood in future.

The politics of the crusades

To understand the politics of the crusades, it should first of all be noted that the word 'crusade' does not originate from the inception of what we have subsequently labelled the First and Second Crusades, for instance. Stemming from the mid-13th century, the term 'crusade' originates from the crosses worn on the vestments of those who fought against the enemies of Christendom. But 'crusade' or 'crusaders' were not terms that characterised the self-understanding of those going to the Holy Land, the land where Jesus Christ was born and buried, to save it from Muslim dominance. The preferred terminology was 'voyage to Jerusalem' (*iter hierosolymatinum*) or 'way to the holy Sepulchre' (*via Sancti Sepulchri*), or as a secondary choice 'passage' or 'voyage to the other side of the sea' (i.e. the Mediterranean). In a more narrow sense, it was an armed pilgrimage directed towards the tomb of Christ in Jerusalem as well as decided by the pope, who granted spiritual and worldly privileges to those who wore the cross and who were more often called pilgrims (*peregrini*) than crusaders (*crucesignati*).

There is more than one factor leading up to the crusades. Economically and socially the 11th century was a period of expansion – and this was true of Italian commerce in particular. Good trading conditions meant demographic growth and a subsequent lack of land, which (although it was not a decisive factor) formed a favourable context for the idea of the crusades. But the crusades as such were caused by the amalgamation of several factors. First and foremost, there is the ideal of pilgrimage to the Holy Land, conceived in the 11th century as a mode of penitence and forced on the peace movement that had evolved. Secondly, there was the idea of a legitimate war evolving into the idea of a sacred war shaped for the defence of the Christians against the infidels, an idea which was particularly common in Spain in the 11th century.

These ideas and ideals gradually merged with pressing problems such as the advancement of the Turks in Asia Minor (the victory in Manzikert 1071) and the appeals to the pope for help launched by the Byzantines (Michel II in 1074; Alexis I in 1095), leading to atrocities against the Christians in Anatolia and persecutions in the Holy Land. Whether these appeals from the Byzantine Empire to the west were heartfelt or not, the popes (first Gregory VII, next Urban II) encouraged an expedition conducted by the church to meet the escalating spiral of persecution of Christians in the Holy Land, which reached its climax after centuries of Muslim aggression against Christians since the Muslims conquered Jerusalem in 638. Urban II's appeal at the Council of Clermont (27th November, 1095) recounts the situation thus:

As many of you have already been told, the Turks, a Persian race, have overrun the eastern Christians right up to the Mediterranean Sea. Occupying more and more of the land of the Christians on the borders of Romania [the Byzantine Empire], they have conquered them…slaughtering and capturing many, destroying churches and laying waste the kingdom of God. So, if you leave them alone much longer they will further grind under their heels the faithful of God.

One month before addressing the Council of Clermont, pope Urban II, former Grand Prior of Cluny, consecrated a new abbey church at the great monastic centre of Cluny – an important act in raising supporters. All in all, much of the propaganda for the crusade took place by way of networking both within the monastic orders and amongst the noble families, two sides of the same coin, since most monks were recruited from the international network of noble families across Europe.

Having proclaimed the First Crusade at the Council of Clermont, calling on western knights to liberate Jerusalem, pope Urban II began his year-long preaching tour of France (1095-96) in order to generate support for the mission. Over the next six years, as many as 130,000 men and women joined the armies leaving for the Holy Land, of whom nobles and knights comprised only about 10 per cent of the total 'army'. Of the several thousand, many of whom travelled independently in small parties, most were not professional soldiers but peasants or townspeople caught up on the wave of popular enthusiasm (Riley-Smith 1991, 28). Many were dedicated to the enterprise and prepared to make huge financial sacrifices (Riley-Smith 1992, 101-108).

For others the crusading atmosphere unleashed less ideal, indeed rather violent emotions. Many crusaders, before they even left for the holy cause of liberating Jerusalem from Muslim occupation (the justification given by the church), began a vendetta against the Jews for the crucifixion of Christ. There were anti-Jewish riots at Rouen in France, in Bavaria and Bohemia. By far the worst outbreaks of anti-Semitism occurred in the Rhineland, where the Jewish community of Mainz, one of the largest in Europe, was annihilated. From a European inner-political perspective, this was probably the worst (even though it was unintended) side effect of every major crusading appeal during the 12th century: they all set off fresh attacks on the Jews. Various churchmen tried with varying degrees of success to stop these outbreaks, which curiously enough also became a cause for recruiting people for a crusade.

The attacks on Jews are part of the violence caused by the often unruly knights which was experienced all over Europe. Apart from the violence attached to the crusading appeals, another reason why knights were recruited for the crusade idea was that monasteries and villages were recurrently attacked and robbed by these knights. With a view to channelling the energy of these violent (and in fact criminal) knights into a holy cause, they were encouraged to obtain indulgence for their plundering and rape across Europe through their new engagement in the crusades.

The fact that one form of warfare was seen as compensation and indeed indulgence for the other is revealed by a charter written by the knight (and later crusader) Nivelo of Fréteval to the abbey of St Peter of Chartres in 1096. Nivelo sees the pilgrimage to Jerusalem as a pardon for his former crimes. Although it is obvious that he is promised more than redemption for his soul, namely a great sum of money, material rewards were not the prime object of the early crusaders.

I, Nivelo, raised in a nobility of birth which produces in many people an ignobility of mind, for the redemption of my soul and in exchange for a great sum of money given me for this, renounce for ever in favour of St Peter the oppressive behaviour resulting from a certain bad custom... I had harshly worn down the land of St Peter, that is to say Emprianville and the places around it, in the way that had become customary, by seizing the goods of the inhabitants there. Whenever the onset of knightly ferocity stirred me up, I used to descend on the aforesaid village, taking with me a troop of my knights and a crowd of my attendants, and against nature I would make over the goods of the men of St Peter for food for my knights.

And so since, in order to obtain the pardon for my crimes which God can give me, I am going on pilgrimage to Jerusalem which until now has been enslaved with her sons, the monks have given me 10 pounds in *denarii* towards the expenses of the appointed journey, in return for giving up this oppression.

Nivelo's wording reflects the mindset of knights and the politics of the crusading spirit. The knights' unholy warlike conduct against the people of Europe is to be transformed into a holy 'pilgrimage' to Jerusalem in order to set free her 'enslaved sons'. The transformation of oppression in Europe into the liberation of the oppressed in Jerusalem also leads to the personal liberation of the knights' enslaved souls. In this way the earthly Jerusalem is linked with the heavenly Jerusalem.

The involvement of the Byzantine Empire and churches in the crusades is an interesting question which I cannot go into here. But let me just point out two important factors in the shaping of Europe and western Latin Christianity. First, that despite their incontestable appeals to the west the Byzantines neither assisted the crusaders nor received them with anything more than a lukewarm spirit (Riley-Smith 1991, 28ff). Second, that the Byzantine church split from the western church in 1054, a few decades before the First Crusade began, after centuries of disagreements. The pronounced and unpronounced disagreements, however fair, seem to me to be of major importance for the problems pertaining to the relation between the east and the Latin west.

Bernard between church and politics

Bernard's part in the Second Crusade and the reason why he entered its politics are questions that are still highly disputed. One question which I would like to pursue here is whether Bernard can be regarded as a political theologian. From a modern perspective, the answer seems to be 'no'. However, it is possible to view Bernard's theological programme as a sort of political theology, which might be perceived as standing in stark contrast to the crusading rhetoric.

Bernard and the Second Crusade

Whereas the First Crusade involved the actual re-entry of Christians into the Holy Land, the Second Crusade was inspired by the plight of the Holy Land. The inner-European political urge for peace and the inner spiritual needs of individual Christians for forgiveness were the same in the two first crusades (or 'pilgrimages', as people called them at the time).

The Second Crusade also started with an appeal from the East. On Christmas Eve 1144, the Muslim ruler of Aleppo and Mosul, Imad al-Din Zangi, captured Edessa, the northernmost of the Christian states in the East which had been held by the Christians since 1098. The Christian leaders in the East appealed to the West, and in December 1145 Pope Eugene III propagated a new crusade. In his letter, *Quantum praedecessores*, the pope is the first to list both spiritual and material privileges to be bestowed on crusaders. At first, despite the privileges being offered, his call was received in silence. Europe as a whole was clearly weary, and the French king Louis VII, on his call to go to the Holy Land, was also met with hostility. It was only when the pope reissued his letter in 1146 and managed to make Bernard of Clairvaux responsible for PR that a concerted recruitment began. On Easter Day 1146 at a meeting at Vézelay between the kings of Europe (the foremost of whom was Louis VII) and the pope, the enactment of the Second Crusade was settled and Bernard was made its prominent preacher.

Apart from preaching successfully for the crusade, Bernard was faced with two other demands which were very similar to those of the First Crusade. He had to combat the anti-Semitic persecution in Rhineland and Bavaria, which he did vehemently in a letter, Ep 363, to the Frankish and Bavarian archbishops (Bernard 1146, 658-661). Peter the Venerable did not do the same – he regarded the Jews as the worst enemies of Christianity, and wrote to the French king Louis VII encouraging him to persecute the Jews rather than combating the Saracens (Prawer 1975, 353-362; Constable 1967, 328). Bernard also had to gain the support of the king of Germany (Conrad III) for the crusade, and this was done at Speyer in December 1146. Bernard thus followed the pattern already laid out in the recruitment for the First Crusade by appealing to individual hopes of salvation and offering the 'mighty men of valour' full remission of their sins in return for taking the cross: "Now, O strong knights and warlike men, you have a place where you can fight without danger, where it is glorious to conquer and profitable to die." (Bernard 1146, 658-659).[3]

As Bernard saw it, this military expedition to Jerusalem was part of the divine plan for human salvation; it was yet another divine gift to help sinners reform.

In Bernard's crusade rhetoric, such an armed pilgrimage was not merely a military operation to protect Christian property and the Christian holy of holies, or to conquer territory from the Muslims. It was first and foremost a matter of personal and collective redemption by giving Christians yet another opportunity to abandon worldly things and turn their will to God by offering themselves for possible martyrdom. On top of that, the armed pilgrimage had the fortunate side effect of providing a necessary strategy for the inner-European peace, as mentioned above, by recruiting unruly knights and savage anti-Semitic persecutors, thereby controlling and channelling their energy towards common goals outside Europe.

However, the crusade soon developed in the wrong direction as various factors added to its complication. In 1147, Pope Eugene III 'by divine dispensation' legalised and gave Saxon leaders permission to attack the pagan Wends (in the bull *Divina dispensatio*) in order to defend Germany's eastern borders against the latter's plundering. Again the pope involved Bernard, who was requested at the Diet of Frankfurt to motivate the Saxons to continue their participation in the crusade. Bernard wrote another encyclical, Ep 457, in which as a preacher of the word of the cross (*verbum crucis*) he called on the Saxon leaders to act jointly against the Slavish tribes and either obliterate (*delendas penitus*) or convert those who attack Christians (Bernard 1147, 890-893). Although the rhetoric sounds even harsher than before, the underlying sentiment is the same – the 'crusade' being equated with the pilgrimage to Jerusalem and concomitantly seen as a matter of redemption. It should be noted, however, that the 'defence attack' on the Wends does not aim at a mission but at real politics. On sober consideration, what Ep 457 says is that at the instance of the Diet in Frankfurt ('*consilio domini Regis et episcoporum et principum, qui convererant Frankonovort*') Bernard gives the Germans a territorial guarantee in order that they, as the letter has it, can go to

---

3   Bernard, at the request of the French king and the pope, wrote this encyclical letter in 1146 to stop the persecutions fired by the monk Rudolf on his preaching the crusade in Rhineland and Bavaria. Here and below I refer to Bernard's letters from Winkler, *Bernhard von Clairvaux III* 1992, in which all the texts are rendered parallel in Latin/German. Translations into English are my own. In connection with Ep 363, it should be noted that historians often refer to Ep 458, a letter to Duke Ladislaus of Bohemia, as Bernard's most significant writing pertaining to the Second Crusade. However, it is disputed whether Bernard is in fact the author of Ep 458. Unlike the crusader scholar Riley-Smith (1991, 48), the Bernard scholar Castaldelli (1992, 1218-1219) holds that Ep 458 was not written by Bernard but by others who copied Bernard's style and rhetoric in Ep 363.

Jerusalem unhindered (Castaldelli, 1218-1219). But at the request of the pope and the Diet, Bernard endeavours to prevent a greater evil (the unruly Germans' slaughter of Jewish communities) by way of a lesser evil (the defence attack on the Wends in order to secure German participation in the real crusade). Persuading the Germans to join the crusade in order to keep them from attacking the Jews in Europe was of paramount importance to Bernard, who strongly supported and defended Europe's Jews. In this light, Bernard's manoeuvre was much more a political strategy than an example of religious zeal.

In the end, none of the kings and their armies followed Bernard's request of acting jointly, and the Second Crusade was a huge failure. It was complicated not only by the aforementioned 'crusade' against the Slavs, but also by other 'crusades' such as the campaign of the Castilian king Alfonso VII against the Moors in Spain, authorised in 1147 by the pope to equate with the crusade. It was a scattered group of crusaders, large armies in the Byzantine and many at sea in the Mediterranean, that eventually resumed its main objective: the recapturing of Edessa. All in all, the personal interests of the leaders and their aspiration to establish their own domination even before their arrival in Jerusalem may explain the failure (see for example Lloyd 2001, 34-65).

The First and Second Crusades had the same theological and political background and goals, but the big difference between the two was that the Second Crusade was led by kings, Louis VII of France and Conrad III of Germany, who did not seem to have quite the same interests as the church leaders in securing the rights of Christians at large. Perhaps the quest for heavenly Jerusalem was not as large in the Second Crusade as Bernard had hoped and preached; and once again the relation of *imperium* and *sacerdotium* proved problematic, as it did throughout the High Middle Ages (1054-1300). Be that as it may, there is no doubt that Bernard was not acting on a whim of his own, but was actually involved in a huge religious-military programme imposed on the narrower project planned by Pope Eugene III.

The two swords

Writing at a time in which the great territorial princes began to consolidate their lands and powers, Bernard witnessed the princes' efforts to enforce the peace and extend their jurisdiction and understood the relationship of secular and ecclesiastical authority through the lenses of late 11th-century's disputes over church reform and investiture. Accordingly, Bernard and the Cistercians as such used the language that (in the Carolingian period) described the concord of the emperor and his clergy to portray a prince as being willing to serve the aims of the church and to maintain peace in his territory. But the Cistercians modified the Carolingian political language in two ways: they applied it to all territorial rulers, not only the king or emperor, and they found evidence of the rulers' service in their behaviour and conscience, not their anointing or birth (Newman 1996, 177).

It is in this light that Bernard's often disputed teaching on the two swords should be understood. The teaching of the two swords had its biblical foundation in Luke 22:35-38, where Jesus says of the two swords: 'That is enough' (*satis est*), and its patristic foundation in (for example) Ambrose's exposition of Luke, *Expositio secundum Lucam*. But in the 12th century, in the aftermath of the investiture and as a consequence of the success of the First Crusade and distribution of political power (the church recognised the first crusaders in 1113), the teaching of the two swords took on a special meaning. The fact that according to God's plan there were two swords was beyond discussion, but it was highly disputed to whom these two swords belonged.

According to Bernard, the two swords both belonged to the church, but he had his own interpretation which was not identical with that of the ecclesiastical powers of his time. Bernard aimed at a reform of the church ministry because in his view the two swords (the spiritual and the worldly) were not being sufficiently divided; and to him the Second Crusade was proof of this fact. In his treatise *De consideratione* (Bernard 1148-1153) – written for Pope Eugene III after the failure of the Second Crusade, with all his disappointment and bewilderment after being blamed for it shining forth in book II (Bernard 1148-1153, 50-52) – he stresses that inasmuch as the two swords both belong to the same church, that is, they are both subordinate to the plan of God, they must be separated. With a biblical grounding in Romans 13:4 and Matthew 22:24, Bernard explains how the spiritual sword is *the word*, which is "drawn by the church ...by the hand of the priest", while the material sword is "drawn for the church...by the hand of the knight". From this, Bernard concludes that in one sense the material sword is also subject to the church, and reminds pope Eugene: "Therefore, this sword also is yours and is to be drawn from its sheath at your command, although not by your hand." But perhaps following Romans 13 he refines the formulation later to "the bidding of the priest and at the command of the emperor." (Bernard 1148-1153, 118).

Bernard thus uses old language, but in a new social and political context. From his letters to various secular rulers, it becomes clear that although he repeats the idea that secular power has a divine source, Bernard does so not only to advocate the merciful exercise of justice but also to stress that rulers should use their powers to serve the needs of the church. We hear a brief echo of this in the above formulations from *De consideratione*. When repeating the Carolingian commonplaces emphasising the partnership of kings and pope, like other Cistercians Bernard actually transforms their meaning from a more dualist understanding to describe cooperation between rulers and churchmen for the sake of the church at large (Newman 1996, 180).

Nonetheless, in his address to Eugene, Bernard reminds the pope that his ministry is a ministry of the spiritual word, not the secular sword, and the main part of *De consideratione* is about the church's spiritual ministry of preaching the word freely without the use of force (see below). In Bernard's perception, the core of the problem concerning the two swords and the crusade lies precisely in the fact that both belong to the church. When the word and the sword are not differently and separately commanded, the church starts acting like a secular power instead of ensuring that the secular power acts in the interests of the church and its concomitant of God's new path to salvation.

The soldiers and servants of Christ

The Cistercian order began the year the crusaders captured Jerusalem, and its monks lived in a society that had already started to incorporate this monastic model for an ideal knight into its culture. Cistercian authors both enhanced the model and shifted its focus by stressing the inner motivation of knights' warfare rather than the conquering of land.

In the crusader theology, the two swords were totally united and not divided as Bernard would have it. With the crusaders and the new orders of knights such as the Knights Templar (papal recognition in 1129) and the Knights Hospitaller, a new synthesis of knight and monk appears on the scene to give succour and protection to pilgrims travelling from Jaffa to Jerusalem and to the holy places in the vicinity. This puts Bernard in a delicate situation when he is repeatedly asked to write a recommendation of the Knights Templar. When he finally writes *In laude novae militiae* (On the New Knighthood) (Bernard 1130)[4], he bases it on arguments and vocabulary that were developed in connection with the First Crusade.

Bernard never preached war, but he had no pacifist ideals. In this vein, he draws a distinction between two kinds of warfare: the spiritual, characteristic of monks and fought against the invisible forces of evil; and the physical, undertaken by knights against terrestrial and material enemies. The Knights Templar, however, fight in both ways, a form 'hitherto unknown'. Bernard emphasises the novelty of the order and calls it a new type of knights (*novum militiae genus*). As a monk's order the Knights Templar are already justified, but Bernard clearly has difficulties in legitimising the order as a knight's order with a military commission. Even so Bernard favours the order, and finds its legitimacy in its contrast to secular knight's orders, in the contrast of secular knights' evil (*malitia*) and the knight-monks' true warfare (*militia*). The Knights Templar have taken the monastic vows to live a life following Christ and to fight for the Christian cause in contrast with the secular knights and their cruel and selfish conduct. And not least important, the order lives as a community with unity and equality as their highest principles, exactly like the Cistercians. For Bernard, this was the best way for a person of any order to progress toward salvation.

In his moral support for the new order, Bernard borrows language from 2 Tim 2:3 to designate the anomaly of the warrior-monks, consequently calling them 'soldiers of Christ' (*milites Christi*) and 'servants' (*ministry*) alike. For when a battle is at hand they, as he has it, "arm themselves on the interior with faith and on the exterior with steel rather than with gold." (Bernard 1130, 47). For when fighting their spiritual and physical war, they simultaneously spread the word of salvation and defend the

---

4   The correct dating of the treatise for the Knights Templar is not known, but it is unlikely that he wrote it before 1130.

Christian faith and its faithful against the enemies of the cross of Christ; and when they die they become holy martyrs (pp. 33-35), (pp. 39-43). The key is motivation, or in Augustinian terms, right intention. Pride, revenge, or even self-defence are unjustifiable reasons for killing; only when the motive is pure can fighting not be considered evil (p. 39).

When Bernard explains why it is legitimate to fight a physical war for the cause of Christ, he draws on Augustine's definition of a just war (*bellum iustum*) – that is, a war fought on proper authority, with right intention, and for a just cause. But mostly he borrows from the crusader rhetoric of pope Urban II (in conjunction with the First Crusade), who, in turn, based his rhetoric on pope Gregory VII's (1073-1085) rather militant understanding of mission (Barber 2000, 12-13). In Bernard's terminology, however, only a defence war is justifiable within the Christian paradigm, not a war of determination, and especially not when it is not for a just cause. If war is not justifiable within the Christian paradigm, it should have been banned by scripture; but instead scripture talks about John the Baptist paying soldiers their due pay (Luke 3:14). Military intervention may also be necessary to defend the Christian heritage, and military power is justifiable when it is directed towards those who threaten Christians, although its primary aim is to provide security for Christians and to secure the holy places in and around Jerusalem. Only then should both swords be employed.

The main part of *In laude novae militiae* is not about warfare. Much of the treatise provides a spiritual geography of the Holy Land. Never having been to the Holy Land, Bernard moves his reader through the places of Jesus' life and death (from Bethlehem to the Holy Sepulchre), giving brief meditations on the feelings and lessons he imagined such places would evoke (pp. 53-80). This itinerary parallelled the process of spiritual development and redemption that formed part of the crusading ideology. And the Cistercian monks, who did not need to go on crusade because they bore an inner cross on their hearts, had the strength to model their lives on the life of Jerusalem and follow the difficult path demanded; whereas crusaders, pilgrims, and even the Knights Templar followed the easier path marked by the hope offered by Jesus' death rather than the demands of his life. Secular life might offer opportunities for spiritual progress and salvation, but the path of greatest merit lay in the monastery, where people were socialised into a life in love.

The church and the ministry of love

It should not be overlooked that Bernard was a prominent leader of the Cistercians, who like other people throughout the 12th century experimented with ways of understanding the links between society and individuals, and individuals separated from one another. The conception of Christian society formulated by the 12th century Cistercians provides an example of how to link the individual and groups, and their spirituality was shaped in the dialectics of the individual and the community, understood as common life. The monks used their idea of love (*caritas*), drawn from a face-to-face society with personal connections and friendships, to unite not only the disparate abbeys in their order and in the larger monastic world but also the church and all of Christendom.

Bernard's theology was based on faith in the God who *is* love, who out of that love came in flesh, lived in the world, endured humiliations and eventually suffered death on the world's worst torture instrument, the cross. In his treatise on the love of God, *De diligendo Deo*, for instance, Bernard taught that true love is formed after Christ, who as a *forma Dei* exemplified, lived and gave humanity his totally unselfish, disinterested love (*amor castus*). Bernard pedagogically outlines the way in which God's love educates and transforms humans, first by love of Christ in his humanity, then by the love of neighbours, and eventually by the love of enemies (Bernard 1128).[5] It is Bernard's point that human life on this earth is a continuous pilgrimage, an ongoing process of acknowledgement. Humans are on their way (*in via*) on a pilgrimage through different stages or forms of love with the aim of attaining the highest form of love through faith and God, who is love. To strive for such an unselfish love for others and to allow space for others, inspired by God's love, is to seek the kingdom of God (Bernard 1128, 26). As can be seen in Bernard's vast authorship, he regarded the monastery as the school of love (*schola caritatis*), a place to learn such a Christ-formed life in love.

In *De consideratione* Bernard resolves the true roles of priests and monks in the church. This is the theme of the treatise, for which the pope had made, as Bernard playfully emphasises, a "request rather than a command" (Bernard 1148-1153, 23). He eloquently links this with the failure of the crusade, which the pope had commanded: "We rushed into this, not aimlessly but at your command, or rather, through you at God's command." (p. 48). According to Bernard, the aim of the crusade was lost as the ecclesiastical ministry was abused and confused with worldly power and dominance. Therefore, with reference to Luke 22:27 he reminds the pope of the substance of the apostolicity (*apostolica forma*), which is responsibility for the churches, not dominion: "This is the precedent established by the Apostles: dominion is forbidden, ministry is imposed." (p. 59). By way of a series of prophetic titles such as "advocate of the poor", Bernard then points out the true theological meaning of church ministry: a prophetic ministry under the grace of God and the power of love. With a clear ironic distance to the pope's actual practice, Bernard urges the pope to consult God, not earthly and secular powers, in his ministry:

Understand what I am saying: the Lord will give you understanding. When power is joined to evil (*malitia*) intent, you must assume for yourself something above your humanity. Let your countenance be against those who do evil (*mala*)' (p. 138).

---

5   It is not clear when Bernard actually wrote this treatise, whether it was in 1128 or not until 1153, shortly before his death.

The ministry of the church implies the power of love, which encompasses not Canon Law or any form of secular power, but the divine commands of love including love of your enemy (p. 60; pp. 175-177).

Bernard's disappointment with the pope looms large in *De consideratione*, written as it is on the background of the Second Crusade's failure and the fact that Bernard was made its scapegoat. He who asked the pope to spare him, when early in 1146 he was pressured to support and to preach the crusade (Ferzoco, 96), now reminds the pope about the prime pastoral responsibility: "If you preach the Gospel willingly you will have glory even among the Apostles. To preach the Gospel is to feed. Do the work of an evangelist and you have fulfilled the office of shepherd." (p. 117). A true *imitatio Christi* lies in the preaching and teaching of the word, for in Bernard's view a *pastor* imitating Christ must speak against the rich and powerful and look after the poor (p. 124). Hence, he defines the task of the one, holy, catholic and apostolic church as that of giving: "peace for the kingdoms, law for Barbarians, quiet for the monasteries, order for the churches, discipline for clerics, a people acceptable to God and zealous for good works (Titus 2:14)." (pp. 125-126).

Conclusion

Bernard had high ideals about both the church and society. Late in his life he employed the self-description '*chimaera*', neither a contemplative monk nor a layperson, busy as he had often been in extra-monastic affairs (Bernard 1147-1150, 334). Even as ecclesiastical officials began to define procedures and laws to determine the merits of a case, the Cistercians continued to rely more on personal connections than on abstract principles and arguments. Hence, Bernard's image of a church bound by *caritas* was very different from the development of an ecclesiastical institution bound by the legal principles of Canon Law. With a focus on the theology of the cross and a Trinitarian love of theology as a socialising model for the whole of humanity, Bernard wanted to reform the church and the world in which it is embedded in quite another direction than both the ecclesiastical and the secular powers of his time.

Bernard expected the crusade to be about the salvation of humanity preached freely and without oppression by a unified church, but discovered that it was about secular power and dominance of land and felt abused by both swords. In his view, the church has many different responsibilities and tasks that are all unified under the ministry of love which belongs to the whole church, and which he wanted to transpose to the whole world. Does this point forward to the views of a president Bush calling for a crusade against terrorism or of a Pope Benedict XVI calling for reason in the enterprise of faith?

Bibliography

Barber, Malcolm 2000. 'Introduction'. In: Malcolm Barber, M. Conrad Greenia (translator), *In Praise of the New Knighthood*. Kalamazoo: Cistercian Publications.

Benedikt XVI 2006. 'Faith, Reason and the University'. On: http://www.vatican. va/holy_father/benedict_xvi/speeches/2006/september/documents/ hf_ben-xvi_spe_20060912_university-regensburg_en.html

Bernard of Clairvaux 1128 (or 1153). 'De diligendo Deo'. In: Emero Stiegman (ed.) 1995, *On Loving God. An Analytical Commentary*. Kalamazoo: Cistercian Publications, 3-42.

Bernard of Clairvaux 1130. 'In laude novae militiae'. In: Malcolm Barber (introduction), M. Conrad Greenia (translator) 2000, *In Praise of the New Knighthood*. Kalamazoo: Cistercian Publications.

Bernard of Clairvaux 1147-1150. 'Ep 250'. In: Gerhard B.Winkler (ed.) 1992. *Bernard von Clairvaux III*. Innsbruck: Tyrolia-Verlag, 330-335.

Bernard of Clairvaux 1146.'Ep 363'. In: Gerhard B. Winkler (ed.) 1992. *Bernhard von Clairvaux. Sämtliche Werke III*. Innsbruck: Tyrolia-Verlag, 649-661.

Bernard of Clairvaux 1147. 'Ep 457'. In: Gerhard B. Winkler (ed.) 1992. *Bernhard von Clairvaux. Sämtliche Werke III*. Innsbruck: Tyrolia-Verlag, 890-893.

Bernard of Clairvaux 1148-1153. 'De consideratione ad Eugenium papam tertiam libri quinque'. In: John D. Anderson, Elizabeth T. Kennan (translators and introduction) 1976, *Five Books on Considerations. Advice to a Pope*. Kalamazoo: Cistercian Publications.

Bush, George 2001. 'Remarks by the President'. On: http://www.whitehouse.gov/news/ releases/2001/09/20010916-2.html

Castaldelli, Ferrucio 1992. 'Anmerkungen und historischer Kommentar'. In: Gerhard B. Winkler (ed.), *Bernhard von Clairvaux. Sämtliche Werke III*. Innsbruck: Tyrolia-Verlag, 1184-1184; 1218-19.

Constable, Giles (ed.) 1967. *The Letters of Peter the Venerable I*. Cambridge Mass: Harvard University Press.

Ferzoco, George 1992. 'The Origin of the Second Crusade'. In: Michael Gervers (ed.), *The Second Crusade and the Cistercians*. New York: St. Martin's Press, 91-99.

Lloyd, Simon 2001 (second edition). 'The Crusading Movement, 1097-1274'. In: Jonathan Riley-Smith (ed.), *The Oxford Illustrated History of the Crusades*. Oxford: Oxford University Press, 34-65.

Newman, Martha G. 1996. *The Boundaries of Charity. Cistercian Culture and Ecclesiastical Reform, 1098-1180*. Stanford: Stanford University Press.

Prawer, Joshua 1975. *Histoire du royaume latin de Jérusalem*. Paris: Éditions du Centre National de la Recherche Scientifique.

Riley-Smith, Jonathan 1991. *The Atlas of the Crusades*. London: Times Books.

Riley-Smith, Jonathan 1992. 'Family Traditions and Participation in the Second Crusade'. In: Michael Gervers (ed.), *The Second Crusade and the Cistercians*. New York: St. Martin's Press, 101-108.

TOTALITARIAN IDEOLOGIES AND THE CHRISTIAN CHURCHES

Jens Holger Schjørring

Confrontation between totalitarian ideologies and the Christian churches indisputably constitutes a basic feature in the church history of the 20th century. Admittedly, as regards a consistent definition of categories, it is a challenge to decide whether catalogues of obvious differences between specific totalitarian ideologies such as German Nazism or Soviet Marxism carry more weight than perspectives that emphasise common essential features. A compromise seems appropriate, to the effect that certain overarching structures are maintained in terms of basic determination of genre, while allowing for contextual variations in terms of time and location.

Notwithstanding their differentiated appearances, it remains fundamentally the case that totalitarian ideologies involved a radical confrontation with the Christian belief of individuals and institutional churches alike. The key issue of conflict was the incompatibility between the exclusivity of Christian monotheism and the first commandment on the one hand, and the totalitarian claim to cover all areas of life, leaving no space for exception or reservation on the other.

No less importantly for a comprehensive assessment of the 20th century, the process of individualisation and privatisation of Christian patterns of life is another decisive leitmotif, not least within the liberal Protestant churches, but also beyond. At first sight, one might be tempted to see only contradiction between the two dynamics: on the one hand mass movements, often defined as atheist from spring to mouth of the torrent, marked by terror and systematic suppression of freedom; and on the other the harvest of enlightenment, the inalienable rights of freedom, which in our part of the world are usually connected with the basic hallmarks of Christianity, at least of the Protestant tradition in north-western Europe.

It is, however, an intriguing reflection that the spontaneous decline of traditional churches based upon historical continuity and ordained ministry seems to have been almost as manifest as the effect of persecution of Christians within totalitarian regimes.

When attention is turned to the question of whether, in an open society, principles of religious belief are admissible in the conduct of public affairs, the complexity of the picture is more fully exposed. Likewise, the need for careful discrimination becomes even more apparent when we begin to examine the historical course of development of the diverse anti-religious reactions displayed by various totalitarian regimes, when viewed alongside the attitudes of Christian churches and individuals confronted by such regimes.

For a historical overview of the past century, it needs to be stated that two distinct sets of state law were adopted at the beginning of the century, both intending to refer religious conviction to the private sphere alone.

The first act was the separation between church and state in France in 1905, a long-term realisation of the watchwords of the French Revolution. To this end, French politicians terminated the status of churches as subjects of state law, instead ordaining that religious communities be seen solely as private associations, and that religious instruction in schools be strictly prohibited. These measures were meant as safeguards of individual freedom, as opposed to the tutelage of the churches during the 'ancien régime' (Burleigh 2005).

The second instance, the set of laws adopted by the Soviets following the Marxist-Leninist revolution in 1917, exhibits a striking similarity. Again, the essential objective was declared to be respect for the individual's freedom of conviction. Behind the benevolence, however, lay a strict privatisation of religion, dissolution of church structures within the communal framework of the state and local communities, cancellation of the right of the churches to receive financial support via taxes, and abolition of religious instruction in schools – in other words, a thoroughgoing invalidation of religious belief within the public sphere. Without questioning the similarity between the two instances, it needs to be added that the respective adoptions took different shapes: in France within the framework of a liberal, open society; in the Soviet Union in a one-party state, soon defined by its totalitarian ideology.

This essay, then, will examine various types of totalitarian ideologies and regimes seen against the background of the role played by Christian churches forced into a struggle for survival as they face the seemingly inexhaustible determination of those in power to eliminate open opposition and even silent reservation. What were the strategies of the totalitarian regimes towards religious communities, and how did the churches react?

Persecution and survival. The conflict between Soviet communism and the churches

It was not long before a contradiction became apparent between the seemingly liberal and neutral laws adopted by the Leninist council of people's commissars in January 1918 and the actual attitude shown by the new authorities. A decree of 23 January 1918 indicated two significant objectives as the background for the immediate measures leading to separation between church and state. The first objective was to prevent any violation of the liberty of conscience and to abolish any privileges or prerogatives attaching to the citizen's confessional membership. The second was an affirmation of the right of citizens to confess any religion or to have no religious conviction. This freedom was accompanied by the abolition of all losses of civil rights penalising particular religious identities or the absence of religious identity. Subsequent paragraphs of the decree ordered that public ceremonies must be conducted with no religious framework. Yet it was also asserted that there should be free access to the performance of religious rites, provided they did not involve any disturbance of public order (Stupperich 1962).

Having stated such general rights of freedom, the following paragraphs went on to indicate major limitations on the traditional role of institutional churches. Civil registration was to become a matter for civil authorities only, thus abolishing the role of the churches in the registration of births and marriages. No less radical was the strict separation between church and school. No educational institution, whether state or private school, had any right to give religious instruction. Such instruction was a matter for the private sphere exclusively. Next, all religious communities were referred to the conditions of common public associations or unions, leaving no space for privileges or autonomy. As a further consequence of this, churches and religious organisations no longer had the right or means to collect or receive taxes or donations. The overall justification for this limitation was the definition of churches as being no longer subjects of public law, and accordingly having no right to possess property. All former church property was subject to annexation by the state – to collectivisation by force. All in all, liberal-seeming objectives went hand in hand with harsh restrictions.

Furthermore, as can be seen from a circular dated December 1918, it soon became evident that not all regional offices had a clear understanding of their administrative duty regarding the implementation of separation between church and state. Judging by the directives issued therein by the law commissars, there can be no doubt that several local officials had gone far beyond their assignment and had committed injustices against not only church furniture and equipment but clergy and employees as well. This kind of conduct caused anxiety among leading officials in central offices, who feared that the violations might generate a serious setback for the new ideas or even provoke renewed sympathy for the churches. The directives made it clear, for instance, that church buildings must be left at the disposal of congregations if such congregations had attained an agreement with the authorities. Moreover, the commissar emphasised that it was entirely impermissible for officials to have confiscated vestments and used them for other purposes. In the case of icons being removed from their place, officials were forbidden from encouraging public celebration of the removal. No less remarkable was the instruction banning the imposition upon clergy and cult servants such punishment as street-cleaning or similar dirty work. The population might well get a misleading impression of the intentions of the party. Indications of this type reveal a picture of a strategy divided between a radical final goal and the reluctant adoption of more cautious preliminary tactics calculated to avoid gratuitously provoking counter-revolutionary efforts.

On the part of the churches similar discrepancies come to the surface. There were some who were determined to resist, even at the cost of martyrdom; while others were more inclined to adjust to certain aspects of the new party ideology, whether this happened out of conviction or was due to a desperate compromise in order to survive. Many determined opponents left the country and went into exile. For those who remained, the church sometimes served as a kind of rallying point for people in opposition to the new authorities. This led the party to organise transportation to penal colonies.

In hindsight, it is striking to observe the lack of consistency in the ideology of the party. In times of famine the policy became milder. This was even more the case during the Second World War, 'the great national war', when Stalin offered an alliance to the Orthodox Church in the hope of creating a united national force against the incursion of Hitler's army.

Taking stock of the communist period between 1917 and 1989, a number of distinctly different periods in the relationship between church and state stand out:

1. A period of initial build-up from 1917 to 1929, comprising a revolutionary beginning, forceful confiscation and partial liberalisation, as well as the consequences of a so-called 'New Economic Policy'.
2. The period of Stalinism from 1929 to 1941, characterised by systematic persecution, purging and destruction of church life, with the effect that Christians, in a struggle for survival, were forced to resort to underground churches or catacombs.
3. The period from the Second World War to Stalin's death, 1941-1953, marked by a certain degree of accommodation shown towards the churches, yet at times also new waves of repression.
4. The post-Stalinist period of thaw during the leadership of Nikita Khrushchev; on the other hand, there were also new excesses including persecutions and deportations.
5. The period under Leonid Brezhnev, marked by continuous atheist propaganda on the one hand, but an increasing public presence for the Russian Orthodox Church on the other.
6. A period with increasing signs of change, glasnost and perestrojka during Mikhail Gorbachev's leadership 1985-1989, with the millennium of the Russian Orthodox Church in 1988 as a peak (Stricker 2002, 63f).

As indicated in this brief survey, a conspicuous discontinuity operates alongside a powerful interventionism which was imbedded in the basic ideology of the communist party. This opaqueness of purpose is an essential aspect of the qualification of Soviet Marxism-Leninism as a totalitarian ideology.

In recent research there has been wide discussion as to whether the approach adopted by those political scientists who emphasise the priority of interpretation of totalitarianism as ideology can in fact hold water. The first point of reservation is directed against the claim that all totalitarian ideologies can be considered under one single framework, whether German Nazism, Italian Fascism, Soviet Stalinism or Islamic fundamentalism. Critics maintain that no single arrangement within a specific category is valid without paying attention to substantial exceptions, given the differences in terms of location, time and circumstances in society and culture. The second point of objection has to do with the inherent risk associated with the systematic definition of totalitarian ideologies, since this carries an implication of a predictable pattern of development, amounting to a kind of historical predestination. The objection to this alleged tendency emphasises the necessity of taking historical contingency into due account. The third objection is no less far-ranging, because it questions the method behind emphasis on the rigidity of totalitarian ideologies. The counter-assertion would stress the interaction between a given set of political ideas and specific sociological and political circumstances.

However, allowing for the weight of such reservations, it seems appropriate to state the view that certain ideological items of totalitarianism were inherent during the Soviet communist period. Among them were not least:

First, the claim of hierarchical political leadership, often by one single leader with 'Führer'-like ambitions, wielding executive political power within a one-party state;

Second, the systematic use of secret police as an instrument of control, for example by spreading fear that the families of those voicing opposition could be killed;

Third, the systematic use of propaganda via mass media, schooling at all levels of the educational system and a widespread network of party-led organisations, as opposed to civic organisations in an open society;

Fourth, a centrally planned and controlled economy;

Fifth, a military machinery of maximum strength, justified by the inherent fear of an alleged enemy said to be waiting for the right moment to extend his military power.

Moreover, the ideological system itself invoked a semi-religious self-representation, more or less openly articulated, depending upon changing political configurations.

Against this background it is no wonder that confrontation with the Christian churches became unavoidable and dramatic. Yet there were fundamental differences within this confrontational situation. The minor Protestant churches were faced with the permanent danger of being stigmatised as alien and unpatriotic, and were therefore frequently forced into an underground existence. However, their status as minority congregations was often combined with a strong inner solidarity, remarkably steadfast and difficult for party and police to infiltrate. On the one hand the Orthodox Church was the obvious enemy for party and state, which was a chief reason for persecution; on the other it could be mobilised as a precious ally in times of threat from an external enemy, as an instrument to stimulate spiritual and social cohesion in society at large. This alliance, however, proved to be a long-term risk for the integrity of the Orthodox Church, because the partnership involved an overt coexistence which rendered the Church vulnerable to intimidation and the loss of remaining bases for autonomy. Historical evidence shows nonetheless that the Orthodox Church maintained an impressive power to survive, an ability which can only be explained in terms of its rootedness in the souls of most Russians. Specific modes of expression have given voice to and visible signs of this perseverance, first of all the biblical narratives related in privacy within the family, but also icons as warrants of divine presence, and – this should not be overlooked – people's familiarity with the divine liturgy.

Church struggle and weak resistance. Nazism and the churches in Germany

The situation of the churches during the twelve years of Nazi reign took a different course. Soon after the initial period when Hitler had seized power as Führer, it became clear that the Nazi ideology and political system, which had been shaped with astonishing speed, was of a character absolutely incompatible with liberal, constitutional democracy.

Nazism was a mass movement, and the way to power was conditioned by unceasing, passionate dismissal of the preceding Weimar Republic, which had been instituted after defeat in the First World War and the subsequent Versailles Treaty. Instead, Nazi ideology assumed the appearance of 'Weltanschauung', i.e. a mass movement, claiming to have deeper roots in the soul and history of the German people than formal democracy, and asserting its relevance to all areas and aspects of society, including the Christian churches. Accordingly, the situation of the churches within the Nazi state was defined not in terms of constitutional paragraphs, but rather by promises given by Hitler in his first speech as Chancellor on 23 March 1933. He referred to the churches as partners in a common cause with the Nazi party and government, namely in the struggle for rebirth of the moral identity of the German people, which had been led astray during the preceding dominance of the powers of godlessness. Provided the churches would live up to their responsibility and assist as midwives at the rebirth of the nation which was desperately waiting to be led to unity and the struggle against inward and outward enemies, they were assured that their rights would be respected by the national government. An additional condition which was part of Hitler's speech attracted less attention at the time: the Führer made it clear that his promises rested upon the assumption that the churches would refrain from any interference in politics (Scholder 1977, 277ff).

The speech was welcomed by the overwhelming majority of the German population, including prominent theologians and church leaders. Yet it was not long before matters of conflict became burning issues in the public sphere, first in the Protestant Church, and subsequently in the Roman Catholic Church as well. However, the bone of contention was not any specific statement made by Hitler personally, nor was it any general aspect of the Nazi 'Weltanschauung'. On the contrary, most Germans remained persuaded that the Führer occupied his office with divine authority. The Nazi seizure of power was seen as the transition from an age of national humiliation to a new era of progress and glory, bringing unity and shared destiny to all Germans, regardless of class and religious identity. This conviction long remained deeply rooted, with the result that for years internal contention was directed against excrescences of the ideology, not against the ideology as such. For instance, the population at large welcomed the application of the Aryan paragraph within the state, which as early as April 1933 excluded non-Aryans from jobs as civil servants. Five months later, a radical group in the Protestant church, called the 'Faith Association of German Christians', demanded the introduction of a church law likewise applying an Aryan paragraph within the Church, as a way of extending the Nazi 'Weltanschauung' from state to church. The same group had already called for the establishment of a central leading office as Bishop for the whole Reich, thereby transferring the Führer principle to the Church. Such initiatives called into being a nationwide resistance movement within the Protestant Church. Initially formed as the Pastors' Emergency League, it subsequently turned into the Confessing Church, founded as the outcome of a national synod held in Wuppertal-Barmen in late May 1934.

For a balanced historical evaluation, it is essential to take into account the remarkable tendencies towards consistent resistance involved in the theological statement adopted at the Barmen Synod (Cochrane 1984, 19ff). The originators of the Confessing Church did not only succeed in setting up a united front against the penetration of 'alien qualifications' into the proper territory of the Church, which ought to be conditioned solely by the Holy Bible and the Confessions (for the first time since the Reformation 400 hundred years earlier, it was possible to create this kind of unity). They also presented a new interpretation of the controversial distinction between two kingdoms, defining it as the responsibility of the sovereign state to safeguard 'justice and peace', whereas it was the office of the Church to proclaim the kingdom of God. However, notably, this pronouncement necessarily implied consequences both for those holding office as rulers and for those subject to their rule alike. Thus the implications were far-reaching, even more far-reaching than was clear to many of the delegates who signed the statement. For the Nazi government, the formation of the Confessing Church was the first decisive defeat, insofar as a body within the state defined a criterion for limiting the authority of party and government.

On the other side of the coin, however, and no less consistent, are the limitations of the Barmen Declaration. The statement did not direct attention towards the totalitarian ideology as such. It allowed the members of the Confessing Church to adhere to a divided identity, on the one hand keeping the integrity of the Church inviolate, on the other remaining loyal to the political leadership, even to the extent in some cases of nurturing enthusiastic endorsement of Nazi ideology.

The lack of consistency inside the Confessing Church can be observed in specific examples. During the same period in the first months of 1934 when the opposition was gaining momentum, one of the leading ideologists of the Nazi party, Alfred Rosenberg, a dedicated spokesman for Germanic paganism, was made director for the ideological training of the entire population. Though this new office within the state system stood in obvious contradiction to Hitler's promises and to other efforts to establish a Church government as an integral part of the foundations for the Nazi state, few protests were directed against it. The bulk of the population remained convinced of the Führer's Christian conviction, a blindness which in point of fact meant that they closed their eyes to the true face of the totalitarian ideology. Moreover, they did not recognise anti-Semitism as a consistent part of the party ideology; indeed, the spirit of Nazi racism was not explicitly addressed in the Barmen Declaration. Also it deserves to be mentioned as a basic aspect of the situation inside the Protestant Church in 1934 that most Germans swept under the carpet criticism from outside Germany, including warning voices from Germans in exile. Even at a later point, in 1936, when members of the Confessing Church reserved no doubt as to the incompatibility between Nazism and Christianity, it remained the convention to observe a sustained national loyalty within the Confessing Church, a kind of apologetic attitude in defiance of manifest facts.

In comparison, the Roman Catholic Church reacted differently in several respects. Above all, she proved better equipped to resist, or at least to avoid being swallowed up by the Nazi totalitarian attempts to secure all-embracing control, because her institutional structure was firm and small-meshed. Opposition from Catholic clerics gained ground as New-German paganism appeared as a dominant impulse in schools and youth organisations. Against all such claims to set up new standards for education and public life, Catholics insisted on the sacred rights of parents and the Church to take responsibility for ethical and religious instruction of the young generation. In addition, the universal character of the Catholic Church turned out to counterbalance some of the chauvinist nationalistic features of the Nazi state. Having stated this, it deserves mentioning that questions of doctrinal integrity were taken up with less trenchancy than was the case in the Protestant Church.

Seen from an international perspective, it seems appropriate to conclude that there are obvious similarities between Soviet Marxism and German Nazism, above all with regard to the use of propaganda including enemy images, the suppression of opposition, the establishment of a monolithic, state-controlled apparatus for public administration, and, not to be overlooked, a state-controlled system of ideological training which asserted its own unconditional validity and therefore entailed displacement of the Christian churches in the public sphere. Yet historians and political scientists have engaged in an animated debate concerning the possibility of a comparative approach to totalitarian ideologies. In particular, those who have focused upon the extermination, carried out with pedantic thoroughness, of millions of Jews during the Second World War, have argued that it is not only misplaced but also a moral insult to assert any parallel atrocity in history. Without unduly compromising, it appears a matter of sound judgment to avoid a false alternative between the two arguments, in the sense that it is possible to adhere to the apparent similarities at the same time as acknowledging specific divergent circumstances in either case, and avoiding relativising any atrocities in both regimes.

Perspectives from outside Europe: Ethiopia and South Africa

Any international survey of totalitarian ideologies and their clash with Christian churches would be disgracefully partial were it not to include perspectives from non-European contexts. Allowing for brevity, a reference to developments in two corners of the African continent, Ethiopia and South Africa, may serve as indication of the complexity of the issues at stake here, acknowledgement of which stands out as a *sine qua non* in any assessment of the past century.

In Ethiopia a *coup d'état* in 1974 introduced a Marxist dictatorship which lasted almost two decades until it was dissolved in 1991, leading to a rather unsettled transitional situation, yet without uncontrolled bloodshed such as has been the case elsewhere in Africa. The Marxist ideology was openly inspired by Soviet and East European predecessors, slightly adapted to African soil. It was centralistic and made use of oppressive methods similar to those seen in previous totalitarian regimes. Reaction on the part of Christian churches, however, took a shape decidedly different from the patterns that had prevailed in Europe. First of all, the strategy of escape into a covert privacy in an attempt to avoid persecution was not adopted so frequently in Ethiopia as had been seen in Eastern Europe. The difference went back to the 'holistic' view which was a consistent aspect of Christian identity in most Ethiopian churches, that is, a view built upon interaction between social justice and development in society on the one hand, and proclamation of the Gospel and Christian salvation on the other. Certainly ethnic conflicts, famine, endless throngs of refugees and vast economic trouble on top of other difficulties ensure that the situation of the churches in Ethiopia in the aftermath of the Marxist revolution allows for no romanticising. Notwithstanding such hardship however, many of the Christian churches have experienced a remarkable growth which was stopped only temporarily during the totalitarian regime. Moreover, Ethiopia is just one of several other examples from the Southern hemisphere that reveal a remarkable dynamic within the churches. Their growth in terms of membership corresponds with their presence on the public scene, where they serve as forerunners for socio-ethical awareness (Eide 2000).

No less remarkable is the situation of the churches in South Africa, where the general political situation signals a similar warning against the painting of any romanticising picture. Apartheid ideology was totalitarian in a sense that was fundamentally different from Marxist dictatorships. In terms of its racist foundation it had more similarity with the Aryan ideology embodied in German Nazism. Opposition to the heresy of racial segregation in South Africa took a different direction from that adopted by the Confessing Church in Germany in 1934. The Kairos document from 1986, in spite of some similarities with the Barmen Declaration, goes further than the rejection of racist oppression and insistence on doctrinal integrity. It declares an interaction between that liberation of the poor and oppressed advocated in the narratives of the Bible, and the liberation from oppressive bonds in society here and now. A direct link appears between this confessional statement and the prominent role played by church representatives in the Commission for Truth and Reconciliation, which has been an integral part of the peaceful transition from a totalitarian apartheid ideology towards the beginnings of an open society. Again, it would be a sign of Eurocentric arrogance were we instantly to dismiss such invocation of Christian standards drawn from the proclamation of the Gospel, on the grounds that it involves an ungodly politicising of the divine message. The process of taking stock after the various instances of showdown between totalitarian ideologies and Christian churches must allow for considerable variation, not only in respect of the different faces of totalitarian systems and ideologies, but also in respect of the diverse patterns of reaction followed by the respective churches.

Concluding remarks

It is one of the hallmarks of modern western societies that religion has been put on trial in the public sphere. Insistence on historical rootedness or metaphysical truth does not count when traditional values and historical church institutions are challenged to stand the test before rapidly changing patterns of values and political ideas of governance, which are themselves no less exposed to transformation.

It has been indicated in this essay that the confrontation with totalitarian ideologies has challenged the Christian churches inside and outside Europe, frequently under dramatic circumstances. This is probably one of the main reasons why this clash has attracted the attention of historians and theologians more than have other aspects of modern church history, such as the slow yet incessant process of privatisation and individualisation of religious belief in western societies.

In a broader historical perspective, the confrontation with totalitarian ideologies might be said to have forced the Christian churches into a trial unparallelled in previous periods of history. The era of Absolutism had similar monolithic systems of government and suppression of opposition. Yet they were different, first of all in the fundamental sense that their foundation was theocratic, insofar as the supreme head of state was seen as God's anointed representative on earth and head of the national church. It is true that some of the modern totalitarian ideologies reveal Christian inspiration in their origins and have sometimes developed into a kind of political religion. Notwithstanding this, their role has been shaped by conditions unprecedented in earlier centuries. First of all, the political leaders of societies built upon totalitarian ideologies have had at their disposal systems of administrative control applying even in remote corners of these societies. Moreover, the mass media have served as channels for propaganda in previously unparallelled ways. As has been shown above, the initial political initiatives taken by the new leaders of the totalitarian regimes of the Soviet Union and the Third Reich in Germany held out the prospects of tolerance. In times of external threat to the state, such offers of tolerance and cooperation were reaffirmed. Yet there was no doubt about the long-term goal: the definitive elimination of any sign of religious presence in the public sphere.

The encounter faced the churches with a choice: either acceptance of the given conditions or martyrdom. In many cases, the result was withdrawal into silent, private conviction, if not surrender in the sense of giving up membership of organised congregations. Still, as history has shown, the churches played an important role as one of the few institutions that were able to set up a limitation to the absolute claims of totalitarian ideology.

The process of taking stock of this process is still in progress, so a final evaluation is premature. It must necessarily be an essential aspect of a comprehensive overview to set any analysis of these confrontations in juxtaposition with a similar analysis of the status of Christian belief and organised churches in liberal societies. Moreover, the inclusion of perspectives from outside Europe should be part of any international statement.

The attention given to Islamic fundamentalism in recent years creates the danger of sweeping the complexities in our own European tradition under the carpet, and claiming that full watchfulness is needed in the face of the Muslim threat arising from non-European civilizations.

Against any such simplistic dualism a self-critical, full-scale, international analysis of the encounter between totalitarian ideologies and the Christian churches seems more appropriate than ever before.

Bibliography

Arendt, Hannah 1951 and later. *The Origins of Totalitarianism.* New York & London: Hartcourt.

Burleigh, Michael 2005. *Earthly Powers: the clash of religion and politics in Europe from the French Revolution to the Great War.* New York: HarperCollins.

Cochrane, Arthur 1984. 'Text of the Barmen Declaration'. In: Hubert G. Locke (ed.), *The Church confronts the Nazis. Barmen then and now.* New York: The Edwin Mellen Press, 19-26.

Eide, Øyvind M. 2000. *Revolution & Religion in Ethiopia. The Growth & Persecution of the Mekane Yesus Church 1974-1985.* Oxford.

Gebremedhin, Ezra 2000. The Ethiopian Evangelical Church Mekane Yesus under Marxist Dictatorship. In: Katharina Kunter/Jens Holger Schjørring (eds.) *Changing Relarions between Churches in Europe and Africa. The Internationalization of Christianity and Politics in the 20th Century.* Wiesbaden Harrassowitz Verlag, 89-108.

Gottlieb, Christian 2003. *Dilemmas of Reaction in Leninist Russia: The Christian Response to the Revolution in the Works of N.A. Berdyaev 1917-1924.* Odense, University of Southern Denmark.

Hobsbawm, Eric 1994 and later. *Age of Extremes. The Short Twentieth Century 1914-1991.* London: Abacus.

Lindt, Andreas 1981. *Das Zeitalter des Totalitarismus.* Stuttgart: Kohlhammer.

Luchterhandt, Otto 2002. 'Die Phase der Errichtung der kommunistischen Herrschaft in der Sowjetunion'. In: Peter Maser & J.H. Schjørring (Hg.), *Zwischen den Mühlsteinen. Protestantische Kirchen in der Phase der Errichtung der kommunistischen Herrschaft im östlichen Europa.* Erlangen: Martin Luther Verlag, 25-62.

Scholder, Klaus 1977 and later. *Die Kirchen und das Dritte Reich.* Bd. I-III. Propyläen, Frankfurt/M, Berlin, München: Propyläen.

Stricker, Gert 2002. 'Die Ev.-Luth. Kirche in Russland im ersten Jahrzehnt der sowjettischen
    Herrschaft (1917-1929)'. In: Peter Maser & J.H. Schjørring (Hg.), *Zwischen den Mühlsteinen.*
    Protestantische Kirchen in der Phase der Errichtung der kommunistischen Herrschaft im östlichen
    Europa. Erlangen: Martin Luther Verlag, 63-120.
Stupperich, Robert (Hrsg.) 1962. *Kirche und Staat in der Sowjetunion. Gesetze und Verordnungen.*
    Witten: Luther.

WHEN FAITHS COLLIDE AND STATES MEET
INTERRELIGIOUS DIALOGUE AS A POLICY INSTRUMENT

Viggo Mortensen

*The collisions of faiths, or the collisions of peoples of faith, are
among the most threatening conflicts around the world.*
(Martin E. Marty 2005)

*Is it possible to develop a theological position mature enough to – critically and construc-
tively – deal with the reigning religious pluralism? When Christianity is analysed as a
translation and contextualisation movement, new tensions arise. How is the relationship
between the civil religion – so important for the cohesion of a given society – and a confes-
sionally defined Christianity – so important for the identity of the church? The question
of the validity of religion and the conflicting truth claims in a multireligious setting is
analysed within the discipline theology of religions, with a focus on the problem of how
to ensure the conditions required for a peaceful religious encounter.*

*When faiths collide and tensions arise dialogue is the prescribed remedy. But how
can interreligious dialogue function between states that are in principle secular? In a case
study, three government-sponsored consecutive interfaith dialogues (Bali 2005, Larnaca
2006 and Nanjing 2007) of the Asia Europe Meetings (ASEM) are analysed. The analysis
of the formal outcome of these dialogues, the Bali Declaration, the Larnaca Plan of Action and the Nanjing Final Statement are read in an attempt to define a common basis
for joint action. When religion enters the battlefield of the general political interests of
states, religion can be treated either as an ideological force or as pure window dressing.
Because both culture and religion are necessary for the identity of people and nations,
it is argued here that interfaith dialogue is of importance when pluralist states organise
their international relations.*

The story goes that when the Danish Prime Minister Poul Hartling visited Chairman
Mao, Mao asked him how many Danes there were. Upon Hartling's response (five
million), Chairman Mao is reported to have exclaimed: "Then we need to protect
you". The Danes and the Danish national state constitute an endangered species! This
is an all too common view among ethnic Danes. In Denmark we have a host of say-
ings indicating that we understand ourselves as a tiny nation prone to cosiness ("Du
puslingland, som hygger dig i smug, mens hele verden brænder om din vugge". Jeppe
Aakjær). But on the other hand we also have a high opinion of ourselves, and are
ready to face the world and give our contribution, as expressed by the Danish national

poet Hans Christian Andersen ("Et lille land, – og dog så vidt om jorden, end høres danskens sang og mejselslag").

The caricature crisis as an example of how faiths collide

The way Danes perceive themselves was severely shaken when the so-called Mohammed or Caricature/Cartoon Crisis hit the country in 2005/06. Without entering into a full discussion of this case, let me just state that this was indeed a steep learning curve for Denmark. And this was the intention according to Osama bin Laden, who commented on the caricatures in his speech *The People of Islam* on April 24, 2006 (Lawrence 2007). Here he stresses that among all the attacks on Islam, the attacks and ridicule of the Prophet and Sharia are the most vicious. They need to be met with the sword. And the sword was indeed applied. It began with the murder of Theo van Gogh, the Dutch filmmaker; and the Danes were perplexed onlookers when the holy rage erupted in the streets of the Middle East and failed to understand how the Danish 'joke' could develop into such an urgent crisis with many killed and diplomatic relations severely hurt. This was a conflict that was ignited because of misunderstandings from both sides. Seen from the vantage point of religious studies, it was a classic example of what is normally termed Orientalism. The West displayed a blatant Orientalism, and was met by equally strong expressions of Occidentalism.[1]

If there is a lesson to be learned from this it can be summarised in three points:

- There is no room for double standards: What is said in the corner will be shouted out from the rooftops.
- Islam is a strong religion.
- The Islamic *Umma* is in place and functioning.

In Denmark the episode led to a very lively discussion of the limits of freedom of expression and the role of religion in nation building and in the public square. The background is that like all European nations Denmark has been through a process of secularisation and modernisation. The result of this process was a naked public square. When religions come back in different forms, as seen in Europe at the moment, there is a temptation to opt (again) for a sacred public square. For many reasons neither of these possibilities is a good one. There is actually a need to develop a civic public square. On the basis of a number of core values and human rights – including freedom of religion, the right to change belief without any repercussions whatsoever, and the

---

[1]   This is a reference to Edward Said's notion of Orientalism perceived as a constellation of false assumptions underlying Western attitudes towards the East. In his book (Said 1978) he argued that a long tradition of false and romanticised images of the Orient had served as an implicit justification for the West's colonial history. As an inversion of Orientalism Ian Buruma and Avishai Margalit (2004) formed the term Occidentalism to signify the equally stereotyped and dehumanising Eastern views of the West.

rights of minorities – the differences should be negotiated to ensure the maximum freedom for the individual.

It has rightly been pointed out that religion can function both in a negative and in a positive way, but that it is always a force to be reckoned with. When religions want to play a part in the nation-building process and thus function as civil religions, they need to tone down their confessional identity and develop structures that allow others to have full freedom of religion. Respecting minority views does not mean that there cannot be a lead culture in a given society, as is the case with Pancasilla in Indonesia and Folk Christianity in Denmark, for instance. Various metaphors have been employed to characterise the multicultural society that is the most likely result of the present process of globalisation: melting pot, salad bowl, symphony and rainbow. I favour two other metaphors: artichoke and Lego. They underline both respect for diversity and the necessary drive towards unity. Diversity and plurality can indeed be celebrated, but can only come into full bloom if they are nourished by and contribute to the common good. The common good is not simply the sum of individual or group interests, but really the good that is common. This can only be worked out through public debate and negotiation. Thus there "is an inescapable 'contextual' dimension to any genuine understanding of the common good".[2] Governments should therefore actively encourage public dialogue among various faith traditions.

The changing European scene

This is not often done in Western secular democracies, but the situation in Europe is indeed changing. In a leading missiological journal the religious situation in Europe is in focus under the heading: *Europe: Christendom Graveyard or Christian Laboratory?* The main articles have titles such as *Godless Europe?* by Philip Jenkins and *Can Europe be saved?* by Lamin Sanneh. The notion of Eurabia is mentioned. Just to give an impression, here are a couple of citations:

Will the rapid pace of dechristianization push Europe to the fringes of the Muslim world as Eurabia? Will Spain revert to Islam? Will Britain become North Pakistan, France the Islamic Republic of New Algeria, Spain the Moorish Emirate of Iberia, Germany the new Turkey? Will Brussels and Belgium become Belgistan? Will Italy and Albania merge to become a new Albanian Islamic Federation? As Libya's president Qaddafi asserts: "There are signs that Allah will grant Islam victory in Europe without swords, without guns, without conquests. The fifty million Muslims of Europe will turn it into a Muslim continent within a few decades" (Sanneh 2007, 121).

---

2   Ramachandra 1999, 161. I am very much in agreement with Ramachandra as he compares his position to that of John Rawls and his talk of 'overlapping consensus'. "In a democratic and pluralist society, social convergence is sought around a set of politico-ethical guides for action in the public square…It is openly acknowledged that no such common foundation exists…I would stress that public civility is cultivated by fostering genuine debate over the truth-values of particular conceptions of human ends. … 'Overlapping consensus' can also enshrine beliefs about a context-specific common good. The important thing, however, is that it must emerge out of actual dialogue and debate, not abstract theorizing." (162).

A more thorough analysis and documentation is presented in Philip Jenkins 2007. This is the third volume of his ambitious trilogy examining religion in a global perspective. The first volume was *The Next Christendom* (Jenkins 2002), followed by *The New Faces of Christianity* (Jenkins 2006). In *God's Continent*, Jenkins seeks to counter what he views as excessively dismal, even alarmist analyses of the future of Europe.

The changes in the European religious scene are obvious, and American observers give us the choice: graveyard or laboratory. Although some people may have a preference for the quietness and calm of well preserved graveyards, to me there can be no doubt. I opt for the noisy and laborious laboratory. So this is what Europe is today: a laboratory where it is possible to experience and study what happens when a formerly monoreligious Christian continent turns multireligious. The options are numerous, and nobody knows what the result will be. Religion may vanish; churches may disappear and be replaced by strong fundamentalist religions – or by a weak form of religiosity that is spread thinly like varnish such as the New Age religiosity already in existence today.

Globally a number of obvious trends can be spotted:

- The traditional confessional churches are in a dramatic decline. Some are desperately trying a variety of remedies to cure the malady, using the technology of the media and marketing transformed through evangelical piety and spirituality.
- Some individual congregations that very consciously invest all their money in one direction (nowadays these are mostly of an evangelical provenance) may experience moderate success.
- There is an overwhelming dominance of independent churches buying into a prosperity gospel. If you want to be rich (and the poor always want to be rich), then make your investment.
- A growth in syncretism and the privatisation of religion, resulting in mix-and-choose religion.

Some of the same trends can be observed in Europe. But because Europe has a specific history and is shaped by Constantinian Christianity, developments here raise some specific issues and questions such as:

- What will a post-secular Europe look like?
- What role will the new immigrant Christian churches play in the European laboratory?
- Can the folk church structures prevail as we have known them in the Nordic countries?
- What is the future of confessional churches?
- What will win: the Protestantisation of religion or the Islamisation of Christianity?

The Protestantisation of religion will let secularisation prevail. The Islamisation of Christianity will create a totally new agenda. How it will all develop remains to be seen. Recently the debate concerning state and religion has been reinvigorated under the catchword of the cohesion of society.[3] Historically speaking, religions have played a pivotal role in several cases in providing for stability and coherence of society. That is why many people, concerned with the cohesion of a given society, are asking now how much diversity a society can include or just tolerate. It is clear that integration is the key. If separation due to globalisation is impossible (the Westphalian principle), and if parallel development is unethical and unsustainable (apartheid), then integration is the only possibility, and integration presupposes tolerance towards the different and a clear position regarding what is not tolerable.

If we do not want to restrict religious and cultural pluralism in our societies, then the different religions in pluralistic societies are confronted with a number of challenges such as:

- How can different religious groups develop the potential in their own religion for an attitude of respect and inclusiveness for adherents of other religions in order to promote peace and harmony in society?
- How can the claims to universality and absoluteness in the religious traditions be handled so that 'the other' is not excluded from participating fully in the democratic processes of any given society?
- How can religions contribute positively to the common good of society? What can be brought to the common table as a gift from the various religious traditions?
- How can different religious communities relate to or contribute to the development of common values and norms in society so that they are not seen as threats to the stability of society but contributors to the cohesion of society?
- How can we do all this and at the same time respect the specific religious identities?

The possible dialogue in Europe

As observed often before, the situation in Europe is a special case.[4] For instance, Philip Jenkins (2007) notices that both Christianity and Islam face real difficulties in surviving within Europe's secular cultural ambience in anything like their familiar historical forms. Europe is a historical phenomenon, and Europe without its familiar historical forms is not Europe. The American author Richard John Neuhaus gives a thorough analysis of Jenkins' book under the heading *The Much Exaggerated Death of Europe*.

---

3   The Danish discussion of this topic was recently invigorated by an article by Prime Minister Anders Fogh Rasmussen and the ensuing discussion documented in Lodberg 2007.

4   See the discussion following Grace Davie (2002)

He explains that to speak of the death of Europe is not to suggest that the continent called Europe will disappear. It is possible that 'Euro secularity' in sustained tension with an Islamo-Christian cultural ambience will flourish, at least economically, for generations to come. But, with the possible establishment of Eurabia or the Maghreb, Europe "in anything like its familiar historical forms" will be a memory. That is what is meant by the death of Europe.

Richard John Neuhaus concludes with the following story:

At a recent dinner party with European intellectuals, I put to an influential French archbishop Daniel Pipes' projection: Either assimilation or expulsion or Islamic takeover. That, he said, puts the possibilities much too starkly. "We hope for the first," he said, "while we work at reducing immigration and prepare ourselves for soft Islamization." Soft Islamization. It is a wan expression. Whether soft or hard, the prospect is that, in the not-so-distant future, someone will publish a book titled Allah's Continent. In fact, several Muslim authors have already published books with very similar titles, anticipating the future of the Europe that was. Needless to say, and historical contingencies being as contingent as they are, I very much hope that they turn out to be wrong (Neuhaus 2007).

How can we sustain a hope that Europe can be sustained in something like its familiar historic form? What is the alternative to islamisation and secularisation? For me the answer lies in dialogue, exchange and conversation on all levels, culturally and religiously. In particular, interreligious dialogue comes into play as a way to bridge the gap between different religious and worldviews. In Hans Küng's famous words: There is no peace between nations without peace between religions; and there is no peace between religions without interreligious dialogue. We have dialogue to further understanding. In the encounter with 'the other' one experiences both alienation and commonalities, and the aim is to incorporate what is different into a common frame of reference or horizon, something which the German philosopher Hans Georg Gadamer calls 'Horizontverschmelzung'. To understand is to change. I am different when I leave a dialogue and exchange than I was before it started. That is why dialogue is a risky business and truly difficult because you are requested both fully to encounter 'the other' and to keep your own horizon of understanding intact. Of the many forms of dialogue (dialogue of life and action, the spiritual dialogue and the intellectual dialogue), those who focus on the more practical issues have the best chance of success. A good starting point is to act together in order to alleviate concrete suffering. If that proves successful, a fruitful framework for a more extended dialogue is created. Interreligious dialogue is a good instrument to dismantle prejudices. The biggest threat to interfaith harmony is the lack of knowledge of 'the other' and an inadequate understanding of one's own position.

When states meet what role can interreligious dialogue play?

My experience of interreligious dialogue has mainly been gained in the context of the government-sponsored organisation Asia Europe Meeting (ASEM). Here I have learned that freedom of religion is the most important and also most highly contested issue within the dialogue. When everybody agrees on the fundamentality of this, the road can be cleared towards a more tolerant society.

The Inter Faith Dialogue (IFD) within the Asia Europe Meeting (ASEM) has met three times so far. It started in 2004 in Bali, where the so-called Bali Declaration was formulated. It continued with a meeting in Cyprus in 2005, which resulted in the Larnaca Plan of Action. The most recent dialogue was conducted in China in 2006, and led to the Nanjing Statement.[5] The dialogue is to continue in June 2008 in Amsterdam.

Globalisation

The goal of such a global dialogue is to respond to a perceived need by many different societies and states, all currently experiencing the challenge of how to deal with religion in the public sphere. Due to globalisation many states are now facing the same problems. So globalisation is the buzzword defining the rapid multidimensional and polycentric transformation process that all societies are encountering at the moment. This is not the place to try to give an exhaustive definition of this phenomenon. It is well known that the global economy and modern technology are the driving forces behind a development leading to enhanced cultural and economic exchanges between regions and nations as well as profound changes in traditional societies. The *economists* continue to advocate globalisation as the tool to increase prosperity. But this is hard to believe for those who are not in the forefront of the globalisation movement, because they experience that globalisation increases disparity and inequality. *Socially*, globalisation can cause many problems. Such diverse factors as the 'brain drain' and 'migration' influence nations both in the South and the North, both in Asia and Europe. *Culturally*, globalisation can be experienced as enrichment, because it offers you the possibility to get to know other cultures better. When it comes to food we are all globalised multiculturalists. But globalisation can also lead to homogeneity – which is sometimes referred to as McDonaldisation[6] to indicate that globalisation promotes uniformity and hegemony. As globalisation is always accompanied by localisation, the resulting culture will often be a hybrid.[7]

Here we will just regard globalisation as a matter of fact and focus on the consequences for culture and religion. What globalisation does first and foremost is to stress the *interdependence* of all people and nations of this earth. Without cooperation we

---

5   A short report and the three texts can be seen http://www.aseminfoboard.org/.
6   The term was introduced by George Ritzer 2004 in order to describe predominant features of modern society such as efficiency, calculability, predictability and control.
7   The British sociologist Roland Robertson introduced the Japanese business term glocalisation to sociological theory to signify the interplay of local, regional and global interactions.

cannot solve the problems we are facing (poverty, environmental problems or cultural clashes alike). Secondly: globalisation leads to increased diversity within different societies and growing inequality among nations.

The final verdict on how we should evaluate globalisation is still pending. It is fair to say that there are both good and bad consequences. Inequality is reigning at the moment, and a growing sense of instability and vulnerability is spreading, symbolised through the fear of terror and the war on terrorism. In addition, climate change also constitutes a very concrete threat to people and the environment. The driving force behind these developments is the tremendous rise in the population, combined with industrialisation. In the year 1900, the globe was inhabited by 1.6 billion people. Now we have reached 6.6 billion. It is foreseen that around the year 2050, China alone will have 1.6 billion people; and India alone 1.6 billion people. 1.6 billion people – that is the population of the entire globe 150 years ago. This huge rise in population puts enormous pressure on all ecological systems. The biggest political challenge is therefore how to master the challenge arising from these demographic and ecological changes.

In order to meet these challenges constructively, it is vital to explore the possibilities provided by our interdependency. In particular, the climate change debate shows that we are all in this together. In order to achieve greater integration, a global culture of understanding is needed. Participation, inclusion, responsibility and belonging are keywords here. Identity is often established through differentiation. I am because I am not you, because you are 'other'. In German they have the following fitting expression: 'Identität durch differenz'. In this there is an element of truth. But this insight needs to be supplemented with the African understanding encapsulated in the notion of 'Ubuntu': I am because you are.

Interdependency

The argument goes like this: Globalisation – apart from anything else – leads to more interdependency for better or worse. This poses the big question: How can we manage this interdependency? Under the influence of modernity, it was thought that an ideology could form a consensus and thus unity could be established. But in late modernity we find (in European countries at least) that we have gone from a situation in which unity was the goal to a situation in which we are content if we can achieve just a little harmony, or (if that is too high an ideal) at least the absence of strife. We are no longer striving for consensus but happy for convergence; we no longer believe in ideology but hope for social cohesion.

When striving for harmony while recognising the differences that exist between people, one has to keep in mind what Heraclitus said a long time ago: harmony can only be established when the tension between opposites is maintained. So when it comes to matters of culture and religion we should not necessarily expect consensus. Diversity is the order of the day, but we should encourage convergence. After the collapse of Communism there is now widespread scepticism with regard to the use of ideology as a means of unifying people. But seeking identity is an extremely basic human instinct, and the establishment of a certain degree of cohesion is important for all societies. The mosaic madness[8] of the modern multi-everything societies has led to renewed interest in the question of social cohesion. Can we establish a new cosmopolitanism? Are all religions in need of a theology of integration?

When it comes to harmony, convergence and cohesion within a given culture, religion comes to the fore. Religion can inspire the worst and the best deeds. On a global scale, one often finds a religious dimension to conflicts and tensions. Sometimes religion is seen as the root cause of the conflict; sometimes religion serves as a badge of identity in order to mobilise nationalist or ethnic passions. If we consider a list of just a few of the current hotspots in the world – Iraq, Afghanistan, Palestine, Lebanon, Nigeria, Sudan, Kashmir, Sri Lanka, Chechnya, Kosovo – I think it is fair to say that most of the conflicts in these areas have a religious and in most cases an Islamic interface. Below the surface there are not only traditional political conflicts of interest but also a collision of globalisation with the traditional values often embedded in religion. To overcome the threat of terror and the deadlock in which the war against terror has placed us, we need a more effective strategy of cultural engagement.

When Samuel Huntington (1996) released his theory of the clash of civilisations, nobody in the intellectual establishment wanted to take it seriously. It is true that the theory has some basic flaws, but it has sustained itself for the last ten years. Huntington noted that religion is the defining element of culture. Many intellectuals in Europe would not accept this assumption, and the consequence is that we have not been able to deal with religious differences; and religious demagogues like Bin Laden and Milosevic have prevailed, because we have failed to understand the way in which religion shapes the worldviews and political aspirations of others.

Core values and commonalities in interfaith dialogue

The interfaith dialogue within the Asia Europe Meetings is – as I see it – an attempt to explore how interfaith dialogue can help establish right relationships between people and nations by focusing on some core values. At the last meeting in the IFD in Nanjing in 2006 I put forward a list suggesting that we should focus on some of the values mentioned here if we wish to encourage more harmony, convergence and cohesion; and I gave reasons why Christianity has a contribution to make to these values.[9]

---

8   It is the Canadian sociologist Reginald W. Bibby that employs this notion when discussing multiculturalism in Canada. See his book *Mosaic Madness. Pluralism without a cause*. Stoddart. Toronto 1990.

9   It is not the intention here to entertain a more philosophical discussion of the contested concept of value. Here I take my starting point in the fact that the concept is widely used also in more practical work in peace building and reconciliation as reported on the website for The International Centre for Religion & Diplomacy. See http://www.icrd.org/, which I draw upon here. This new trend in 'faith-based diplomacy' is introduced in Thomas 2005.

- Pluralism. Here a distinction is in order. Plurality is an existential reality, but pluralism is a core value in which ethnic and cultural diversity is seen as a gift and a blessing. Pluralism means that we should show respect for distinctiveness while focusing on the basis of common ground. Because there are limits to plurality in a society that should function effectively, pluralism demands that we define the common ground and seek unity in the midst of diversity.
- Toleration & inclusion. Confronted with people who are 'other' than us in respect to ethnicity, class, culture or religion, the first natural reaction may very well be *exclusion*. In the wake of the enlightenment the idea of *toleration* was born. To tolerate what seems unacceptable, it must first be clear what cannot be tolerated. And this is constantly debatable and can only be solved in an open discourse. For instance, freedom of speech is indispensable for a tolerant society. Sometimes it is said that we should move beyond tolerance. And there could be some truth in that because the highest point is *inclusion* and embrace. Overcoming hostility by practising unconditional love is an ideal demand that is built into several religious traditions. In Christianity the Greek word Agape stands for such compassion, charity and self-giving love. This cannot be realised in society as such, but as an idea it can indirectly inform the legislation of a given society.
- Peace. In Christianity there is a very realistic understanding that people are not always as good as they should be. So sin is part of human nature, and the ensuing consequence is strife and conflict. Now, conflict could also present an opportunity to explore differences and go deeper into relationships. A commitment to peace means that we always seek the peaceful solution to strife and violence.
- Social justice. We cannot have lasting peace and reconciliation without social justice. Faith-based social justice means that it is legitimate to argue in the political realm on the background of an ethical stance asking for the common good and seeking to transform the soul of a given community.
- Forgiveness. Forgiveness is or should be at the core of all human relationships. Exercising forgiveness and repentance in order to create a better future is a very powerful tool because it can change lives and transform societies.
- Healing. Not only individuals need healing, but wounded communities and nations must sometimes go through a process in which painful historical memories, suffering and injustice can be acknowledged, repented and healed. Healing the wounds of history through acknowledging suffering and injustice can be a necessary process in order to reach
- Atonement. Human beings are spiritual beings. So we humans are on a spiritual quest towards a deeper understanding of three basic questions: Where did I come from? Why am I here? Where am I going? We never get to the bottom of these questions, which is why we experience alienation. Atonement is a process in which I am reconciled and find peace with God, my neighbour and myself.

This list of values is of course not exhaustive. Others can be added; but it is my allegation that all the major religious traditions can contribute to these core values. I can vouch for Christianity in this respect. And I am eager to learn from other religious traditions how they can illuminate these same values. Because the starting point for any meaningful interfaith dialogue will be what we have in common. The common reality that cuts across all the divisions that separate us is that we all live on this vulnerable globe; and globalisation makes our interdependence more obvious.

In addition we realise that we are all human beings. We suffer together. When I cut myself, I bleed. When my Muslim neighbour cuts herself, she bleeds too. When my Buddhist neighbour cuts himself, he bleeds as well. When we experience loss we grieve. We are bound to give different interpretations of these facts. Although culture and religion can form our experiences, underneath the different interpretations there is this common fact: We are one world and we belong to one humanity. We can give our commonalities different forms and outlooks, but, beyond all the cultural and religious differences, we need to be aware of the commonalities that come with the fact that we are all humans; humans endowed with dignity and certain inalienable rights.

As we have seen above, globalisation means that faiths meets faiths. This article was prefaced with a quote from Martin Marty indicating that this meeting between faiths does not always pass off peacefully. On the contrary – there may be clashes, and these collisions of peoples of faith are among the most threatening conflicts in the world. Efforts to understand what is happening are the first step to overcome tensions. The next is to invent and practise forms of pluralism that make it possible to live together with differences, in a unity of reconciled diversity. In his book Marty argues that we should move beyond mere tolerance, and he advocates a strategy of aggressive risk-taking on behalf of hospitality. The most important thing we can do is to be hospitable, to find reasons for and to practise hospitality. "Faiths will continue to collide, but those individuals and groups that risk hospitality and promote engagement with the stranger, the different, the other, will contribute to a world in which measured hopes can survive and those who hope can guide." (Marty 2005, 179). It seems to me that this could be the starting point for a fruitful interfaith dialogue – also in the area of globalisation.

Bibliography

Buruma, Ian & Margalit, Avishai 2004. *Occidentalism. A Short History of Anti-Westernism.* USA: Penguin.

Davie, Grace 2002. *Europe: the Exceptional Case. Parameters of Faiths in the Modern World.* London: Sarum Theological Lectures.

Huntington, Samuel P. 1996. *The Clash of Civilizations and the Remaking of the World Order.* New York: Simon & Schuster.

Jenkins, Philip, 2007a. 'Godless Europe?'. *International Bulletin of Missionary Research. IBMR* 31/3, July 2007, 115-120.

Jenkins, Philip 2007. *God's Continent. Christianity, Islam, and Europe's Religious Crisis.* Oxford: Oxford University Press.

Jenkins, Philip 2006. *The New Faces of Christianity. Believing the Bible in the Global South.* Oxford: Oxford University Press.

Jenkins, Philip 2002. *The Next Christendom. The Coming of Global Christianity.* Oxford: Oxford University Press.

Lawrence, Bruce 2007. *Budskap til Verden. Osama Bin Ladens brev og taler.* Norge: LSP forlag.

Lodberg, Peter (ed.) 2007. *Sammenhængskraften. Replikker til Fogh.* Højbjerg: Univers.

Marty, Martin E. 2005. *When Faiths Collide.* Oxford: Blackwell Publishing.

Neuhaus, Richard John 2007. 'The Much Exaggerated Death of Europe'. *First Things: A Journal of Religion, Culture and Public Life.* http://www.firstthings.com/article

Ramachandra, Vinoth 1999. *Faiths in Conflict. Christian Integrity in a Multicultural World.* Leicester: Inter Varsity Press.

Ritzer, George 2004 (Revised New Century Edition). *The McDonaldization of Society.* London: Sage Publications.

Said, Edward 1978. *Orientalism. Western Conceptions of the Orient.* New York: Vintage Books.

Sanneh, Lamin 2007. 'Can Europe be saved? A Review Essay'. *IBMR* 31/3, July 2007.

Thomas, Scott M. 2005. *The Global Resurgence of Religion and the Transformation of International Relations. The Struggle for the Soul of the Twenty First Century.* London: Palgrave.

THE MYSTERIOUS PRESENCE OF THE DIVINE
ON THE ROLE OF RELIGION IN SOCIETY

Ulrik Nissen

"Denn ich mich schier rhümen möchte, das sint der Apostel zeit das weltliche schwerd und oberkeit nie so klerlich beschrieben und herrlich gepreiset ist, wie auch meine feinde müssen bekennen, als durch mich." (WA 19, 625, 15ff.). These are the words of the reformer Martin Luther in 1526. Unabashedly and without hesitation he proclaims himself as the one who most clearly has described temporal authority since the days of the apostles. Today we might be somewhat reluctant to agree with Luther on this assessment of his own *grandeur*. Admittedly, there can hardly be any doubt that the Lutheran Reformation has had an immense influence on the history of political thought. In the classical work on Luther's political thought, this importance is rightly pointed out (Thompson 1984, 9). But this is not the same as Luther being clear in his political views. Many would argue that the lack of a systematic presentation of his thought also entails a lack of an inner coherence. In a well-known history of political thought Luther is given up as a political thinker due to his lack of a systematic account of his thought and frequent self-contradiction (Allen 1977, 15). Even if it may be correct that Luther was no political thinker, the influence of his thought still gives us a good reason to continue to explore new meanings and dimensions of his theology and ethics. But at the same time, the lack of clarity in Luther also provides us with the stimulus to look into other parts of the Lutheran tradition when we wish to reflect on Lutheran ethics in a contemporary setting.

In the present essay this is precisely what we will do. Our main concern is to reflect on the role of the church, democracy and ethics in the light of the Lutheran tradition. The starting point of this contemplation will be taken in the so-called 'Cartoon Crisis' in Denmark in 2006. This will lead us to the second part of the essay, where we will ask if Luther's understanding of temporal authority entails that religion should play a subordinate role in contemporary society. It will be argued that this appears not to be the case. In the third part of the essay we turn to Dietrich Bonhoeffer and his understanding of the mystery of reality. As we shall see, this idea holds concrete political implications. In the fourth and last part of the essay we will bring together the main ideas in Luther and Bonhoeffer. This will make it possible for us to see that Luther and Bonhoeffer argue for a mysterious role of religion in society. Arguing for the mysterious role of religion, the last question – which can only be touched upon – will be if this makes any difference. If religion only has a mysterious role, does it then have any significance at all?

The Cartoon Crisis – and the role of religion in society

In December 2005 the Danish newspaper *Jyllands-Posten* published a series of cartoondrawings depicting the prophet Muhammad. The reactions immediately after publication were only very limited. But after a delegation of representatives of Danish Muslims had travelled to the Middle East and informed people about these drawings, an immense outcry arose causing what has been called the biggest international crisis for Danish society since World War 2 – the so-called 'Cartoon Crisis'. This crisis also gave rise to various discussions on freedom of speech in Western-European countries, the role of the media in a democratic society, the place and role of the Muslim religion in Danish society, and the relation between religion and politics in general. As part of this discussion the Danish prime minister published an article in the Danish newspaper *Politiken* with the title 'Hold religionen indendørs' ('Keep religion indoors'. Fogh Rasmussen 2006a). In this article Fogh Rasmussen argued that religion should be a private matter. Religion was something that should be kept indoors, and should remain a personal and private affair. Religion should not play a role in the public debate. As part of this position, Fogh Rasmussen endorsed the idea of social cohesion (sammenhængskraft), which he believed was vital in Danish society.

If society is to be characterised by inner cohesion, religion can only be seen as part of the private sphere. This is the point where this debate becomes interesting for our present concern. In the discussion of the relation between democracy, church and ethics this question is at the very core of our concern. If these three spheres are to be understood in relation to each other, how can religion be understood as a purely private matter? In the present article it will be argued that these three notions do indeed relate to each other. So the article will question Fogh Rasmussen's claim that religion must be a personal and private matter. Even if Fogh Rasmussen (Fogh Rasmussen 2006a) admits several ways in which religion can play a role in public life – e.g. in having an influence on a person's views and actions – the whole aim of his article is to argue that religion should play a minor role in the public sphere. Fogh Rasmussen mentions four points that are important:

- Individual believers must refrain from demanding that people not of their faith should follow the religious requirements of this faith in the public sphere.
- It must be maintained as a principle that there is no one authority that can speak on behalf of the Danish Evangelical-Lutheran Church (Folkekirken).
- All citizens in Denmark have equal rights and duties irrespective of religious convictions.
- A societal order must be maintained in which laws and rules are above and neutral with respect to different religious views.

Even if all four principles are debatable, the first and the third principle are the least controversial, which is why they will not be discussed here. The second and the fourth principle, however, are more problematic and call for a comment.

The second principle can very easily be read as a dubious attempt to silence possible critics. It is not in itself a question of the relation between religion and politics. Rather, it may very well be seen as a purely political and strategic attempt to silence voices that may be undesirable. In principle such voices could come from anywhere. But in both a historical perspective and in the light of the debates in recent years, it is very pragmatic for Fogh Rasmussen to silence the voice of churches and other religious communities and groups. But for this very same reason we should be hesitant in approving of this principle. Perhaps it is precisely this attempt by Fogh Rasmussen that should make us more interested in ensuring that the Danish Evangelical-Lutheran Church should have a voice with a higher profile. This is even more the case when we take a look around us at the various churches in countries close to Denmark. Most countries close to Denmark would be justifiably surprised to learn that the Danish Evangelical-Lutheran Church did not hold an opinion on various political and ethical issues.

The fourth principle may also lead to some reservations. When Fogh Rasmussen held a constitution-day speech (grundlovstale) on 5 June 2006 he expressed a similar idea, emphasising that the Bible, the Qur'an and other holy writings were not above the laws of the parliament (Fogh Rasmussen 2006b). This is a position with which it is easier to agree. But even here some reservations seem justified. The understanding seems too simplified. It must be recognised that there are many Christians and Muslims who base their outlook on the Bible or the Qur'an. And to the extent that this outlook partly shapes their reasonable participation in the public debate, one can hardly claim that there is anything wrong with this. In the article in *Politiken* quoted above however, the fourth principle is something that simply cannot be endorsed from the perspective of a consistent Christian political ethic. It cannot be affirmed that a Christian religious conviction is subordinated to the laws and rules of the political society. When Fogh Rasmussen writes that the laws and rules of the political society must be above religious convictions, this implies a subordination of religious outlooks. Without inflating the rhetoric too much, this may well be the place to remind ourselves of examples in the history of Christianity in which it was only too clear that subduing Christian and other religious views never does any good. Rather than seeing them as groups of opposition, Fogh Rasmussen could have included them in a respectful and mutual conversation. Religious outlooks and views should not be subdued, but rather integrated and taken seriously in the public debate.

Even though Fogh Rasmussen's view has already been debated from a variety of perspectives (Lodberg 2007), the debate is still so recent and raises so many fundamental issues that it may still serve as the point of departure for the more general debate on church, democracy and ethics. Lutheran theology and ethics is one place where this debate is interesting for several reasons. Apart from Fogh Rasmussen actually referring to Luther in support of his position (Fogh Rasmussen 2006a), the debate on Luther's actual intention and the meaning of his social ethics also motivates our enquiry into his thought.

Martin Luther and temporal authority

When we turn to Luther's understanding of the role of religion and politics, we need to remind ourselves that this question is in itself anachronistic. The concepts of 'religion' and 'politics' are not found in Luther. But even though we do not find exactly the same terminology, we still find a concern with important implications for our contemporary debate. In Luther we find this concern in his understanding of law and temporal authority.

In Luther there are two uses of the law: (i) a political use and (ii) a theological use. The notion of the two uses of the law is found, for instance, in one of the most central writings of Luther – his commentary in 1535 on Paul's letter to the Galatians. Closely related to Luther's understanding of the double use of the law is his double concept of justice: (i) outer, political justice (coram hominibus) and (ii) inner, spiritual justice (coram Deo). Apart from being found in the commentary on Paul's letter to the Galatians, the distinction between the two concepts of justice is also found in *De servo arbitrio* and – above all – in his *Von weltlicher Oberkeit*.

With the political use of the law (also called the first use of the law), Luther understands the law in its function within political society. The law is understood as having a political function and use when compelling people to good works (seen from the outside). In this function the law aims at outer, civil justice (iustitia externa/civilis). According to Luther's understanding, this first use of the law is a precondition for the political and public coexistence of human beings. In addition to the political use of the law, Luther also speaks of the theological use of the law (the second use). In this function the law is understood as driving people to justification by faith. Here the law is understood as driving people to Christ. The law in this sense aims at a form of justice which cannot be gained by outer, good works. The law in its theological use aims at the justification which is given – the passive and alien justice (iustitia aliena). The law does this by demonstrating the insufficiency and incompleteness of the human being's righteousness before God if it were not to receive the justification by grace.

This distinction between two uses of the law and two notions of justice is closely related to Luther's understanding of the two governments (Regimente) or kingdoms (Reiche) – worldly and spiritual. The worldly government is instituted by God in order to uphold the world. This government is part of God's *creatio continua*, i.e. God's continuous presence and creative work within creation. The purpose of worldly government is to punish the wicked and protect the pious. In this respect the law is understood as the law of punishment. It is within the worldly government that the law has its political use. The spiritual government is upheld by the word. It is the kingdom of mercy and compassion. In this kingdom love (and not law) is the ruler. Here the law assumes its theological use.

This double understanding of law and the two spheres of God's way of governing the world can be misread and interpreted dualistically. Luther's views on temporal authority have been used to argue for the separation of religion and politics in a contemporary context (Fogh Rasmussen 2006a), even though this is a misreading of Luther (Nissen 2003). A proper reading of Luther would take note of the fact that God is behind both concepts of the law and both spheres of governance. In Luther we do not find an 'empty space' where God has no say. Even though Hugo Grotius argued about hundred years later that natural law has its validity even if God is not there, we do not find this in Luther. In Luther there is no dimension of reality existing independently of God. Everything *is* in relation to God. Worldly reality in all its dimensions cannot be understood separately from God as its creator. So the whole of reality is marked by God's mysterious presence.

Dietrich Bonhoeffer's mysterious concept of reality

Just as we could argue that Luther endorses an idea of God's mysterious presence in the whole of reality, we can also argue that Dietrich Bonhoeffer resembles Luther – perhaps he actually follows him – in a mysterious understanding of reality. In this similarity Bonhoeffer is also critical of the potential misreading of Luther. Even though Luther does not endorse a dualist conception of God's relation to the world, he can be read in this way. This could imply a dichotomy in the notion of reality – a dichotomy ultimately denying God as creator and the recreation in Christ. We may, therefore, follow Bonhoeffer in his critique of this dichotomy. Bonhoeffer argues that the reconciliation of man and God in Christ implies that there cannot be a separation between two kinds of reality. There is only one reality, i.e. a reality reconciled with God in Christ. In Bonhoeffer the whole of reality is seen in its relation to God. There is no reality separable from this relation. As God is seen as the ultimate reality (letzte Wirklichkeit), any attempt to ignore this relation would be an empty abstraction.

Alle Dinge erscheinen ja im Zerrbild, wo sie nicht in Gott gesehen und erkannt werden. Alle sogenannte Gegebenheiten, alle Gesetze und Normen sind Abstraktionen, so lange nicht Gott als die letzte Wirklichkeit geglaubt wird (DBW 6, 32).

As such, the good in the world (das Gutsein der Welt) cannot be separated from God's good (das Gutsein Gottes). God's good is revealed in Jesus Christ, therefore the question of the good can only be determined in Jesus Christ (33). Consequently, the basis of Christian ethics is the revelation of God's reality in Jesus Christ. The source of Christian ethics is this reality of God.

Der Ursprung der christlichen Ethik ist nicht die Wirklichkeit des eigenen Ich, nicht die Wirklichkeit der Welt, aber auch nicht die Wirklichkeit der Normen und Werte, sondern die Wirklichkeit Gottes in seiner Offenbarung in Jesus Christus (33).

Bonhoeffer's idea that the whole of reality is to be seen in relation to God and that this relation is revealed in Jesus Christ also implies for him that there is only one reality, i.e. the one and only Christ reality (Christuswirklichkeit) (43f.). In Jesus Christ, however, the reality of God and the reality of the world are reconciled. The reality of God and the reality of the world are both confirmed. Neither can be separated from nor understood apart from the other. The reality of the world and the reality of God are necessarily related to each other in Jesus Christ.

In Christus begegnet uns das Angebot, an der Gotteswirklichkeit und an der Weltwirklichkeit zugleich teil zu bekommen, eines nicht ohne das andere. Die Wirklichkeit Gottes erschließt sich nicht anders als indem sie mich ganz in die Weltwirklichkeit hineinstellt, die Weltwirklichkeit aber finde ich immer schon getragen, angenommen, versöhnt in der Wirklichkeit Gottes vor (…) Es geht also darum, *an der Wirklichkeit Gottes und der Welt in Jesus Christus heute teilzuhaben* und das so, daß ich die Wirklichkeit Gottes nie ohne die Wirklichkeit der Welt und die Wirklichkeit der Welt nie ohne die Wirklichkeit Gottes erfahre (40f.).

The understanding of the reality of God and the reality of the world as reconciled in Christ implies for Bonhoeffer that he rejects the traditional understanding of a separation between two spheres which has been upheld and defined variously throughout Christian tradition (41f.). For Bonhoeffer there is only one reality.

Bonhoeffer's understanding of the Christ reality also means for him that reality as such cannot be understood separate from Christ. To understand reality separate from the real one (der Wirkliche) makes no sense and leads to a senseless life.

Alles Faktische erfährt von *dem* Wirklichen, dessen Name Jesus Christus heißt, seine letzte Begründung und seine letzte Aufhebung, seine Rechtfertigung und seinen letzten Widerspruch, sein letztes Ja und sein letztes Nein. Die Wirklichkeit ohne den Wirklichen verstehen zu wollen, bedeutet in einer Abstraktion leben, der der Verantwortliche niemals verfallen darf, bedeutet Vorbeileben an der Wirklichkeit, bedeutet endloses Schwanken zwischen den Extremen der Servilität und der Auflehnung gegenüber dem Faktischen (261).

In Christ the whole of reality is affirmed and reconciled with God. Therefore, to act according to reality (wirklichkeitsgemäß) is to act in Christ.

Weil in Jesus Christus, dem Wirklichen, die ganze Wirklichkeit aufgenommen und zusammengefaßt ist, weil sie ihn [zum] Ursprung, Wesen und Ziel hat, darum ist nur in ihm und von ihm aus ein wirklichgemäßes Handeln möglich (262).

For Bonhoeffer this also means that action is to be seen as acting in Christ. So it is no wonder that Bonhoeffer also draws concrete implications of this understanding.

Does it make a difference?

Having seen how both Luther and Bonhoeffer argue for a mysterious understanding either of God's ruling of the world or Christ's unity with the world, the immediate question arises – does it make a difference? In the concrete ethical stance one has to take in a political context, does it lead to any difference in one's decisions or actions? I will reply to this question in the light of Bonhoeffer, even though a similar reply could be made on the basis of Luther.

In the understanding of the Christological mystery of reality we have a double-sided nature of the Christian ethics. On the one hand the common dimension is maintained, and on the other the emphasis is on the more specific identity. These two dimensions of Christian ethics are not seen as being in conflict with each other. Rather, they are seen as being related to each other in the same way as the two natures of Christ are related to each other. In this sense we could say that Bonhoeffer argues for a Chalcedonian model for a Christian social ethic (Nissen 2006). The double-sided nature of the Christian social ethic also means that each of these dimensions can be asserted without seeing this as a neglect of the other. One can argue for a common and a more specific understanding of Christian ethics at the same time. In Bonhoeffer we find the implications of this view in his understanding of pacifism and resistance, for instance.

This is not the place to go into a detailed theological analysis of Bonhoeffer's motives for both pacifism and resistance or of his move from one to the other, as this has already been done elsewhere (Nissen, 2009). But it is important for our present concern to note that one of the theological arguments that Bonhoeffer draws on in his arguments for resistance is the understanding of Christ. It is particularly in the section 'History and Good' that we find Bonhoeffer's arguments for participation in the resistance. Here Bonhoeffer develops four themes: Vicarious representative action (Stellvertretung), correspondence with reality, taking on guilt, and freedom. These themes are all developed in his wish to explain the concept of a responsible life (DBW 6, 256ff.). And for Bonhoeffer the notion of responsibility is linked to his understanding of reality (262f.). But here it is important that this is understood as an affirmation of worldly and human reality. It is precisely because the Christological understanding of reality affirms the worldly reality that Bonhoeffer can argue for this approach to reality.

Wirklichkeitsgemäß ist das christusgemäße Handeln, weil es die Welt Welt läßt, weil es mit der Welt als Welt rechnet und doch niemals aus den Augen läßt, daß die Welt in Jesus Christus von Gott geliebt, gerichtet und versöhnt ist (263.).

Therefore, the world remains a world loved by and reconciled with God in Christ. As such the world is the space of concrete responsibility (266). However, this responsibility is limited by human conditions. But this limitation also raises a responsibility. Christian responsibility is linked to the creaturely conditions (267ff.). So even if this means that Christian responsibility is creaturely and humble, it also entails that in extreme situations in which 'necessities of life' are threatened, the responsible action may protect the necessities. In these situations the responsible action may protect nothing more than life itself, transcending law and normal morality in order to do this.

In Bonhoeffer an important basis for his justification of resistance lies in his understanding of the world as reconciled with God in Christ. Even if this follows from a Christological understanding of reality, it is important in Bonhoeffer that this is still understood as an affirmation of the world in itself. The world is affirmed as itself in Christ. This self-affirmation of the world in Christ also means for Bonhoeffer that he can find support for his 'worldly' responsibilities in these Christological deliberations. If Bonhoeffer did not have this Christological basis for his social ethics, he would not be able to argue for the same kind of responsibility. His understanding of the mystery of Christ with relation to reality would fall apart. This would lead him to a position where he would easily fall into a separation of reality into two spheres. Bonhoeffer saw this approach much too clearly in contemporary Lutheran theologians, and understood that it made it impossible for them to develop a Christian response to the political authority that challenged the credibility and authenticity of Christian faith and confession. But rather than taking a path where he developed a highly profiled and specific reply (which would also tear apart the notion of reality), Bonhoeffer argued for a double-sided view of reality which made it possible for him to reply with a specific Christian stance and yet maintain this as an affirmation of common human reality.

It can be argued that this double-sided understanding of reality and the notion of a mysterious presence of a Divine reality within human reality is important for a contemporary reflection on the role between church, democracy and ethics. This double-sided view entails an affirmation of democracy as the best possible condition of the political realm within human reality. But at the same time it also points to the limits of the political realm. It maintains that human reality finds its affirmation outside itself and can never be separated from this Divine affirmation without losing its own meaning. This limit also holds both the sources of the critical response that makes a difference, and the continuous reminder of the mysterious presence of the Divine within the whole of human reality. The church is the place where the identity of the mysterious dimension of reality is proclaimed. As such the church holds an important role in society as the place where the political realm is reminded of its true character and the limits of its authority.

Bibliography

Allen, J.W. 1977 (1928). *A History of Political Thought in the Sixteenth Century*. London: Methuen.

Bonhoeffer, Dietrich 1944 (1998). *Ethik. Dietrich Bonhoeffer Werke*, Band 6 (DBW 6). Gütersloh: Chr. Kaiser/Gütersloher Verlagshaus.

Fogh Rasmussen, Anders 2006a. Fogh: 'Hold religionen indendørs'. *Politiken*, 20 May, 3. sektion: 6.

Fogh Rasmussen, Anders 2006b. 'Grundlovstale 2006'. Terndruplund. http://venstre.dk/fileadmin/ venstre.dk/main/files/afr_grundlov06.pdf (24.6.2008)

Lodberg, Peter (ed.) 2007. *Sammenhængskraften. Replikker til Fogh*. Højbjerg: Forlaget Univers.

Luther, Martin 1526 (1897). *Ob Kriegsleute auch in seligem Stande sein können* (Martin Luthers Werke: Kritische Gesamtausgabe). Weimar: Hermann Böhlau (WA 19, 623-662).

Nissen, Ulrik 2003. 'Between Unity and Differentiation. On the Identity of Lutheran Social Ethics'. In: Ulrik Nissen, Svend Andersen, Lars Reuter (eds.), *The Sources of Public Morality – On the Ethics and Religion Debate*. Münster: LIT Verlag, 152-171.

Nissen, U.B. (2009). "Dietrich Bonhoeffer: A Journey from Pacifism to Resistance", i Dosenrode, S. (red.) *Christianity and Restistance in the 20th Century*, Brill Academic Publishers, Leiden and Boston, s. 147-174.

Nissen, Ulrik 2007. 'Sammenhængskraft og luthersk socialetik. Inspirationen fra Dietrich Bonhoeffer'. In: Peter Lodberg (ed.), *Sammenhængskraften. Replikker til Fogh*. Højbjerg: Forlaget Univers, 141-151.

Nissen, Ulrik 2006. 'The Christological Ontology of Reason'. *NZSTh*, 48, 460-478.

Thompson, W.D.J. Cargill 1984. *The Political Thought of Martin Luther*. Brighton: Harvester Press.

ABOUT THE AUTHORS

Johannes Adamsen, PhD. Has worked on religion in modernity. Articles in Danish, English and German. Has published *Skorpionens gift. Vilh. Grønbechs kritik af kristendom og kultur* (2002). Concentrates on democracy and religion with special interest in citizenship and the importance of history.

Lars Albinus PhD is an Associate Professor in Systematic Theology at the Faculty of Theology, Aarhus University, Denmark. Has recently published: "Wittgenstein og respekten for det religiøse" in: A.M. Christensen (ed.) 2006. *Om religion og religiøsitet.* Aarhus University Press; and 'Tolerancens problem: den vanskelige balance'. *Religionsvidenskabeligt Tidsskrift* 48.

Vagn Andersen is an Associate Professor of the Philosophy of Religion at the Department of the Study of Religion, Faculty of Theology, Aarhus University, Denmark. In 1980 he acquired a PhD in theology for his dissertation on hermeneutics and ideology critique. Since then his research has primarily been concerned with Kierkegaard, German idealism and 20th-century German philosophy, and he has recently completed a monograph on the consequences of Jürgen Habermas' thinking, viewed from the perspective of the philosophy of religion.

Morten Brænder is a PhD fellow at the Department of Political Science at Aarhus University, Denmark. He has a Master's degree in the History of Ideas and Comparative Religion. In the autumn of 2007 he was Visiting Research Student Collaborator at the Center for the Study of Religion and the Department of Sociology, Princeton University. In his dissertation Morten Brænder analyses the presence of civil religious notions in milblogs, which are internet diaries written by American soldiers in the field in Iraq. He has previously written articles on civil religion and co-edited the book *Antiterrorismens Idehistorie, Stater og Vold i 500 år* (Aarhus University Press, 2007).

Henrik Reintoft Christensen is a PhD fellow at the Department of the Study of Religion at the Faculty of Theology, Aarhus University, Denmark. He is a graduate in the study of religion and political science from the universities of Aarhus and Uppsala. He is currently working on a project on public religion in Scandinavia. He has previously written on the relationship between religion and secular society in a number of working papers and articles, for instance 'Om kræfternes ikke helt frie spil', 'May the Forces be with us: The Battle for the Hearts or Minds of the Danish People', and 'Sikkerhedsliggørelsen af Islam'.

Per Ingesman Dr.phil. is an Associate Professor of Church History at the Faculty of Theology, Aarhus University, Denmark. His main area of research is Danish and European ecclesiastical history in the late medieval and early modern period. Dr. Ingesman has written numerous articles and two books: *Ærkesædets godsadministration i senmiddelalderen* (1990), and *Provisioner og processer. Den romerske Rota og dens behandling af danske sager i middelalderen* (2003). He has co-edited fifteen anthologies on a wide range of topics within medieval and modern history and Church history.

Karen-Lise Johansen Karman is a PhD fellow at the Department of the Study of Religion, Aarhus University, Denmark. Her dissertation focuses on the giving of fatwas (non-binding legal advice) by fatwa councils to Muslim minorities in the West. She has published one article on this, 'Intellectual Influences between the West and the Muslim World: Religious Authority in Transnational Interaction.' In: *Women, Gender & Research* (2007). She has previously studied religious renewal among young Muslims in Denmark, and published *Muslimske stemmer. Religiøs forandring blandt unge muslimer i Danmark* [Muslim Voices: Religious Transformation among Young Muslims in Denmark] (2002).

Peter Lodberg is an Associate Professor of Systematic Theology at the Faculty of Theology, Aarhus University, Denmark. He earned his PhD degree at Aarhus University for a thesis on Ecclesiology and Ethics in the work of the World Council of Churches in 1992. His area of research includes Palestinian theology, State and Church, political theology and ecumenism. His recent publications include: *The Beacon of Hope. Inspiration from Desmond Tutu* (Unitas, 2007), *Von Kaj Munk zu Desmond Tutu. Der Widerstand der Kirchen gegen Apartheid und Ungerechtigkeit in Afrika* (Duisburg, 2006), and *For All People. Global Theologies in Context* (Eerdmans, 2002).

Viggo Mortensen Dr.theol. is Professor in Systematic Theology at the Faculty of Theology, Aarhus University, Denmark, where he holds a chair in Global Christianity and Ecumenical Concerns and is director of the Centre for Multireligious Studies, director of the Danish Pluralism Project, and coordinator of the European Network for Religious Innovation and Pluralism in 21st century Europe (RIPE). He served in 1991-1999 as director of the Department of Theology and Studies at the Lutheran World Federation in Geneva, and is presently chair of the board of the Nordic Institute for Missiology and Ecumenism (NIME). He has recently published: *Kristendommen under forvandling. Pluralismen som udfordring til teologi og kirke* (Christianity Changing. Pluralism as a Challenge to Theology and the Church) (Univers, 2005). 'Global Christianity is changing: how do these changes influence conflict and peace?' In: T. Yates (ed.), *Mission and the next Christendom*. Cliff College Academic Series 2006. Religion & Society. Cross-disciplinary European Perspectives (Univers, 2006).

Johannes Nissen is an Associate Professor of New Testament Exegesis and Practical Theology at the Faculty of Theology, Aarhus University, Denmark. He has published a number of books and articles, especially on the Bible and ethics, the New Testament and mission, hermeneutics, and practical theological issues. His recent publications include *New Testament and Mission: Historical and Hermeneutical Perspectives* (Peter Lang, 1999, 2007, 4th. ed.), *Bibel og etik: Konkrete og principielle problemstillinger* (Aarhus University Press, 2003), *Bibel og økumeni: Essays om enhed og mangfoldighed* (Aros forlag, 2006), and *Diakoni og menneskesyn* (Aros forlag, 2008).

Ulrik Nissen PhD is an Associate Professor of Ethics at the Department of Systematic Theology, Aarhus University, Denmark. He is also Director of the Centre for Bioethics and Nanoethics, Aarhus University. His PhD dissertation is from 2001 on *Nature and Reason. A Study on Natural Law and Environmental Ethics*. Among more recent books he has co-edited *Mysteries in the Theology of Dietrich Bonhoeffer* in 2007, and *The Sources of Public Morality – On the Ethics and Religion Debate* in 2003. He is currently working on Dietrich Bonhoeffer's ethics with relation to the question of the relation between religion and politics in contemporary society.

Else Marie Wiberg Pedersen is an Associate Professor of Systematic Theology at the Faculty of Theology, Aarhus University, Denmark. She earned her doctoral degree at Aarhus University for a thesis on Beatrice of Nazareth and her vernacular theology. Her areas of research include Cistercian theology, ecclesiology, women's issues, Mariology and ecumenism. Her recent publications include: *Om nåden og den fri vilje* (Anis, 2006), *Cracks in the Wall* (Peter Lang, 2005), *For All People. Global Theologies in Contexts* (Eerdmans, 2002), and Bernhard af Clairvaux. Teolog eller mystiker? (Anis, 2008)

Jens Holger Schjørring Dr.theol. is Professor of Church History at the Faculty of Theology, Aarhus University, Denmark. Among his recent publications are (ed. with P. Kumari and N.A. Hjelm): *From Federation to Communion. The History of the Lutheran World Federation 1947-1997*. Minneapolis: Fortress 1997 (also German ed. same year); (ed.): *Nordiske folkekirker i opbrud. National identitet og international nyorientering efter 1945*. Aarhus: Aarhus University Press. 2001; (ed. with P. Maser): *Zwischen den Mühlsteinen. Protestantische Kirchen in der Phase der Errichtung der kommunistischen Herrschaft im östlichen Europa* (Erlangen: M. Luther 2002; (ed. with H. Lehmann): *Im Räderwerk des "real existierenden Sozialismus". Kirchen in Ostmittel- und Osteuropa von Stalin bis Gorbatschow*. Göttingen: Wallstein 2003; (ed. with P. Maser): *Wie die Träumenden? Protestantische Kirchen in der Phase des Zusammenbruchs der kommunistischen Herrschaft im östlichen Europa*. Erlangen: M. Luther Verlag 2003; (ed. with K. Kunter): *Die Kirchen und das Erbe des Kommunismus. Die Zeit nach 1989 – Zäsur, Vergangenheitsbewältigung und Neubeginn. Fallstudien aus Mittel- und Osteuropa und Bestandsaufnahme aus der Ökumene*. Erlangen. M. Luther Verlag 2007; and (ed. with K. Kunter): *Changing Relations between Churches in Europe and Africa. The Internationalization of Christianity and Politics*. Wiesbaden, Harrassowitz 2008.